The
BURNING
of the
VANITIES
SAVONAROLA AND THE BORGIA POPE

DESMOND SEWARD

SUTTON PUBLISHING

For
John and Caroline Hervey-Bathurst

First published in the United Kingdom in 2006 by
Sutton Publishing Limited · Phoenix Mill
Thrupp · Stroud · Gloucestershire · GL5 2BU

British Library Cataloguing in Publication Data
A catalogue record for this book is available from the British Library.

ISBN 0-7509-2981-2

Typeset in 11/14pt Sabon.
Typesetting and origination by
Sutton Publishing Limited.
Printed and bound in England by
J.H. Haynes & Co. Ltd, Sparkford.

Contents

iv   *Contents*

Preface

Of so great a man we must speak with reverence.
                    Niccolò Machiavelli, *Discorsi*

In the priory of San Marco at Florence there is a painting by an
unknown artist of an execution in the city's Piazza della Signoria.
Dating from about 1500, scarcely more than folk art, the painting
has a disturbing quality that for me verges on the sinister –
reminiscent of the irrational fear felt when reading ghost stories.
Clearly the work of an eyewitness, it tells a tale in three parts. First,
three figures in long white shirts kneel before a group of dignitaries;
next, each figure flanked by men in black hoods, they are led down
a timber platform to a gibbet in the middle of the Piazza; finally,
they hang in chains over a great fire – the executioners are bringing
faggots to make the flames burn higher. Some of the spectators in
the scene look on with fascination, others run away in dismay. Such
a death in so beautiful a setting seems peculiarly cruel and
unnatural; but it was this painting, *Supplizio del Savonarola*, that
made me want to know more.

Another motive has been a wish to appreciate George Eliot's novel
Romola, which was inspired by Savonarola's life and times. Eliot
explains, accurately enough, that 'Savonarola appeared to believe,
and his hearers more or less waveringly believed, that he had a
mission like that of the Hebrew prophets, and that the Florentines
among whom his message was delivered were in some sense a
second chosen people.'[1] Eliot thought *Romola* the finest of her
books, as did Henry James, but today most readers find it
inaccessible unless they are familiar with Savonarola's story.

Generally Savonarola is remembered only for his 'burning of the
vanities' – *bruciamente della vanità* – which Tom Wolfe used as the
title for a novel, translating '*bruciamento*' as 'bonfire'. But this was

not so in the nineteenth century. 'A man whose nature seemed made of fire,' Jacob Burckhardt wrote of him.[2] 'Savonarola's eloquence is the expression of a lofty and commanding personality, the like of which was not seen again until the time of Luther.' Pasquale Villari's *History of Girolamo Savonarola*, dedicated to Mr Gladstone, became a Victorian best-seller,[3] while in 1886 the *Encyclopaedia Britannica* claimed 'The roll of Italian great men contains few grander names than Savonarola.'

Savonarola prophesied with eerie precision the French invasion of Italy and the death of his enemy Lorenzo the Magnificent and many others. Dominating Florence for over three years, he not only reformed its citizens' way of life but gave them a genuinely representative government. Among contemporaries who admired him were scholars such as Pico della Mirandola, historians such as Guicciardini, artists such as Botticelli and Michelangelo. Even opponents respected him. When Lorenzo lay dying, he sent for 'the Frate', as Savonarola became known, while Machiavelli, once hostile, came to regard him with veneration.

Much of Savonarola's influence came from his predictions, so accurate that he himself came to believe he possessed the biblical gift of prophecy. But because of his determination to reform the Church he fell foul of Alexander VI – well summed up by George Eliot as 'a lustful, greedy, lying and murderous old man, once called Rodrigo Borgia'.[4] 'Rome has confused all the scriptures, all the vices, everything,' declared Savonarola, adding that the Borgia pope was a criminal, illegally elected, who had to be deposed. In response, Alexander brought pressure to bear on the Florentines to overthrow him, and then encouraged his murder.

Some historians tend to see him as a forerunner of Martin Luther, others as a philistine who rejected the Renaissance. Far from being an Italian Luther he was a herald of the Counter Reformation, and had he prevailed over Alexander VI there might have been no Protestant Reformation. The number of scholars and artists among his friends shows that he was scarcely a foe of the Renaissance.

One reason why he casts a spell down the ages is his ability to peer into the future. Even today there are people – especially in Florence – who suspect that his writings contain a secret message that may be of vital importance for the entire world.

Acknowledgements

I would first of all like to thank Gianozzo Pucci, with whom two short conversations at Florence changed my entire approach to Savonarola. My next debt is to two scholars I have never met, Claudio Leonardi and Lorenzo Polizzotto – the first for his insights into Savonarola's gift of prophecy, the second for the later history of the Savonarolean movement. I am particularly grateful to Jeremy Musson for showing me his unpublished thesis on the circulation of Savonarola's publications in contemporary England; and to Fr Aidan Nichols and the Dominicans of Blackfriars, Cambridge, for their hospitality and the use of their library.

I have to thank, too, Anna Allemandi (Anna Somers-Cocks) for drawing my attention to the intaglio portrait of Savonarola by Giovanni delle Corniole; Damian Thompson for reading the typescript; Hugo Lesser for tracking down references to Ivan Illich; Sara Ayad for obtaining the plates; and my cousins Hugues de Montelambert and Chantal Hoppenot for, as always, their unfailing encouragement.

I also have to thank the staffs of the British Library, the Cambridge University Library and the London Library.

My best thanks, however, are due to my extraordinarily patient and understanding editor, Elizabeth Stone.

The Savonarola of Ferrara

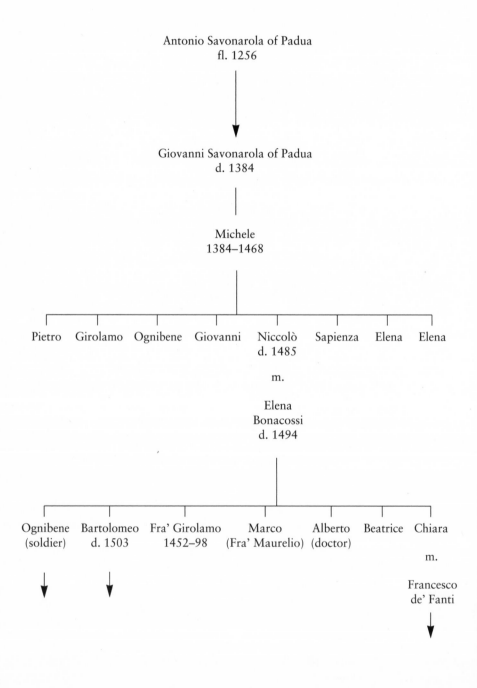

Antonio Savonarola of Padua
fl. 1256

Giovanni Savonarola of Padua
d. 1384

Michele
1384–1468

Pietro   Girolamo   Ognibene   Giovanni   Niccolò   Sapienza   Elena   Elena
d. 1485

m.

Elena
Bonacossi
d. 1494

Ognibene   Bartolomeo   Fra' Girolamo   Marco   Alberto   Beatrice   Chiara
(soldier)   d. 1503   1452–98   (Fra' Maurelio)   (doctor)

m.

Francesco
de' Fanti

The Estensi (simplified)

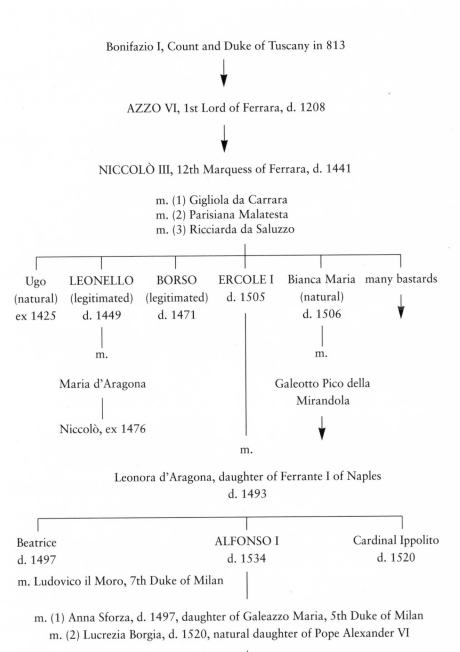

Bonifazio I, Count and Duke of Tuscany in 813

AZZO VI, 1st Lord of Ferrara, d. 1208

NICCOLÒ III, 12th Marquess of Ferrara, d. 1441

m. (1) Gigliola da Carrara
m. (2) Parisiana Malatesta
m. (3) Ricciarda da Saluzzo

Ugo (natural) ex 1425

LEONELLO (legitimated) d. 1449

BORSO (legitimated) d. 1471

ERCOLE I d. 1505

Bianca Maria (natural) d. 1506

many bastards

m.

Maria d'Aragona

Niccolò, ex 1476

m.

Galeotto Pico della Mirandola

m.

Leonora d'Aragona, daughter of Ferrante I of Naples
d. 1493

Beatrice
d. 1497

ALFONSO I
d. 1534

Cardinal Ippolito
d. 1520

m. Ludovico il Moro, 7th Duke of Milan

m. (1) Anna Sforza, d. 1497, daughter of Galeazzo Maria, 5th Duke of Milan
m. (2) Lucrezia Borgia, d. 1520, natural daughter of Pope Alexander VI

Put Savonarola to death, even if he is another John the Baptist
Pope Alexander VI

ONE

The Tyrants

Duke Borso – medal of 1460

The word 'tyrant' means a man of utterly evil life, of deeper wickedness than most, a usurper of other men's rights, a murderer of his own soul and of the souls of others.

Savonarola, *Prediche sopra Aggeo*

Girolamo Savonarola was born at Ferrara on 21 September 1452, in the same year as Leonardo da Vinci. Known as the 'Great Lady of the Po', the city lay under the shadow of a stronghold, which remains today. Linked to the now long-vanished Palazzo del Corte by a fortified bridge over a deep moat, it had been built by the Estensi as a protection against their subjects.

Ringed by water, defended by bastions and towers – notably the tall Torre Marchesana – entered only across drawbridges and lacking the extra storey, loggias and turrets that have softened its grim outline, the Castello d'Estense looked far more sinister in Girolamo's time.

'A rattle of chains and the groaning of men in agony drifted up from the dungeons and could be heard amid the feasting and revelry overhead, above the ring of silver plate, majolica and Venetian glass' is how Pasquale Villari, Savonarola's first modern biographer, imagines life at the Ferrarese court.[1] In reality, the court occupied the Palazzo del Corte, only moving into the Castello in times of danger. Yet its courtiers were well aware of the cells under the Torre Marchesana, lapped by the moat. Even today when the cells are brightly lit, entering through the waist-high doors can be unnerving – each has a tiny, tunnel-like window high up, barred by four gratings, save for the smallest which is without any window at all and whose floor used to be under water. Many men and even women died in these cells.

In 1452 Ferrara was the capital of a flourishing state that covered nearly 9,000 square kilometres, stretching across Italy from the Mediterranean to the Adriatic. It included Modena, Reggio, Adria, Comacchio and Polisene di Rovigo on the Venetian frontier, together with a string of castles.

The city had grown rich from exporting salt and corn: the flat, melancholy surrounding countryside consisted not only of intensely cultivated farmland but of impenetrable marshes and lagoons not yet drained. Its 20,000 inhabitants never went short of bread, since the rulers stockpiled reserves of flour in case of bad harvests. As luxurious in its own way as Milan or Florence, its wealthier citizens were envied for their fine clothes and for eating game – the period's luxury food – from silver platters. Those not so rich ate at excellent taverns, such as the Hosteria del Chiuchiolino in Via Gorgadella.

At the beginning of the century Niccolò III had laid out an entire new quarter on the south side, with the city's one broad thoroughfare, Via di San Francesco, but most of Ferrara was crammed into twisting, narrow streets behind high walls. A few rich nobles lived in *palazzi*, such as the Casa Romei in Via di San Francesco, built in the 1440s and only a few yards down the road from the Savonarola family, although most people inhabited unlit alleys of the sort that still exist today in the area around Via delle Volte – in Girolamo's time the business centre – whose cleansing was left to the rain and foraging pigs. They were dangerous alleys and not just at night, since the city's wealth attracted criminals, while young noblemen fought murderous duels in Via Pergolato.

The citizens were more afraid of their rulers than robbery or duellists, even if the chronicle known as the *Diario Ferrarese* cringingly refers to the Estensi as mirrors of virtue. Admittedly, they were not jumped-up tyrants like the Sforza or the Medici. A hundred years after Girolamo's day, Torquato Tasso wrote in *Gerusalemme Liberata* of a magic, mirror-like shield in whose reflection the family's Roman forebears might be glimpsed – including 'Foresto, the Italian Hector', who vanquished Attila the Hun in single combat.[2] However, their real ancestors were the Lombard Obertenghi, by the ninth century already mighty feudal lords and since the twelfth rulers of the city. The Ferrarese were proud of their time-honoured blood.

Fifteenth-century Estensi were colourful figures. Niccolò III, father of the rulers in Girolamo's day, was a fat, jolly man who was said to have slept with 800 women and sired 800 bastards – although when he learned that his young wife Parisiana Malatesta was sleeping with his eldest son Ugo, he had the pair beheaded in a cell under the Torre Marchesana and ordered the execution of every unfaithful wife in Ferrara. He liked to impress his subjects by regularly processing through his capital in cloth of gold with an escort bearing flaming torches, or by jousting on the main Piazza.

Niccolò dazzled his subjects with pomp. Whenever he visited another prince or a prince came to Ferrara, he was accompanied by a cortège of richly dressed courtiers on extravagantly caparisoned horses. On certain days, the '*Illustre Marchese*', preceded by trumpeters, processed through his capital, gleaming in cloth of gold or silver, with an escort bearing flaming torches. Jousts took place regularly on the main piazza while there were balls and banquets at the Palazzo del Corte.

Setting aside his legitimate heir, Ercole, as too young to rule, Niccolò bequeathed Ferrara to two bastards in succession, both of whom were legitimised by the Pope. Despite a splendid court, the Marquess Leonello (1441–50) took little interest in display – save for the foible of choosing the colour of his clothes according to the position of the planets – and made his capital a centre of Greek studies, attracting scholars from all over Italy and abroad, including England. He was also a keen patron of the arts, inviting Roger van der Weyden to Ferrara and commissioning medals by Pisanello. But his real passion was humanist learning.

Humanist scholars were convinced that they could rediscover the lost wisdom of ancient Greece and Rome through a better understanding of the Classics. 'After the darkness has been dispelled,' Petrarch had written in the previous century, 'our grandsons will be able to walk back into the pure radiance of the past.' Enormous hopes were placed on Latin manuscripts found in dusty monastery libraries or on Greek texts bought at Constantinople before it fell to the Turks. A new approach towards art and science was emerging, even towards pleasure. Yet the revival of Greek (and, to some extent, of Hebrew) was welcomed by churchmen, who believed it would give them deeper understanding of the Scriptures. Although this particular hope was strongest north of the Alps, in the Northern Renaissance, it was also widespread among the Italian higher clergy.

In 1442 Leonello reopened the *Studium generale* or university that his grandfather had founded at Ferrara, establishing chairs for humanists, architects, mathematicians and astrologers. By modern standards it was minute, with, at most, 300 students. But a chair of medicine was specially created for an academic from Padua who had settled at Ferrara: this was Girolamo's grandfather, Ser Michele Savonarola, who belonged to an old Paduan noble family and was a graduate of the famous school of medicine at Padua University.[3] No doubt the school lacked any proper knowledge of anatomy or surgery, but it possessed the works of Galen and understood the Hippocratic oath, and Michele was a surprisingly good doctor. He wrote books that circulated widely after the invention of printing: his *Practica de aegritudinibus de capite usque ad pedes* (or *Treatment of Diseases from Head to Foot*) was quoted as late as 1628 by Robert Burton in the *Anatomy of Melancholy* – reflecting Michele's opinion that the only difference between melancholy and madness is one of degree. Other books included treatises on gynaecology, fevers and children's diseases, a guide to healing wells and hot springs, and a manual on how to distil aqua vitae.

Michele also wrote a treatise on bodily sicknesses caused by mental disturbance, stressing the medical importance of the patients' state of mind, including their dreams. His best known prescription – which explains his popularity as a physician – was to tell patients they should drink plenty of wine if they wanted to banish melancholy and the other evil humours.[4]

Since much of the surrounding country was marshy, the city was mosquito-ridden and malarial in summer, damp and foggy in winter. The Po frequently burst its banks during the winter months, flooding the city – sometimes the courtyard of the Castello was eight feet under water. In consequence, the citizens were afflicted by agues and fevers, coughs, colds and depression. It was understandable that Marquess Niccolò should invite a distinguished doctor to be his personal physician. When Michele arrived in 1440 he was given two houses by the Marquess, one in the city and another in the country on the far side of the Po, with a salary of 400 gold ducats. Besides ministering to Niccolò and the court, he lectured, gaining such a

Ferrara in 1490. From A. Sardi, *Annotazione istoriche dal MDLVI al MDLXXI (Modena, Biblioteca Estense Universitaria)*

reputation that Pope Nicholas V summoned him to Rome to treat an 'incurable' illness. He healed the pontiff so quickly that he was made a knight of the Holy Sepulchre.

Michele's main house, where Girolamo spent the first two decades of his life, stood in Via di San Francesco – today called Via Savonarola – the only wide street of the new quarter and then the most fashionable thoroughfare in Ferrara. Not far from the ducal pleasure palace of Schifanoia (meaning 'shun boredom'), the house faced the priory of the Gesuati, whose church was dedicated to St Girolamo – no doubt the inspiration for his grandson's name. Now part of the university, built in the local red brick with a plain, narrow frontage, it is roomier than it looks and has a vaulted gateway opening into an enclosed courtyard.[5]

When Leonello d'Este succeeded Niccolò, he confirmed Ser Michele Savonarola in his post, later creating the university's chair of medicine for him. In 1450, just before his death 'from a dreadful headache' (presumably a brain tumour) that not even Michele could cure, Leonello gave him a small estate, increased his salary and freed him from all duties save 'healing our body, that of our brother, the illustrious lord Borso, and those of members of our House of Este of either sex'.[6]

Although the next marquess, Borso d'Este, was no intellectual and could not read Latin, let alone speak it, Michele remained in favour. 'Borso was a man of fine physique and more than average height with beautiful hair and a pleasing countenance,' writes Pope Pius II in his memoirs. 'His talk was full of blandishments mingled with lies.' In the faded frescoes at the palace of Schifanoia, he is the epitome of *bonhomie*. Perpetually smiling a tight-lipped grin, he dispensed good justice, so long as it did not inconvenience him, and listened patiently to the humblest petitioner who accosted him. Despite spending most of his time hunting or with his jesters, he was an able ruler, and by staying closely allied with Venice, avoided involvement in the petty wars that plagued Italy.

Borso's court had a mysterious reputation for vice. Some historians imagine orgies during which young noblewomen danced naked, but this seems unlikely since the Duke preferred his own sex. Not the slightest hint is given by the chroniclers of his contemplating marriage or taking a mistress, while they mention unusually close male friends, and the sexuality of more than one prominent courtier in the Schifanoia frescoes looks distinctly ambiguous. All the indications are that Borso was homosexual, if firm proof is lacking. The rumours must have shocked his subjects in an age which sent men of lesser rank to the stake for sodomy.

Determined to cut a fine figure, for a vast sum Borso bought the title of duke from Emperor Frederick III and presented Florence with a statue of himself, to be erected in the city's main piazza. Even when hunting he dressed in gold brocade sewn with jewels. 'During his reign,' says the *Diario Ferrarese*, 'he bestowed gifts of coin and raiment valued at 400,000 ducats or more.'[7] But in a secret satire on court life, *De Nuptiis Battibecco et Serrabocca*, Ser Michele comments that 'giving robes, horses, land and money to jesters and worthless men lessens the people's love'.[8] Michele composed a public eulogy of Borso's career, *De felici progressu illustrissimi Borsii Estensis ad marchionatum Ferrariae*, crediting his patron with every virtue, telling how the 'senate' – his flattering term for the twelve *Savi* or 'Wise Men' of Ferrara – elected Borso to succeed his brother: they had no choice. He gives a glowing account of Emperor Frederick creating Borso Duke of Modena in the Piazza between the Palazzo del Corte and the Duomo, describing how the Germans marvelled that so many Ferrarese were dressed in cloth of gold and that everyone shouted so enthusiastically, '*Borso! Borso! Duca! Duca!*'

Michele wrote on other subjects besides medicine and public affairs. One book was a strange study of the prophecies of St John the Baptist. Sometimes his writings are more like the reflections of a Carthusian hermit than those of a professional courtier – he warns his readers to stay away from court if they want to serve God – while his preferred reading was the Bible or Thomas Aquinas.

His son Niccolò married a Mantuan lady of good family named Elena Bonacossi, a descendant of the lords of Mantua. It is likely that Ser Michele wrote *De regimine praegnantium* for his daughter-in-law, who gave birth to seven children. They included five sons, the third being Girolamo.

There has always been speculation about Girolamo's childhood, based on a statement of the early biographer who goes under the name the Pseudo-Burlamacchi, that he had been, 'sparing in conversation, spending the greater part of the time withdrawn and alone'.[9] Yet all we know about Savonarola as a boy is that he must have been intelligent, sensitive and highly strung, and, judging from his letters as an adult, fond of his family. 'Reaching the age for learning manners and letters, his grandfather being still alive, he made no small progress at grammar and Latin,' the Pseudo-Burlamacchi tells us.[10] After nursing so many children through sickness, old Michele was well equipped to teach. He taught him to read, write and speak Latin fluently – not the convoluted Latin of the humanists but the simple, colloquial Latin that was the idiom of every scholar. It is likely, too, that he gave him a smattering of Greek and, just possibly, a very little Hebrew, if no more than the alphabet. In addition, he gave him lessons in the period's primitive geography. According to Girolamo's first biographer, his friend and disciple Fra' Benedetto da Firenze, he learned quickly, while the Pseudo-Burlamacchi says he 'studied night and day'.[11] Benedetto adds that for relaxation he enjoyed drawing and playing the lute.

Above all, Michele gave the boy a love of Aquinas. One of Girolamo's modern biographers, Roberto Ridolfi, says that Michele 'belonged entirely to the fourteenth century, not only by birth [he was born in 1385], but also by outlook and education – to that fourteenth century which was as remote from humanism as it was steeped in scholasticism'.[12] This view should be questioned, however, since scholasticism – the philosophy of Aquinas – remained in fashion throughout the fifteenth century and most humanists continued to be Thomists.

It is probable, too, that Girolamo attended at least some of the lectures at Ferrara's university given by Battista Guerino, a renowned humanist and teacher of Greek. Girolamo himself says he had 'frequented the schools of the poets', meaning that at the university he studied the Classical authors, and wrote a commentary on Plato's *Dialogues* that he later destroyed.[13] But his grandfather may have warned him to be on his guard against the wilder revivals of Greek and Roman attitudes.

Girolamo had been not quite seven when on 17 May 1459 Pope Pius II visited Ferrara during a progress through Italy to summon a crusade that would rescue Constantinople from the Turks, who had stormed the city only six years before. Duke Borso rode to meet him, accompanied by the city's nobles and richer citizens. Among the prelates who accompanied the Pope was his vice-chancellor, the 28-year-old Cardinal Rodrigo Borgia, a burly, virile Catalan. At about this time, his former tutor, Gaspare da Verona, described Borgia: 'A handsome man with a cheerful face and charming conversation, he wins the affection of any woman he fancies, attracting ladies as a magnet does iron filings, but seemingly goes no further.'[14] The only thing people disliked about him was the incomprehensible language he spoke to kinsmen, a Valencian form of Catalan. He owed his career to his uncle, Pope Calixtus III, who made him a cardinal and Archbishop of Valencia (the richest see in Spain) when he was twenty-two, and then vice-chancellor of the Roman Church – which meant he was the Pope's most powerful minister.

During the conclave that followed Calixtus's death, Borgia's astute manoeuvring secured Pius II's election. The new pontiff always remained grateful, if a little shocked by the Cardinal's love of dancing and passion for hawking and boar-hunting. That a man as upright as Pius should like Cardinal Borgia reveals the agreeable side of Borgia's personality. Someone with such a magnificent presence as the ebullient Cardinal of Valencia must have stood out during the papal visit to Ferrara. No doubt he was at Pius's side when the Pope blessed the citizens from a tribunal outside a window of the Palazzo del Corte – the crowd in the Piazza below 'so great that a crumb falling from above could not have reached the ground', says the *Diario ferrarese*.[15]

Not everyone was happy about the way the pontiff was welcomed at Ferrara, a welcome more suited to a Roman general than the Vicar of Christ. Pius rode in through the Porta San Pietro along flower-strewn streets lined with naked statues of the gods and goddesses of pagan antiquity, while a pornographic Venus was borne at the head of a procession that included ten cardinals and sixty bishops. It made some Christians fear that religion was being undermined by humanism – sexuality was becoming freer and easier, homosexuality increasing. The lascivious statues were brought out again when Pius passed through Ferrara the following year.

When Pius died in 1464 Cardinal Borgia backed an outsider in the ensuing election, the Venetian Pietro Barbo. The new pontiff was the first Renaissance Pope, keeping a concubine and collecting jewels, so proud of his good looks that he wanted to take the name '*Formosus*' ('Handsome') but settled for Paul II. Suspecting the humanist scholars at his court of planning to replace the papacy by a Roman republic, he had them tortured. Yet he always retained confidence in his vice-chancellor, Rodrigo Borgia.

In 1468 Michele Savonarola died, aged eighty-three. The new head of the family, Niccolò Savonarola, was very different. His career as a banker had failed since he recklessly underwrote loans without security while he hung about the court and acquired expensive friends – Girolamo's godfather, Francesco Libanori, was Duke Borso's chancellor. After squandering Michele's legacy and his wife's dowry, eventually he had to be supported by his brother-in-law. But the spendthrift Niccolò and the warm-hearted Elena gave their family an affectionate home.

No Ferrarese could escape from the Estensi's shadow. Anybody who criticised them vanished into the Castello's dungeons, and as a boy, Girolamo must always have been aware of their menacing presence. Their emblem, a white eagle, was on countless buildings, while the gate of the Palazzo del Corte opposite the Duomo was flanked on each side by an Este in bronze – Niccolò I grasping a general's baton and Borso seated on a judge's throne. After a single visit to the Palazzo – he was taken by his parents when a child – Girolamo refused to set foot in it ever again.

TWO

St George's Day at Ferrara

Borso and his court – fresco at Palazzo Schifanoia

*Go forth out of thy country, and from thy kindred, and out of
thy father's house, and come into the land that I shall show thee.*
Genesis 12: 1

After graduating as a master of arts, Girolamo began reading
medicine. He planned to become a doctor like his grandfather
– certainly not a priest like his younger brother Marco. Of the older

Savonarola brothers, Ognibene became a soldier and Bartolomeo an architect. The youngest, Alberto, also wanted to be a doctor, despite being a wild youth whose behaviour worried his parents.

There is a description of Girolamo in his thirties. If ugly, he was a person whom people remembered meeting. Very thin and of medium height, he wore his long, curly, dark red hair down to his shoulders. He had a big, hooked nose, a large mouth with thick, compressed lips and strange, grey-green eyes 'flecked with gold', that were shaded by odd, light-red eyelashes. His most striking features were beautiful hands, long and etiolated, and a sudden, radiant smile that transformed him.

We have no details of his master of arts degree course, but it included philosophy, which meant Plato, Aristotle and, above all, Thomas Aquinas. He read everything available by Aristotle, while becoming expert in the use of syllogistic logic, mainly by way of Aquinas. Yet this was far from being the narrow, 'dry as dust' education it sounds to modern readers. Admittedly, Thomism too often degenerated into the logic-chopping of the 'schoolmen', who forgot that the philosophy began from a position of near agnosticism. Yet Dante was a warm admirer of Aquinas and his achievement, writing in the *Paradiso* of '*La gloriosa vita di Tommaso*',[1] and when properly approached Thomism has a perennial freshness. G.K. Chesterton wrote that 'in reading Aquinas's philosophy, I have a very peculiar and powerful impression analogous to poetry'.[2] Thomism combines philosophy with religion, ethics with revelation, and to medieval men seemed to explain almost everything. Byzantines produced a Greek version of Thomas's *Summa Theologica* (a compendium of doctrine) while rabbis translated some of his philosophical books into Hebrew. If he went out of fashion in the next century, at this date Western scholars were still Thomist. From an early age Girolamo was fascinated by the writings of the 'Angelic Doctor'. 'I have always loved and revered him,' he wrote of Aquinas, looking back in later life.[3]

Like every literate Italian of the period, and judging from the verse he produced from time to time, Girolamo read Petrarch's *Canzonieri*, absorbing a melancholy that he is unlikely to have recognised as Classical and pagan. It seems, too, from his own future writings, that he was familiar with Dante's *Divina Commedia*. But other than these we cannot even hazard a guess about the books he read outside his studies.

When still in his teens he fell in love, says his disciple Fra' Benedetto, who heard the story from his brother, Marco Savonarola.[4] In Palazzo Strozzi next door there lived a young girl, Laodamia Strozzi, a bastard daughter of Roberto Strozzi, a member of a great Florentine family who had taken refuge at Ferrara, where Roberto's brother, Lorenzo, was Duke Borso's dearest friend – according to the *Diario Ferrarese*, '*suo principal homo e compagno*'.[5] Benedetto tells us that Girolamo and Laodamia flirted with each other from their windows, while later writers say he bought himself fine clothes and serenaded her with his lute. He asked her to marry him. But the girl laughed that no Strozzi would allow her to marry anyone so low as a Savonarola, to which Girolamo retorted that no Savonarola would let him marry a bastard.

The episode must have taken place when Savonarola was no more than twenty, since in 1472 Niccolò Savonarola, running short of money, sold the house to the Strozzi. The episode reveals that despite their ancestry his family was no longer regarded as noble – indeed the Florentine historian Guicciardini describes Girolamo as belonging to a '*famiglia popolana e mediocre*'.[6] It also shows that as a young man he had no intention of entering the Church and knew the pull of the flesh. However, the Pseudo-Burlamacchi tells us that 'One night while sleeping he felt as if his body was being drenched by cold water which woke him and, after wondering why this had happened, he made up his mind to shun the glory of the world and all its vanities.'[7]

The Castello d'Estense loomed more menacingly than ever during the summer of 1471. In a final blaze of ostentation, escorted by 500 noblemen in cloth of silver and with an entourage that included gyrfalcons and leopards, Borso had visited Rome to be created Duke of Ferrara by the Pope, fulfilling his greatest ambition; now he ranked, in his own estimation at least, with the Doge of Venice and the Duke of Milan. On his way home, he fell dangerously ill at one of his country palaces, raising the spectre of civil war. There was no law of succession: Ferrara would pass to whichever Este could seize it, and there were two determined claimants, Niccolò III's youngest legitimate son Ercole and Leonello's bastard son Niccolò – the former's followers were known as *Diamanteschi* after his device of a diamond, and the latter's as *Veleschi* from his '*vela*' or sail. Borso had wanted Niccolò to succeed him, but disillusioned by the young man's rakish habits, he chose Ercole instead.

In July, when it looked as if Borso was dying, Niccolò installed himself in the Castello d'Estense. A battle then broke out in the streets of Ferrara between the *Diamanteschi* and the *Veleschi*, with many killed or wounded: it ended in stalemate. Niccolò appealed to the Marquess of Mantua and the Duke of Milan for help, whereupon they moved troops up to the Ferrarese frontier. At the same time, Ercole's Venetian friends sent ships along the Po, filled with men-at-arms. Rallying, Borso had himself carried to the Palazzo del Corte, from where he ordered Niccolò to withdraw from the Castello to Mantua and Ercole to return to his residence at Modena.

But the Duke quickly grew worse. He was obviously on his deathbed and when he lost consciousness the *Diamanteschi* took over the Castello and every stronghold in the duchy. Borso died on 19 August. On the following day, Ercole, a former *condottiere* and an experienced soldier, marched into Ferrara at the head of several thousand troops while his Venetian allies landed on the riverbank. Much more popular than his nephew Niccolò, Ercole was immediately proclaimed Duke by the Ferrarese, who showed genuine enthusiasm, everyone crying '*Viva il Diamante!*'

The bloodshed was far from over, however. An attempt to poison Niccolò in his refuge at Mantua failed, as did numerous *Veleschi* plots – the conspirators were hanged or beheaded in front of the Castello. In 1476 a coup by Niccolò and 600 *Veleschi* failed disastrously. Corpses filled the streets in heaps or swung from the Castello's battlements. Caught as he fled, Niccolò was beheaded in a dungeon the night after his capture and then, his head sewn back on his trunk, buried by torchlight among his ancestors in the family vault at the church of San Francesco. Reprisals against the *Veleschi* went on for weeks, resulting in many executions.

Long before Niccolò's death, in *Canzone de ruina mundi*, a poem that reflects his horror, Girolamo referred to a 'bloody saturnalia of Ferrara'. The lines 'Happy is he who lives by rapine/And who feeds on another's blood' can only refer to Duke Ercole who, ironically, would one day be his ally. The *canzone* was about more than the Duke's coup, however, even if Girolamo warns his readers to 'Flee from palaces and halls'.[8]

The poem, written in 1472 when Girolamo was still only twenty, attacks what is wrong with the world, with Italy and with the Church. 'Here they admire God's enemies,' Girolamo laments. 'The

sceptre has fallen into the hands of a pirate – down goes St Peter.'
He continues, 'The earth is burdened with such a weight of vice that
it cannot stand upright – down goes its leader, Rome, who will never
regain her former eminence.' Far from being the work of a callow
young man revealing 'the dreariness of his thoughts', as his
nineteenth-century biographer Villari believed, the *canzone* shows
that he was remarkably mature.[9]

Some of his dismay at the condition of the Church was prompted
by the new pope, Sixtus IV, a Franciscan of humble origin from
Liguria, whose extravagance had been on a colossal scale since his
election in 1471. His papal tiara cost one-third of his first year's
income as pontiff, and he was also spending huge sums on building
the Sistine Chapel. In addition, six of his nephews were created
cardinals and others given vast estates – according to rumour,
several had begun their careers shipping onions by felucca along the
Ligurian coast. Piero Riario, elevated to Patriarch of Constantinople
and Archbishop of Florence at the age of twenty-six, died from
debauchery within two years. On the other hand, another nephew,
Cardinal Giuliano della Rovere – who gave up life on board a
felucca to become a friar when his uncle became General of the
Franciscans – was outstandingly able; yet he, too, was insatiably
avaricious and did not hesitate to keep mistresses.

In 1473 or 1474 Girolamo wrote another *canzone*, *De ruina
ecclesiae*, this time entirely about the Church. He describes meeting
Mother Church in the form of a beautiful, wounded virgin in tears,
who has fled from Rome and hidden in a miserable cave where she
can only weep, after being driven out of the city by 'a false, proud
harlot, Babylon'. But when he asks her what he can do to help, she
merely tells him, 'Weep and stay silent'.[10]

While men who became monks or friars normally took their vows
at a young age, Girolamo was in his twenties before he entered
religion. On May Day 1474, still intent on a career in medicine, he
went for relaxation to Faenza. In the market place he heard organ
music coming from the church of Sant' Agostino, and, going inside,
found an Augustinian friar about to preach. For his text, the friar
took a passage from the Book of Genesis, 'Go forth out of thy
country, and from thy kindred, and out of thy father's house, and
come into the land that I shall show thee.' Girolamo was haunted by
these words.[11]

It took him a year to make up his mind. On the night of 22 April 1475 his mother Elena heard him singing a melancholy song, accompanying himself on his lute. 'My son, you're playing a farewell,'[12] she said sadly, but he told her not to worry. However, he was shaking, and dared not look her in the eye.

The next day was St George's Day, the feast of Ferrara's patron, celebrated by the Ferraresi with enthusiasm. Via Lunga was turned into a race-course for the city's *palio*, with Barbary horses and their riders careering madly through the streets to win the coveted banner of gold brocade. There were other races, for four types of horses in the morning, men in the early afternoon, donkeys in the late afternoon and women in the evening – the prizes being bales of valuable cloth. There was a boating regatta on the Po, and a cross-bow contest in the Piazza.

While the Savonarola family was busy watching the fun, Girolamo slipped out of the city and walked though the flat, dreary countryside to Bologna, twenty-five miles away. When he arrived, he went to the Dominican priory, where he told the friars he wanted to join them. 'Not since I was born have I known such pain and agony as I feel at leaving my own flesh and blood, finding myself among strangers,' he wrote to his father next day. He gives some of his reasons for wanting to become a friar, but not all. He hopes that he will atone for 'the great miseries of the world and man's iniquities, for lechery, and adultery, robbery, pride, idolatry and vicious blasphemy'. He says that in tears he has often repeated to himself a line from Virgil, 'Alas, flee from this cruel land, flee from these greedy shores'. He adds, 'It was because I could no longer bear the sheer wickedness of the blinded people of Italy, since everywhere I saw virtue despised and vice honoured . . . you must blame me for leaving you so secretly, for almost running away. I should like you to know, however, that I was in such a terrible state that, if I had revealed just how much I was suffering at the prospect of leaving you, I think my heart would have broken and that I could not have gone on with it. . . .' Finally, he asks his father to comfort his mother.[13]

Girolamo had left behind him a bitter, short essay headed *Dispregio del Mondo* ('Contempt for the World'). In this he writes that not just Ferrara but Venice and Rome, together with the whole of Italy and the entire world, have gone wrong. 'Our hearts are vanishing away, rapt in thought', by which he apparently means they are being rotted by humanism. He compares Ferrara with Sodom and Gomorrah, saying that it is a corrupt city whose young men are without ideals, whose old men think of nothing but luxury. He expresses deep revulsion for the Ferraresi as a whole, a people who blaspheme and equate wisdom with robbing widows and orphans and making as much money as possible. He demands sardonically:

Who is considered cleverest of all in Ferrara? The man who has invented some new and more diabolical method of torturing a fellow human being, or the man who has plotted and carried out a crime that is even more despicable?[14]

Niccolò and Elena Savonarola were deeply upset. While genuinely fond of their son, they had no doubt been counting on the desperately needed income he might have brought home had he become a doctor like his grandfather. They sent a letter to the priory at Bologna, complaining that he had deserted them. Girolamo wrote back, this time impatiently: 'Why tears, you blind ones, why so much wailing and why all this grumbling, you people too far from the light?' He told them they ought to be grateful God was making him a doctor who was going to look after souls instead of caring for bodies. 'Leave me alone!' he cried.[15]

THREE

The Hounds of the Lord

A hound of the Lord – German, fifteenth century

I will raise them up a prophet from among their brethren . . .
                                        Deuteronomy 18: 8

Already a handsome city with the oldest university in Europe, Bologna, like Ferrara, was ruled by a *'tiranno'*, Giovanni II Bentivoglio. Although the Bentivoglio's palace, stretching endlessly along what is now Strada San Donato, was demolished in the sixteenth century, were Girolamo to return to the *'citta rossa'* today he would recognise the shopping arcades, the Piazza Maggiore, the two leaning towers, the clock tower of San Giacomo Maggiore and the great, unfinished basilica of San Petronio.

Above all, he would know the great priory of the Dominicans, which had been begun in 1223, two years after St Dominic's death in Bologna. The saint's bones rest here in a shrine known as the Arca di San Domenico, carved by the famous Niccolò Pisano with bas-reliefs of his miracles. As a novice, Girolamo must often have visited the chapel housing the Arca, since each night the friars gathered round it to pray to the 'preacher of the truth'. Another chapel contained Dominic's head, encased in silver. There was also a portrait of Thomas Aquinas by Simone da Bologna, an artist who was supposed to have seen Thomas with his own eyes, even if born after the saint's death.

Entering a religious order has similarities to joining a crack regiment. Not only is there a uniform and a programme of basic training, but each order possesses its heroes, battle honours and traditions. For the Dominicans the ultimate hero was their founder, the Spanish priest Domingo de Guzmán (1170–1221), whose mother dreamed before his birth of a black dog running through the world with a torch in its mouth. Dante includes Dominic in the *Paradiso*, calling him '*l'amoroso drudo*' and the '*agricola*' (the 'loving champion' and the 'farmer').[1] Combining learning with poverty, Dominic and his followers had tried to convert the Albigensians, with the result that in 1216 the 'Dominicans' had been recognised as an order of the Church. Like monks, they took vows of poverty, chastity and obedience, but not the monks' vow to remain within a single monastery, since they needed freedom to preach. The 'friar preachers' were a familiar sight all over Western Europe, wearing white habits and hoods over which they wore a hooded black mantle – hence their nickname, 'black friars'.

Intellectuals who identified with the poor, the Dominicans attracted many of the best minds of the time and took a prominent part in university life. In some ways they anticipated the Jesuits (although, unlike Jesuits, they believed men were saved more by faith than good works). They also ran the Inquisition – hence their nickname, '*domini canes*', 'hounds of the Lord' – but it employed only a few friars. Their most influential member was Thomas Aquinas (1225–74), who wrote in his *Summa Theologica* that the highest form of practical goodness is 'giving to others the fruits of contemplation'.[2]

This was Girolamo's inspiration. Savonarola was in no way Chesterton's false contemplative, 'the mystic who shrinks from the world and lives only in his mind'.[3] For him a true Dominican was someone like the thirteenth-century Jordan of Saxony, remembered for the advice, 'Be kind, be kind, and you'll all be saints', so reassuring that ermines ran up to him in the snow. But at first he was less balanced, going without food for days on end and if he slept at all it was under a sack. Looking like a ghost, he worked in the kitchen and the garden or mended clothes, insisting he did not wish to become an 'Aristotle in the cloister'.[4] However, when his novitiate was over, he was made to resume his studies.

Among the outstanding Dominicans of recent years had been Fra' Antonino Peruzzi, prior of San Marco at Florence, a house that became famous all over Italy. An outstanding canon lawyer whose counsel was sought by other lawyers, he was much admired for his preaching, while in times of famine or plague he led a donkey through the streets of Florence laden with food and medicine; he also founded a society to help the 'honest poor' (those ashamed to

Sant' Antonino. From *Curam illis habe*, Florence, 1493

beg) – an early form of distressed gentlefolk's association. He converted the guild of the Bigallo from heresy hunters into carers for orphans. After becoming archbishop – the painter Fra' Angelico had nominated him to the Pope – he endeared himself to its merchants by a sympathetic understanding of their need to make a living. When he died in 1459, his death was regarded as a calamity.

But 'Sant' Antonino', as he was already known (although not canonised until the next century), was not admired unreservedly. He had obtained permission from the Pope for the brethren of his friary to own property and be paid an allowance, although St Dominic had stipulated that friars must always support themselves by begging. The Bologna priory belonged to the Lombard congregation, which observed the original rule, and this suited Fra' Girolamo's uncompromising temperament.

Every Dominican priory is 'a school for the brethren', but Bologna was outstanding and had recently been made a Studium generale because of the high standard of its teaching. When Girolamo began his new studies he concentrated on theology, the 'queen of the sciences', based on Thomas Aquinas and the Bible. His first tutor was a distinguished theologian, Fra' Pietro da Bergamo, who had a name for bringing out the best in pupils, and Girolamo made such rapid progress that within three years he was appointed an assistant lecturer. As the priory formed part of the University of Bologna, his post was not unlike that of a don.

In 1479 Fra' Girolamo Savonarola was sent to the order's priory at Ferrara, of all places, in order to continue his training and try his hand at preaching. By then he had been ordained as a priest, learning to say Mass in the Dominican way with his arms stiffly outstretched as though nailed to the cross.

Meanwhile, Italy was convulsed by futile little wars and a rash of assassinations. In the year of Niccolò d'Este's abortive coup, Galeazzo Sforza, Duke of Milan, was stabbed to death while hearing Mass. At Florence in 1478 two priests bribed by the Pazzi family knifed Giuliano de' Medici in the cathedral during the elevation of the Host and only just failed to kill his brother Lorenzo. In the ensuing reprisals the Archbishop of Pisa, one of the conspirators, was lynched – hanged from a balcony, during his death agony he sank his teeth into a fellow plotter's naked corpse. There were rumours that Pope Sixtus had been the plot's instigator.

When Fra' Girolamo arrived, the Dominican house at Ferrara was known as the '*casa degli angeli*', from its preoccupation with Thomist angelology – Aquinas's investigation of angels in the *Summa Theologica*, of those timeless, bodiless beings who consist of pure intelligence and act as God's instruments of providence. In 1480 Girolamo became master of novices. During his stay, he avoided his family, although their house was only a few minutes' walk away. Presumably they came to hear his sermons, but his first efforts were disappointing. Years later he still remembered his failure in a rueful letter to his mother in which he quotes Christ's words from the Gospel, '*Nemo propheta in patria sua*' ('No prophet is accepted in his own country').[5] Even so, his superiors sent him out to preach all over northern Italy, at Mantua, Brescia, Genoa, Modena, Piacenza and other cities, where he lodged in the local friaries, while retaining Ferrara as his base.

There are indications that he had developed a commanding presence. An early biography by someone who had known him recounts how, during his Ferrara period, while on a journey to Mantua by boat along the Po, he saw a group of soldiers, who were killing time by gambling. Ignoring the young friar in his black and white habit, they continued so curse and swear; but when Girolamo told them to stop blaspheming unless they wanted to go to hell, instead of throwing him into the river, a dozen of them knelt at his feet to beg forgiveness.[6]

Fifteenth-century lecturers and scholars – from *Lectura super v libros Decretalium*, Basle, 1477

After marrying a Neapolitan princess, Ercole d'Este had allied with Naples, abandoning Ferrara's traditional allies, Rome and Venice. In 1481, needing money to pay for his extravagances, he accepted, in return for a huge salary, an invitation to become Lieutenant-General of the armies of Naples, Milan and Florence, which infuriated both the Serenissima and the papacy. Ercole had forgotten that Ferrara's existence depended on Venetian goodwill, and that the lordship was a fiefdom of the papacy.

The following year the War of Ferrara broke out, at first a petty dispute between Venice and Duke Ercole over salt dues. However, when the Venetians invaded Ferrarese territory in strength, Pope Sixtus tried to secure the duchy for a nephew. Claiming to be Ferrara's feudal overlord, he offered to give Modena and Reggio to the Venetians if they would install Riario in place of Ercole, and sent papal troops to help them. Besides being attacked by land and by water, the city was stricken by famine and plague. After falling dangerously ill, Ercole was saved only by the arrival of a Neapolitan army, and then by Sixtus's decision to change sides when he realised that Venice meant to annex the entire duchy.

Ferrara was lucky to escape being razed to the ground, so great was the Venetians' hatred. The struggle had dragged on for two years, the Pope's intrigues involving all Italy – Genoa and several minor states on the side of the papacy and Venice, with Naples, Florence, Milan, Mantua and Bologna supporting Ferrara. Girolamo had been astonishingly perceptive in writing in the *Canzone de ruina mundi* at the very start of Sixtus's reign, that the papacy had 'fallen into the hands of a pirate'.

The War of Ferrara left the duchy intact save for the loss of Rovigo, but it was years before it regained its prosperity. The war probably completed the ruin of the Savonarola family. Girolamo did not suffer although at the outbreak of war the university closed down and his superiors ordered him to leave the city, with most of the other Dominicans in the '*casa degli angeli*'. In any case, the chapter general at Reggio had chosen Girolamo to be the chief lecturer at the priory of San Marco in Florence.

FOUR

The Duke and the Count

The Estense eagle – Florentine, sixteenth century

He was wont to be conversant with me and reveal to me the secrets of his heart . . .

Savonarola on Count Giovanni
Gianfrancesco Pico, *The Life of Giovanni Pico della Mirandola*

No human beings could have resembled each other less than the *condottiere* Ercole d'Este, Duke of Ferrara, and the scholar Count of Mirandola, who would both play key roles in Savonarola's career, one as a supporter from far off, the other as a close friend. Ercole d'Este was an archetypal Renaissance tyrant. His brother-in-law, Giovanni Pico della Mirandola, was the finest mind of the day.

Born in 1431, a handsome man with aquiline features and thick, prematurely white hair, Ercole walked with a stick after being lamed by a war wound. Dosso Dossi's portrait shows a wry face that gives away little.[1] Yet Ercole knew how to enjoy himself. No less extravagant than his brother Borso, even in middle age he rode through the streets during the carnival with boon companions to throw eggs at pretty girls, besides giving masked balls in the Palazzo del Corte – at one of which an elephant was brought into the Sala Grande. Until the end of his life, he remained fond of banquets and masquerades, of jousting, hunting and fishing, while he had an insatiable love of cards and chess.

'Had their buildings, paintings and sculptures, which we now know only from documents, actually survived and remained in Ferrara to the same extent as in Florence, then the Estensi would probably enjoy the same mythical aura that surrounds the Medici,' writes Thomas Tuohy in his study of the city, *Herculean Ferrara*.[2] But their architectural glories have been devastated by earthquakes, their collections long since dispersed.

While not a truly great man, Duke Ercole I was the most creative of the Estensi, a patron of the arts who transformed Ferrara into one of the finest, best planned capitals in Europe. (Burckhardt claims that he created 'the first modern city'.[3]) Although no scholar, he had the comedies of Plautus and Terence performed in the Sala Grande besides building the earliest purpose-built theatre in Italy. He showed rare tolerance for his time by inviting a group of Jewish refugees from Spain to come and join the small Hebrew community at Ferrara, where, unusually, there was no ghetto.

A ruler of Shakespearean complexity and in his earlier days a professional *condottiere*, the Duke had more crimes on his conscience than the murder of his brother. Abroad a ruthless opportunist, at home he employed corrupt ministers who taxed the Ferraresi to the bone. Often he seemed to think only of pleasure, while he was obsessed by astrology and necromancy.

Yet at the same time Ercole was sincerely religious. He heard a sung Mass and Vespers every day, regularly attending sermons and theological debates; if going on a fishing expedition, he heard three Low Masses instead before setting out. He had Passion plays staged in the main piazza during Lent, while his confessors were Dominicans of the strict sort. He built or rebuilt over a dozen churches and monasteries, paid for the refurbishing of many others, and gave lavishly to every religious house in Ferrara, especially to convents – as he valued the prayers of nuns above all others.

The Duke was spectacularly charitable. From the very start of his reign he went through the streets of Ferrara, accompanied by drummers and trumpeters, to knock at doors and ask householders to give him food for the poor. On one occasion, he did so in the midst of a snow storm. Every morning he gave food and money to twelve beggars brought in from the street by his chaplain, while he provided the city hospitals with beds. Each Maundy Thursday he held a banquet for 150 poor at the Palazzo del Corte, with fifteen tables placed in the Sala Grande. Thirteen of the guests sat at the main one in a re-enactment of the Last Supper, presided over by a poverty-stricken priest who symbolised Christ. Bare-headed, Ercole and his sons served them with food and wine, washed their feet and then gave them new clothes.

He was also a keen patron of religious music, keeping a famous choir to sing in the chapel of the Palazzo del Corte and commissioning a superb Mass from Josquin des Prez – set around the vowels of 'Hercules Dux Ferrariae'. He himself wrote a motet, *La Corona della Madonna*.

On the death of the duchess in October 1493 it was rumoured that he had poisoned her after learning that her father King Ferrante had told her to poison him. In fact, he mourned deeply for the saintly 'Madama Leonora', her death making him more devout than ever.

A youthful prodigy born in 1463, Giovanni Pico was a younger son of Giovanni Francesco, Prince of Mirandola (a minuscule state about thirty miles west of Ferrara) and of a daughter of the Ferrarese poet Boiardo.[4] The family was rich and indisputably aristocratic – although one may doubt its claim to direct descent from the Emperor Constantine – and connected with the Este by marriage, Giovanni's brother Galeotto having married Duke Ercole's sister, Bianca Maria. Since 1311 their huge palace-fortress had dominated Mirandola, a small city on the road between Modena and Mantua. *Condottieri* for generations, the Pico had acquired a name for savagery and greed.

Giovanni did not take after his kindred. Regarded from his youth as the most brilliant intellect in Italy, he was strikingly handsome, a tall, well-built young man with fine features, large grey eyes and thick yellow hair, whom contemporaries called the 'phoenix' – in Renaissance belief, a creature of dazzling beauty. The Tuscan poet Angelo Poliziano, who often met Pico, said that he possessed every conceivable gift of mind and body: 'there was something almost godlike in his appearance'.

Besides a complete command of Latin and Greek, of Classical literature and philosophy, Pico was fluent in Hebrew, Chaldean and Arabic, which only a handful of European scholars could read. He claimed to be familiar with twenty-three languages, if in some cases he knew barely more than their alphabet. A passion for theosophy and mysticism, and for the cabbala, led him along some very strange paths indeed. He visited every university in Italy and France, looking for books to increase his knowledge – he once said he had spent 7,000 gold coins on amassing his library.

There was a less admirable side to this paragon, however. He had an affair with the wife of a grocer from Arezzo, and when the grocer died, his family forced his wife, Margherita, to marry, against her will, a local tax official, a poor relation of the Medici. In May 1486 Pico rode with twenty armed men to Arezzo where his mistress was waiting at the city gate and then galloped off with her, pursued by the city guard. Fifteen men were killed during the ensuing scuffle. Although Pico, Margherita and his secretary escaped they were arrested in Marciano and taken back to Arezzo. Lorenzo de' Medici intervened, declaring it was impossible for any woman to be unfaithful to a Medici, that Margherita must return to her husband and Pico be set free – everything had been the secretary's fault. No doubt, Lorenzo was influenced by an elegant *Apologus* written by Marsilio Ficino, who compared the incident to the rape of a nymph by some hero of antiquity.

Later in the same year, apparently unshaken by his adventure at Arezzo and the loss of his mistress, Pico staged a 'philosophical tournament' at Rome. He published 900 theses in every area of philosophy and theology, which he offered to debate publicly with all comers – he even offered to pay their travelling expenses. As a manifesto for his tournament, he wrote his famous oration on the dignity of man, *De Hominis Dignitate*, in which he claims a central place for man in the universe, arguing that unlike other earthly creatures man has no nature to determine his behaviour – instead, he has complete freedom of choice, enabling him to do everything and be everything, which is why he is the image of God. (This was Savonarola's view, also.)

In the oration Pico dwelt on what he saw as the basic unity behind every expression of the human mind, stressing the agreement between the Pythagorean notion of the essential harmony of all human thought and the Christian concept of redemption by the *logos*. He rejected any ultimate antithesis between Plato and Aristotle, while he insisted that the Bible and nature were books by God – who for him was poet as well as creator.

He went too far in one of the theses, in suggesting that no science yields better proof of the divinity of Christ than *magia* (knowledge of the secrets of the heavenly bodies) and the cabbala. Yet what upset most people was his attack on astrologers. Almost the first scholar to do so systematically, he argued that their methods derived from the pagan diviners of antiquity, that Mars and Jupiter were credited with astral influences because such influences had been attributed to them as gods on Mount Olympus – an examination of the effects of radiation would show that neither planet could possibly shape the lives of men and women.

In March 1487 a papal commission condemned seven of Pico's theses (although not *De Hominis Dignitate*) but tried to spare the author, describing him as 'this amazingly learned man'. Pico hastily submitted, publishing an *Apologia* in May. His new book only made matters worse, infuriating the Pope, by that time Innocent VIII. What particularly angered Innocent was Pico's contempt for astrology. In August he condemned all 900 theses, threatening to excommunicate the author unless he retracted everything he had written during his entire career.

Pico refused, fleeing to France, but at the nuncio's request was arrested by the French authorities in January 1488 on a charge of heresy. Confined in the castle of Vincennes, he faced an investigation by the Sorbonne that might end in imprisonment for life or being burned at the stake. He was fortunate to be set free in March and expelled from French territory after the Duke of Milan's intervention. Lorenzo de' Medici then persuaded Pope Innocent to put the case on hold. Under the circumstances, Pico was understandably reluctant to return to Rome.

Luckily he had dedicated the *Apologia* to Lorenzo, who felt deeply flattered. 'He took a most extraordinary fancy to any man who was pre-eminent in his branch of art [or learning],' Machiavelli says of Lorenzo. 'And this explains why Count Giovanni Pico della Mirandola, a man gifted by God, finally said farewell to the many other countries of Europe that he knew so well and, charmed by Lorenzo's generosity, preferred to come and live in Florence.'[5] When he got there, Pico stopped womanising and led an austere life

A theological debate in Duke Ercole's presence led by Savonarola's friend, Vincenzo Bandelli. From *Disputatio solemnis de conceptione B. Virginis*, Barcelona, 1502

devoted to scholarship. He received a warm welcome, not just from Lorenzo but from Poliziano and Marsilio Ficino.

Fra' Girolamo may first have met the 'Phoenix of Genius' at Ferrara in 1480, when Pico, still only sixteen years old, was taking part in a celebrated theological debate. He certainly encountered him in April 1482 at Reggio, where the Dominicans of Lombardy had assembled for their chapter general and where Pico had gone to hear their theologians debate. He is known to have been impressed when Girolamo launched a passionate attack on the Church's decadence and corruption. The link between the two dates from this meeting at Reggio. It says a lot for the solitary, unknown friar that at such an obscure stage of his career he should make friends with a man whom everybody wanted to know. As will be seen, it was a friendship which, indirectly, would change the entire course of Savonarola's life.

FIVE

Florence

Florence – *Supplementum chronicarum*, 1486

Rome's most beautiful and celebrated daughter, Florence
Dante, *Il Convivio*

May 1482 found Girolamo trudging along the road from Ferrara. Leaving the flat plain, he took the road over the Apennines, from where he caught his first glimpse of Florence. In those days her walls were six miles in circumference, buttressed by sixty square towers and eleven gates with barbicans. Entering, he found unusually wide thoroughfares paved with stone with gutters on each side that kept the city free of mud. The broadest of the four bridges, all supported by massive piers, was the Ponte Vecchio, which had houses and shops on it, including those of goldsmiths and money-changers, as also had the Rubaconte Bridge (or Ponte alle

Grazie). But there was only a hospice on the Ponte Santa Trinità and no buildings at all on the narrow Ponte alla Caraja.

Four of the city's *campanili* were especially impressive, such as the battlemented black tower of the Palazzo della Signoria, which was 330 feet high and housed the mighty bell known as La Vacca – when it rang, people said, '*la vacca muglia*', 'the cow is lowing'. Almost as tall was the Podestà, the bell-tower of the police headquarters. The bell-tower of the church of La Badia was more elegant, while the most graceful was that built by Giotto in the preceding century for the cathedral of Santa Maria del Fiore.

The Duomo, covered with pale grey, green and rose marble, was the building of which the Florentines were proudest, and what they admired most about it was Brunelleschi's great dome, an octagonal cupola resting on a drum. Completed in 1436, this was the first such dome in Europe, an extraordinary feat of architecture for the fifteenth century. In 1469 the dome had been surmounted by a ball and cross. There were 180 other churches. Many belonged to one of more than a hundred religious houses, including another Dominican priory besides San Marco, Santa Maria Novella, whose friars followed the relaxed observance – their basilica was among the finest. The Franciscans, too, possessed a magnificent church, dedicated to Santa Croce.

The later fifteenth century was a busy period for building palaces, and among them was Palazzo Rucellai at the corner of Via della Vigna Nuova and Via del Palchetti, near Santa Maria Novella. The Rucellai, whose fortune came from dye-making, were among Florence's richest merchant families and, as will be seen, one of their members would be a devoted follower of Fra' Girolamo. The beautiful, shady Oricellari gardens around it were a favourite meeting place in hot weather. Yet palaces like this, with their massive stone walls and small, barred windows, gave certain streets a gloomy, oppressive air. There were slums as dreadful as in any other city since much of the wealth derived from sweated labour. During high summer the sun created an intolerable heat, while primitive drainage made the city stink. In winter, it was sometimes so cold that the Arno froze from bank to bank.

In 1472 a Milanese, Benedetto Dei, estimated the population of Florence at 70,000, but the real figure was nearer 90,000 or even higher. In contrast, London's population was 50,000 at about this time. The Florentines' wealth came from silks and wools, and from banking; Dei noted that there were thirty-three banks. The Florentine gold florin, often called a ducat, was the most respected currency in Europe. The city was not governed by the nobility in the feudal sense of the term, but by a rich commercial oligarchy, whose members' coats of arms were prominently displayed over their palace doors. If they did not openly rule the city, they comprised the mere three or four thousand citizens who were eligible for election to public office. Banking and commerce made them unusually cosmopolitan, many having travelled abroad or lived in other countries, especially France, where there was a large Florentine colony at Lyons. In 1452 a delegation from Florence visited the French King, to remind him of the close links that had existed between their countries for over two centuries.

The republic's executive body was the Signoria, whose members were elected for only two months, and consisted of the *Gonfaloniere* (or chief magistrate) with eight *Priori* who represented both the guilds and the city's four main districts. The Ten, elected for six months, looked after foreign policy, and the Eight of the Guard, elected for four, administered justice. In addition, there were the sixteen captains of the city's militia, and the twelve *Procuratori*. In practice, a Council of Seventy decided on appointments to all these posts.

Dante had called Florence 'Rome's most beautiful and most celebrated daughter',[1] and by now her citizens thought her even more so. Endowed with an odd, Messianic streak, its citizens were convinced that a wonderful destiny awaited them. An old legend told how after being destroyed by a 'Scourge of God' in the form of Goths she had been refounded by Charlemagne, while a more recent legend claimed that, born again, the Emperor would return to Italy and renew the Church, then conquer Jerusalem and convert the Turks, creating a universal monarchy – and that he was going to give Florence a share in his glory by making her a second Rome. The 'Charlemagne legend' was reinforced by St Bridget's *Revelationes*, first printed in 1455, which promised that, while old Rome and Milan would suffer terrible calamities, a reborn Florence would enjoy unheard of prosperity. A belief in a glorious future was encouraged by the city authorities,[2] and by the time Girolamo arrived, prophets – whether anchorites in hermitages or friars in pulpits – were predicting not only Florence's renewal but the Church's reform. At the same time, her citizens were always ready to experiment with new ideas. While it is nonsense to talk of a clean break between the Renaissance and the Middle Ages, fifteenth-century Florentines recognised that the world had changed after Dante and Petrarch.

'They outdo all other nations in everything at which they try their hand,' Benedetto Varchi, wrote proudly but not without reason, early in the sixteenth century. 'Besides the commerce on which their city is founded, they have a reputation for being most distinguished and gifted men, no less expert in the arts of painting, sculpture and architecture which they practise abroad as well as at home.' Late fifteenth-century Florence contained more geniuses than any other city in Europe. Among artists working there, to mention only the famous, were Botticelli, Filippino Lippi, Antonio Polaiuolo, Verrocchio, Piero di Cosimo Ghirlandaio and the della Robbias. Leonardo da Vinci had only just left, while Michelangelo would soon arrive.

However, the Florentines considered their glory to be their humanist scholars. For this city of hard-faced businessmen had become the most vibrant centre of humanism in all Italy. 'It was they who revived the study of Greek and Latin,' says Varchi, again with some justice. 'It has always astonished me to see how people who since childhood have been used to handling bales of wool and baskets of silk, who spend the entire day and a fair part of the night at looms or spindles, should at the same time develop such high, uplifted intellects.' And there were a substantial number of humanist friars in the city – among the Franciscans at Santa Croce, the Augustinians at Santo Spirito and the Dominicans (of the relaxed observance) at Santa Maria Novella.

The Florentines believed they had rediscovered Classical civilisation and were about to rescue the world from barbarism. A Platonic academy had been established under the influence of the late Gemistus Plethon, a Greek who detested Aristotle and taught what was virtually paganism – referring to God as Zeus. Humanist scholars such as Plethon were idolised in Florence. During the 1480s the best known humanist in the city was Marsilio Ficino, famous for translating Plato into Latin. He venerated Plato as a saint, burning a votive lamp before his bust and celebrating the supposed anniversary of his birth as a feast day of the Church, while in his sermons at San Lorenzo (where he was a canon) he addressed the congregation as 'Dear brethren in Plato'. He was deeply hurt when the Pope rejected a request to canonise his idol.

Ficino's very peculiar form of Platonism had been influenced by the neo-Platonism of Plotinus, and by Pythagoreanism, Zoroastrianism and the cabbala, while he published a translation of the *Pimander* of Hermes Trismegistus, the mythical wand-bearing seer from ancient Alexandria, whose supposed works were so popular with alchemists and magicians. Ficino preached a *pia philosophia*, a 'universal religion' which tried to reconcile the Christian revelation with paganism, claiming that Plato, the Sybils and Virgil had prophesied Christ's coming, and that the gods of Mount Olympus had in their own way borne witness to him. In Ficino's opinion, Plato had possessed a purer spiritual vision than St Paul, while Venus (as goddess of love) should be honoured no less than the Virgin Mary.

These sorts of beliefs were not confined to Florence. At Rome curia officials spoke of Diana when they meant the Madonna, or referred to God the Father as *'Jupiter Optimus Maximus'*, echoing the bulls of the pagan emperors – and giving substance to the jibe (in the seventeenth century) that the papacy was 'none other than the ghost of the deceased Roman Empire, sitting crowned upon the grave thereof'.[3]

In addition, Ficino was an enthusiastic astrologer, who like most humanists had an unquestioning belief in astrological prediction and wore amulets and charms to guard him against adverse planetary influences, relying on the protection of a topaz, a lion's claw or a toad-stone. He dabbled in the magic arts, translating into Latin the *Corpus Hermeticum*, that magician's bible attributed (wrongly) to Hermes Trismegistus. In the 1490s this nearly caused his ruin when enemies denounced him to the Pope as a wizard.

His conviction that a fundamental harmony existed between the beliefs of pagan antiquity and Christianity was widespread among intellectuals, resulting in a strange, half-hearted religion. The wistful, underlying melancholy that accompanied it can be sensed in some of the earlier canvases of Botticelli, when he, too, was a Platonist. Yet it also induced a new confidence in the abilities of mankind, which was evident in every field of art and literature.

There were some fine poets, notably Angelo Poliziano, who wrote in Greek and Latin besides Italian and who, like Ficino, was a cult figure when Savonarola arrived. His lyrics in his own language have stood the test of time and are exquisite, as in *La Giostra* (Stanzas for the Joust) or in his drama, the *Orfeo*. Luigi Pulci, popularly known as Gigi, was the author of a burlesque epic, the *Morgante Maggiore*. In certain moods these two enthusiastic humanists were neo-pagans, especially Pulci, who dabbled in magic, questioned the teaching of the Church and doubted the soul's immortality; significantly, he was refused Christian burial. Yet in some ways they were totally medieval. In 1483 Poliziano, no lover of the female sex, gave a lecture on women, whom he believed had the power of changing into snakes, physically as well as mentally. Poliziano, who had been made a canon of the cathedral, typified the city's unsatisfactory clergy. Pleasure loving, semi-pagan and homosexual, he was the sort most disliked by Savonarola.

Florence was also the pleasure city of Italy, a place of luxury and enjoyment, with many cheerful taverns, such as the Bertucce (the Monkeys) or La Lumaca (the Snail), just off the Mercato Vecchio – 'I place all my trust in good wine, and think that he who believes in it will be saved', wrote Pulci in the *Morgante*,[4] but most Florentines despised drunkenness. The preferred wines were white, Trebbiano or Vernacchia. On the whole, food was fairly simple, based around bread and pasta, although the rich had their game in season, and in particular, hares, quails and ortolans.

Florentine women were famous for their low-cut gowns of damask or brocade with long trains, for spectacular jewellery and for painting their faces. Young men spent as much as women on clothes and scent, wearing short doublets and mantles with skin-tight hose. Only when older did they put on the Florentine *lucco*, a long, voluminous silk or velvet tunic, generally black but sometimes brightly coloured and often trimmed with fur, that reached down to the ankles. Men of all ages never went out of doors without a hat, either the *becchetto* (tied to the doublet by a scarf) or a red cap shaped like a fez.

Communal amusements included racing in the form of the *palio* – similar to the *palio* still to be seen at Siena – on a course that ran through the city from the Porto al Prato gate on one side to the Porto Santa Croce on the other. There was also a water *palio* on the Arno. Jousting was another popular spectator sport, drawing huge crowds, while fights were staged in the public squares between lions and stags or wild boars and dogs. There was even a primitive form of football, the *calcio*. The great time for pleasure was carnival, the days before Lent, with colourful processions. Some of the floats, such as those of Leda and the Swan or of Bacchus and Ariadne, were pornographic, accompanied by masked satyrs, nymphs and bacchantes who sang obscene choruses. A particularly unpleasant carnival custom was the savage stone-throwing between rival gangs of boys, which often resulted in serious wounds or death.

All the vices were much in evidence at Florence. On every street corner men gambled with dice for sums of money that were large

Florence at the end of the fifteenth century. From H. Delaborde, *L'expédition de Charles VIII en Italie*, Paris, 1888

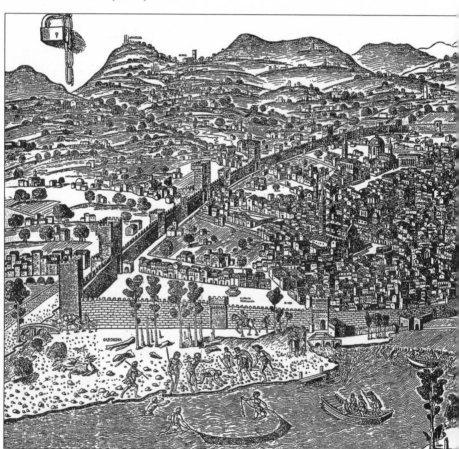

enough to ruin them. The extensive red-light quarter near the Mercato Vecchio included lanes like the Chiasso de' Buoi ('Alley of the Bulls') that overflowed with yellow-veiled prostitutes (whom Savonarola called 'pieces of meat with eyes', meaning they had been dehumanised by their trade) while the biggest brothel, the Frascato, contained over fifty rooms to entertain their customers. The Frascato was not without competitors; and there was a big scandal in 1490 when some nunneries were discovered to be little better than whore-houses.

Sodomy was so rife that the city's authorities thought it was reducing the birthrate. In 1403 an office called the Onestà had been set up to counter (in the words of its charter) 'the filth of that abominable, unnatural, evil and shocking crime'.[5] Still active in Savonarola's time, the Onestà promoted female prostitution in order

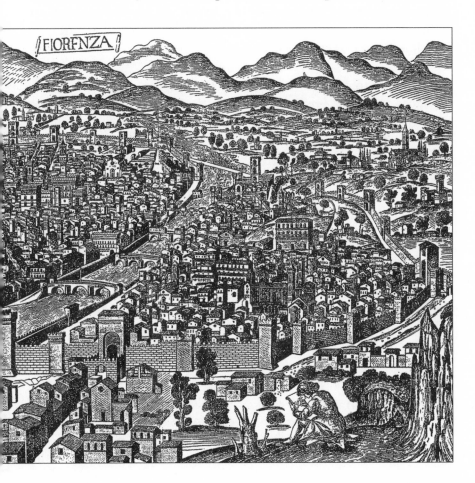

to provide a therapeutic alternative, encouraging girls from abroad to come and work in the brothels. However, we know from the records that the whores began to cater for sodomites, wearing short hair and dressing in men's clothing, and in 1464 the Onestà erected a pillory to shame women who 'lent their bodies to depraved and unnatural usage'.[6] There were also male prostitutes, pursued by an 'Office of the Night'.[7] What upset Girolamo most was the prostitution of young boys.

Villari describes life in Florence at this time as 'a continuous scene of revelry and dissipation',[8] arguing that the regime encouraged pleasure-seeking to stop people asking awkward questions about the way they were governed. As a modern historian puts it, 'The tyranny of the Medici had led not only to the political but also to the moral enslavement of the Florentines.'[9]

Girolamo's new home was the priory of San Marco, in the heart of the city. In his early days the new lecturer is described as sitting in the cloister and discussing a problem of theology 'under a damask rose tree'.[10]

Compared to those at Bologna and Ferrara, the church was small. As in other friaries, brethren no longer slept in dormitories but were housed in a gallery of tiny, whitewashed cells on the upper floor, each with a little window, barred but unglazed, that looked on to the cloister, a wooden shutter keeping out the rain. The prior's apartment consisted of three rooms of this sort, although Girolamo had to be content with a single, minute cell.

Formerly a decayed Benedictine monastery, the priory had been rebuilt in 1437–43 by the famous Michelozzo Michelozzi and paid for by Cosimo de' Medici to provide a Florentine house for strict Dominicans of the Lombard congregation. Cosimo had given the friars vestments and chalices, with a collection of extremely valuable books for which he built a library. Close links still existed between the priory and the founder's family.

Inside, the walls were covered with frescoes. 'Never, perhaps, were the attractions of the monastic life set out more persuasively in paint,'[11] comments the art historian Sir Michael Levey. Many were the work of a mystic, Giovanni da Fiesole, known to history as Fra' Angelico, who had died sixteen years before Savonarola's arrival. He had painted the cloister, refectory and house with crucifixions or scenes from the Life of Christ. There was a fresco inside most of the cells, an episode from the Passion or the Life of the Virgin, and also a Transfiguration and a Resurrection (with the dead bursting forth from caverns, and a demon crushed beneath a door broken down by the risen Lord). Saints were shown in many of them, including Dominic himself and Peter Martyr, and, of course, Thomas Aquinas. 'Fra' Angelico would never use his brushes without praying', the historian Vasari was informed in the sixteenth century by an aged friar. This was Fra' Eustachio, who had joined the community at San Marco when Savonarola was prior. 'Whenever he painted a crucifixion, he did so with tears streaming down his face,'[12] the old friar told Vasari.

The magnificent, many-panelled altarpiece in the priory church was also by Angelico, while there were several choirbooks which he had illuminated with miniatures – one portraying St Dominic meeting St Francis. Indeed, to live here must have been not unlike living inside an illuminated manuscript.

As has been said, the vow of poverty was slightly relaxed, but the community was fervent enough and contained some unusually able men. Among these was the prior, Fra' Vincenzo Bandelli, who would one day be Master General of the Order. He may have met Girolamo at Bologna or Ferrara, while he would certainly have done so during the recent chapter general at Reggio. (Ridolfi thinks it likely that Bandelli was responsible for moving him to Florence.[13])

The new lecturer, whose job was essentially to explain the Bible, proved an immediate success: he was academically impeccable and so inspiring that he brought tears to the eyes of his audience. Only a few months after his arrival he was given the key post of novice master. He became not merely a valued but a popular member of the community, while his views on a stricter observance of the vow of poverty were heard with increasing respect.

Yet Savonarola grew uncomfortably aware that outside San Marco life was very unfair. 'You rob your neighbour of all his goods, you aren't interested in fair dealing, you evade the law and oppress other citizens,' Piero de' Medici had said just before his death in 1469, according to Machiavelli. 'I don't believe there is anywhere else in Italy where one finds so many cases of robbery and extortion as in our city. Did your homeland give you birth in order that you might steal from her?'[14] Little had changed since Piero's day.

Girolamo was shocked at finding Florentine intellectuals so pagan, at their questioning the entire Christian revelation by attributing the pagan classics to divine inspiration. 'Some people have made their minds so narrow, strait-jacketing them with the chains of Antiquity, that they refuse to speak except in the way the ancients spoke and won't say anything that hasn't been said already by the ancients,' he commented. 'Just what sort of reasoning is this, what new kind of logic? If the ancients didn't say something, aren't we allowed to say it ourselves? If a good deed wasn't done by the ancients, are we really supposed not to do it?'[15]

Savonarola was equipped for arguing with humanists, having written a *Compendium totius philosophiae* ('Compendium of all Philosophy'). Published after his death, this work shows that his own position, derived from Aquinas, was basically Aristotelian. He had also produced a compendium, now lost, which summarised the works of Plato as well as Aristotle. But if he wanted to combat neo-paganism from the pulpit, he must preach effectively.

The most popular preacher in Florence was an Augustinian friar, Fra' Mariano da Genazzano, whose sermons at the church of Santo Spirito were tailored to flatter humanist taste and were much admired by the fashionable. Although he spoke in Italian, his elegant discourses, modelled on Ficino's Latin orations, were filled with quotations from Classical authors, while he took care to stress that Christianity had much in common with Platonism. In a famous letter written in April 1489, Poliziano extolled Fra' Mariano: 'When he begins to speak, I am all ears to that musical voice, the well chosen words, the grand sentences,'[16] enthused Poliziano. 'Then I notice his clauses, recognize his periods and am thrilled by their perfect harmony and cadence.' Savonarola, on the other hand, hearing Fra' Mariano at Santo Spirito, while conceding that he spoke with elegance and charm, noted disapprovingly how the Augustinian quoted the poets of ancient Greece and Rome rather than the Bible. He observed that Fra' Mariano should confine himself to the word of God.

At first, he found it difficult to reach his listeners, although an adequate lecturer. After preaching to a convent of nuns, the Murate (still much as he must have known it) and then at small churches, in 1484 he was asked to give the Lenten addresses at Brunelleschi's vast basilica of San Lorenzo. He had not yet found his voice as a preacher and, according to a future biographer Fra' Placido Cinozzi, who was present, his congregation dwindled steadily until by the end of Lent he was speaking to no more than twenty-five people, including children brought by their parents.[17]

Cinozzi tells us Fra' Girolamo was so disheartened that he thought of giving up preaching. Ten years later he himself referred to his shortcomings: 'Everyone who knew me then,' he admits frankly, 'realized I lacked the delivery, enthusiasm and style for preaching.'[18] He adds that in those early days only the simple-minded listened to him. He had not yet developed a voice powerful enough to fill a big church, while his Ferrarese accent – nearer to Venetian than Tuscan, with soft *g* pronounced like *z* – sounded uncouth in a city that prided itself on its own, elegant version of Italian.

Pope Sixtus IV died in August 1484, supposedly of rage at failing to conquer Ferrara. As pontiff Sixtus had been greedy and ruthless, bringing war to all Italy in pursuit of his ambitions for his family; according to Machiavelli, he 'had shown himself to be a wolf rather than a shepherd'.[19] A conclave met at Rome to elect a successor, contemporaries believing that no pontiff could be worse, a belief that they would find mistaken. There was vicious squabbling, until Rodrigo Borgia bought enough votes for his candidate, the colour-less Cardinal Cibo – who according to a Florentine observer looked like a rabbit.

Apart from attacking Naples at the start of his pontificate, Innocent VIII was too indolent to involve Italy in another full-scale war. Devoted to the pleasures of the table – especially ortolans – his one claim to fame was to be the first pontiff who publicly acknowledged his bastards – all seven of them – and he lavished papal funds on his eldest son. He paid no attention to law and order, to such an extent that every morning dead bodies were found lying naked in the streets of Rome and the cardinals had to hire armed guards to defend their palaces. He was notoriously avaricious and had few qualms about selling dioceses to would-be bishops, and allowed justice to be bought in the Roman courts. He also set up a form of bank in the Eternal City for the convenience of sinners, who found they were able to buy a pardon for every imaginable type of sin, if very expensively and according to a fixed tariff. His chamberlain commented piously: 'The Lord desires not the death of a sinner but his purse.' And all Italy was aware of how much gold had changed hands in order to procure the pontiff's election.

Fra' Girolamo was so discouraged that he began writing verse again, begging God to

> *socurri a la Romana*
> *tua santa chiesa, che 'l demonio attera.*

('Rescue your holy Roman church that the Fiend is pulling down.')

In another poem, he adopts, for the first time, a note of menacing prophecy:

> *Vidi l'Italia in guerra*
> *e la carestia grande:*
> *la pestia idio disserra*
> *e suo iudicio espande:*
> *queste son le vivande*
> *de la tua vita . . .*

('I have seen Italy at war and a great famine: He has unleashed plague and has sent down a judgement [on us]: these are the wages for your way of life.')

Interestingly, he blames the humanists for the mess that the Church and Italy are in, with what sounds like a reference to Ficino and Fra' Mariano and their friends:

> *Astrologi e profeti,*
> *omini dotti e santi,*
> *predicator discreti,*
> *t'han preditti i tuo' pianti:*
> *tu cerchi suoni e canti,*
> *perche sei stolta:*
> *nei vizi involta,*
> *in tù virtu non è . . .*

('Astrologers and prophets, all you learned and holy men, you tactful preachers, your weeping is foretold: in your stupidity you look [only] to music and song: given up to vice, there is no health in you.')[20]

The whole of this strange poem seems to demonstrate that its author is obsessed with impending doom. He was only too ready for a revelation of some sort – and the revelation came.

At the end of his life, when on the rack, Girolamo told his torturers how he and a friend, Tommaso Strada, had gone to the convent of San Giorgio in Florence where Fra' Tommaso's sister was a nun: probably this was at some time towards the end of 1484, when Pope Innocent's shortcomings were beginning to be appreciated. While waiting in the churchyard outside and thinking about how he should write a new sermon, there suddenly entered his mind 'many reasons, at least seven of them, which showed me that a scourge of the Church must be at hand'.[21] He was unable to get the idea out of his head. He only wished he had a voice sufficiently powerful to be heard across the entire world so that he could warn everybody in time.

SIX

'Brescia is going to be drowned in blood'

The Triumph of Death – *Predica dell' arte del bene morire*, 1496

And the Lord said unto me, Behold, I have put my words in thy mouth.

The Book of the Prophet Jeremiah 1: 9

In 1485 Savonarola was sent by his prior to give the Lenten addresses at San Gimignano, up in the hills between Florence and Siena. The churches here are less daunting than San Lorenzo, and his sermons must have been a success because he was invited to preach again for the following Lent.

During his stay, he received a letter from his mother, informing him that his father had died. His reply, which has not survived but is known from another letter, tells Elena to stop thinking of him as her son since his family is the Dominican Order and his father is Jesus Christ. Other letters to her are not so harsh, such as one he sent in December 1485. She had written saying she was penniless, because of the death of her brother Borso who had been supporting her, and could not give her daughters dowries. Girolamo advises her not to worry about being poor and to keep her mind fixed on the next world by copying 'that holy Jewish woman, who watched her seven sons being tortured and killed without shedding a tear; on the contrary, she encouraged them to die'.[1] With less otherworldliness, he asks her to forgive him for having nothing more than prayers to help his poverty-stricken family, because he is a friar without any money, but at least he insists that he remains devoted to them.

Girolamo's Lenten sermons at San Gimignano in 1486 have survived, in scribbled Latin drafts, discovered by Roberto Ridolfi in 1935. They mark the beginning of his role as prophet, following the revelation in the churchyard of San Giorgio. The theme of his San Gimignano sermons was that the Church would shortly be punished and then completely renewed: 'We all have to accept that some sort of scourge – antichrist, a war, a plague or a famine – is about to come and probably at any moment.' He denied that he was in any way a prophet, however: 'I am not warning you of this because I'm a prophet, but simply because I can tell from the Bible that a scourge of the Church is imminent.'[2]

Fra' Girolamo gave his congregation eight reasons why this was so. First, the intolerable amount of crime. Second, the Church's evil 'shepherds'. Third, God sending prophets to warn mankind – although Girolamo did not number himself among them. Fourth, the power of good being a spent force among all classes. Fifth, the decline of religious faith in countless human hearts. Sixth, the Church's corruption. Seventh, contempt for the saints. Eighth, people ceasing to go to church. He went into detail about crime, singling out murders, lust – especially sodomy and the prostitution of boys[3] – idol-worship and spells used by astrologers. He also mentioned simony, which in 1486 was an obvious reference to the bribery during the recent papal election.

The San Gimignano sermons anticipate those he delivered in his prime, and contain the first hint of prophecy. Yet we have no record of the reaction to them, nor did they make any stir in Florence – if

Florence ever heard of them. They in no way upset his superiors, since in 1487 he was appointed to the important post of Master of Studies at San Domenico at Bologna. In 1488 he was sent back to the priory at Ferrara, where he stayed for two years, re-establishing regular contact with his mother. From there he visited cities all over northern Italy, including Mantua, Modena, Brescia, Piacenza and Genoa, which entailed exhausting journeys. It appears that he did plenty of preaching, possibly in the apocalyptic manner that he had used at San Gimignano.

Savonarola undoubtedly preached several sermons at Brescia during Advent in 1489. According to the Pseudo-Burlamacchi, on St Andrew's Day in November he delivered a dramatic sermon on the Apocalypse, during which he pictured the three and twenty ancients, sitting clothed in white garments around the throne of God, arising from their seats to announce that a great scourge is coming upon Italy and especially upon Brescia, where 'in the streets fathers shall see their children slaughtered together with other torments'.[4] Years later, when the French had massacred six thousand men, women and children in the city's streets, the Brescians are said to have recalled the friar's warning – although it has to be admitted that none of their chroniclers had mentioned his sermon at the time.

Writing to his mother from Pavia at the end of January 1490, he blames his long silence on the infrequent postal service, an apology which implies that by now he had acquired the habit of writing regularly to Elena. He says that he has to travel to many cities, 'preaching, exhorting, hearing confessions, reading [the Gospel] and counselling': obviously his mother had been grumbling at his leaving Ferrara, which indicates that in recent months she had seen quite a lot of him. In his letter he argues that a man of religion can seldom achieve anything in his own land, which is why the Scriptures command us to 'go forth out of thy country' (the phrase that had first inspired him to become a Dominican). He adds that wherever he goes outside his own country, when he leaves the place 'men and women shed tears and place great value on what I have been saying to them', and that he tells her this not as a boast but to show why he has to be away from Ferrara so often. It also indicates that he was becoming an effective preacher.[5]

For the past two years Savonarola had been convinced he would return to Florence, to fulfil a great mission. This, claims the Pseudo-

Burlamacchi, was because of a revelation he experienced at Brescia – described as 'strange portents'. The catalyst turned out to be his friend Pico.[6] Pico arrived in Florence in the summer of 1488. 'The Count of Mirandola has come and settled here,' Lorenzo de' Medici wrote in June the following year. 'He leads a most holy life, just like a monk.' He adds that Pico is writing books on theology, reads the priests' breviary daily and keeps the prescribed fasts, besides staying chaste. It was Pico who suggested that his host should invite Savonarola to Florence. Girolamo's outspoken criticisms of Rome and the Pope may have been a factor, but in any case Pico genuinely liked and admired the man. Lorenzo could see no objection. 'So that I can convince you that I really want to be of use to you,'[7] he told Pico when he made his request, 'your lordship shall write the letter just as you please, then my chancellor will copy it out and seal it with your seal.' The letter was sent to the Master General of the Dominicans, and as soon as the Vicar and the chapter general of the Lombard congregation had formally agreed to his transfer, probably in May 1490, Girolamo set out for Florence.

The Pseudo-Burlamacchi has a curious story about his journey, no doubt heard from Fra' Girolamo himself.[8] Travelling on foot, he had found the hot, dusty roads and beating sun exceptionally tiring. Increasingly exhausted as he trudged up into the mountains, when he reached Pianoro – still only in the foothills – he collapsed at the roadside, feeling unable to walk a step further. A stranger also travelling on foot along the same road made him get up and stagger on until they reached a monastery, where he was forced to swallow some food. After he had recovered, the stranger walked with him over the Apennines to Florence, to the San Gallo gate. Saying goodbye, he added, 'Don't forget what God has sent you to do in Florence.' Savonarola never saw the stranger again and regretted not having asked his name. He seems to have suspected that he was an angel, of the sort who helped Tobias.

SEVEN

Lorenzo de' Medici

Lorenzo de' Medici – medal of 1478

The Lord sent me to prophesy against this house and against this city all the words that ye have heard.
The Book of the Prophet Jeremiah 26: 12

For three generations the Medici, a rich banking family, had been tyrants of Florence in all but name, through a discreet use of patronage and bribery. Since 1469 the republic had been ruled by Lorenzo de' Medici, who bore no title, held no office and did not even rank as a nobleman – he once informed a foreign embassy that he was just a simple citizen. In practice, he controlled every aspect of politics and administration.

A tall, ungainly man with a sallow, lined face, a nose that had been broken and knocked sideways, and a jutting jaw, Lorenzo's ugly looks were redeemed by a charm and fascination few could resist. He enjoyed unfailing high spirits, singing everywhere he went in a cracked falsetto voice. Guicciardini, who as a child had lived under his regime, tells us that if you could not avoid being governed by a tyrant, then you could not imagine a better or a pleasanter one.[1]

Lorenzo was the ultimate Renaissance tyrant, in many ways an attractive figure. Not merely a politician and statesman of genius, he was also an aesthete and a patron of the arts, an enchanting poet, a writer of beautiful songs and perfectly phrased letters. 'Prudent', 'eloquent and subtle', 'prompt and bold', are the words applied to him by Machiavelli, who adds, 'he was favoured to an extraordinary degree by fortune and by God, so that all his enterprises of state succeeded and all his enemies met with an unhappy end'.[2] His splendid way of life, political shrewdness and sheer good luck were admired by every Italian prince, even by the diabolical Ferrante of Naples, and by other European rulers such as the King of Hungary and the Sultan of Turkey.

Machiavelli was particularly impressed by Lorenzo's foreign policy. For the last five years of his life Florence enjoyed peace thanks to an alliance with Innocent VIII – whom Lorenzo dominated from a distance – and preventing Milan and Naples from fighting each other in a war which might have dragged in all the other Italian states. Machiavelli defines his domestic policy as 'keeping the city prosperous, the people united and the rich respected'.[3] Like the Este at Ferrara, Lorenzo was always busy beautifying an already magnificent Florence, or giving splendid entertainments.

During the festivities of carnival and May Day he paid for pageants that became famous throughout Italy. He organised them himself, distributing costumes and torches to anybody who wanted to take part, in an attempt to turn Florence into what Athens might have been like during the festivities of Dionysus, god of wine. Lorenzo enjoyed the celebrations as much as anyone, roaming the streets in a mask in search of pretty girls. During former carnivals masked men had accosted every good-looking woman they saw by singing her a single, traditional song. Lorenzo not only introduced the custom of wearing fancy dress as well as masks, but composed many songs in place of just one, melodious ballads that occasionally verge on the pornographic, although they tend to be not so much obscene as suggestive – a modern critic says they 'snigger rather than laugh'.[4] Younger Florentines sang these *canti carnescialeschi* (songs of fleshly love) with enthusiasm.

Machiavelli, slightly shocked by the great man's 'puerile amusements', comments that 'beholding his grave side and his frivolous side, you saw two people in him'. He adds with no less distaste that Lorenzo had 'an amazing addiction to amorous intrigue', meaning he was a notorious womaniser.[5]

Yet if Florence was the pleasure city of Italy, it was also Italy's capital of learning, and Lorenzo was the supreme intellectual among Italian tyrants, spending huge sums on books and Classical manuscripts. He was an avid collector of Greek and Roman coins, of antique sculptures, bronzes and gems. Above all, he was a dedicated humanist who never read the Bible for fear the simple language of the Vulgate translation might spoil his elegant Ciceronian Latin. 'He favoured the learned', observes Machiavelli, his preferred companions being men such as Ficino, Pico and Poliziano – whom he rescued from near destitution by making him tutor of his children – and Landini, the translator of Aristotle. He enjoyed giving parties for them in the gardens of his villas outside Florence, or taking them on hawking expeditions of the sort recalled in his enchanting poem, *La Caccia col Falcon*. Someone who could recognise genius as soon as he saw it, he took the young Michelangelo into his household, treating him as a son. As if by instinct, he filled the role of a Maecenas, employing painters like Pollaiuolo and Ghirlandaio. His entourage included what amounted to an academy of music, under the guidance of a celebrated organist, which performed quartets with stringed instruments.

Despite his love of Ciceronian Latin Lorenzo was an admirer of the Italian language in its Tuscan form. His '*poesie volgari*' is exquisite, with a wistful love of life and beauty, as in an often quoted masque song from his *canti carnescialeschi*, when, if he cries, '*Viva Bacco, e viva Amore!*', he laments the flight of youth and the approach of death. The melancholy frequently recurs, as in one of his sonnets:

> *Quanto sia vana ogni speranza nostra,*
> *Quanto fallace ciaschedun disdegno . . .*
> ('How every hope of ours is raised in vain
> How spoiled the plans we laid in vain . . .')[6]

He also wrote religious verse with an appearance of deep feeling – prayers, lauds and a hymn to the Virgin Mary.

Beyond question, Lorenzo de' Medici could be delightful company, yet he was far more of a tyrant than Ercole d'Este, more subtly devious, more ruthless. Often he could be pitiless under a pretence of legality, confiscating his opponents' homes and property by decree or condemning them to death by judicial murder, if sometimes he preferred to arrange for their assassination. When Volterra, a dependency of Florence, rose in rebellion he tricked it into surrender, then let his mercenaries loose on the city, slaughtering the entire population. A group of Florentines caught plotting against him were hanged first by their necks, then by their feet, while over 270 people perished during his reprisals after the Pazzi conspiracy. In 1480, suspecting that a pilgrim who begged for food at the Medicis' villa in the country might be an assassin, by way of interrogation Lorenzo had the soles of the man's feet roasted until the fat ran, after which he was made to walk over coarse salt – dying as a result.

Bored by banking, and although usually a shrewd judge of men, Lorenzo relied on surprisingly incompetent managers to run the Medici bank. When ruinous losses – such as that incurred by Edward IV defaulting on loans made by the London branch during the Wars of the Roses – left him short of money, he stole. He appropriated 50,000 florins from the estate of two young cousins who were his wards besides blatantly plundering the Monte delle Fanciulle, whose function was to provide the penniless girls of Florence with dowries, depriving them of any chance of marriage and driving many into prostitution. He then used the money to buy landed property, which he decided was more secure than banking.

At San Marco Girolamo began to lecture again, this time on logic. The lectures, given in the cloisters under the damask rose tree, were so much appreciated by the community that they asked him to preach in the priory church. Mounting the pulpit, he made a curious announcement: 'I am going to preach for eight years.'[7]

He gave his first sermon, one of a series, on 1 August 1490. By now he had developed a voice that reached everyone in the building. He did not worry about elegance or graceful language, only about sincerity – there were no affectations, no humanist frills, no smart quotations from the Classics. Nobody could have been more different from the smooth-tongued Fra' Mariano at Santo Spirito.

When a friendly critic protested that his bluntness, Ferrarese accent and ungraceful use of his hands invited unfavourable comparison with Genazzano, he agreed: 'All the same, you'll see Fra' Mariano's grace and fluency losing favour, and my simplicity being applauded.'[8]

'I am the hailstorm that's going to smash the heads of those who don't take cover', is how he describes his method.[9] He spoke on the Apocalypse, applying it to the present day, dwelling on three key themes – the need to reform the Church, the punishment of the Church, and the certainty they would happen soon. He made striking use of quotations from the Scriptures. Next day, all Florence was talking about the friar preaching at San Marco. Savonarola continued with sermons like this, preaching on the Apocalypse, for the rest of Advent and until after Christmas. He attacked the vices of the age, the selfish rule of princes, the corruption of priests (especially of those who preached flattering sermons), rebuking the philosophers and poets for paganism and frivolity, warning that terrible punishments were about to fall on them all. The Florentines were fascinated, flocking to the sermons. Even humanists abandoned their lectures and libraries to listen to him.

It is impossible to recapture the thrill of his preaching, yet a Victorian parson, Frederick Myers, made an attempt worth quoting:

> The manner in which an Italian – a Dominican – preaches, I cannot convey to you; so fervid, so forcible, so full of action and of passion; often as if he would pour out his very soul with his speech, and if not attended to would expire on the spot. But this is the kind of sermon with which Savonarola wrought upon the mind of the people at Florence. Day after day, an outpouring of mixed doctrine and emotion, of exhortation and prayer: speech full of force, though not of grace: surging up, as it were, from hot-springs in his heart, and flowing forth from his eyes, his hands, his features, as well as from his lips, rendering him unmindful of all but his subject, and his audience unmindful of all but himself.[10]

His targets were Florentine society in general and Lorenzo in particular. 'You're doing yourself no good, jousting in this way,'[11] Pico warned him, but he took no notice.

Many rich Florentines with a stake in the Medici regime – merchants, higher clergy, office holders – were outraged by the sermons.

Those who applauded were the poorer, especially anyone impoverished for political reasons. The former called him 'the preacher of the no-hopers'. He retorted that it was they who should despair.[12]

Arrangements had been made for Fra' Girolamo to give the Lenten addresses for 1491 in the Duomo itself, the cathedral of Santa Maria del Fiore. Before he started, he was warned by the ever watchful Lorenzo, through agents who refused to reveal who sent them, that he must not be controversial or say anything about the future. 'Are you trying to pretend that no one has sent you?' Savonarola told the men who brought the warning. 'Well, I say somebody has! You can go and tell Lorenzo he ought to start atoning for his sins now, because God has every intention of punishing him and his whole crew.'[13]

Friars at San Marco pleaded with him to be less aggressive. For a short time he wondered if he ought to take their advice, but at the end of April he heard a miraculous voice: 'You fool,' it said. 'Don't you see that it's God's will you should preach like this?' Fra' Girolamo then went into the cathedral pulpit and gave what he himself called 'a frightful sermon' ('*terrificam praedicationem*'). He accused the clergy of being obsessed with money and the ceremonial aspect of religion while ignoring the spirit: 'I warn you, a time is coming when . . . you'll feel the edge of the sword.' The poor were ground down into the dust by unjust taxes while the rich paid nothing because taxes were arranged for their benefit. He condemned their vicious way of life: 'Be careful, rich men, affliction shall come down on you. Your city will no longer be called Florence but a den of thieves, depravity and bloodshed. Then, every one of you is going to be poor . . . I warn you that unheard of times are coming.'[14]

He denounced gamblers as 'Worse than infidels, ministers of the Evil One who celebrate his rites . . . Avaricious, blasphemers, slanderers, calumniators, fault-finders, they are abhorred by God, thieves and murderers who are full of evil.' As for sodomites, they 'declare their sin as did Sodom, they hide it not'. He was no less savage about bankers: 'Every day avarice increases, widening the whirlpool of usury.'[15]

'This sort of preaching did not exactly please Lorenzo,' Guicciardini informs us, 'and it touched him on the raw, because when he had decided to expel Fra' Bernardino da Feltre, a man of saintly reputation, from Florence [a few years earlier] he made himself very unpopular with the people.'[16] Bernardino had attacked the banking system, which bled the poorer classes white by charging them enormous interest for small loans, demanding its replacement by a Monte della Pietà or 'people's bank'. After a Jewish money-lender was attacked and robbed, Bernardino had been thrown out of the city before he could cause any further trouble.

However, Lorenzo may have been afraid of Girolamo, perhaps for some arcane astrological reason – it is quite likely that his friend Ficino had cast the friar's horoscope with daunting results. And no doubt Pico was constantly putting in a good word for him. In addition, so Guicciardini tells us, Lorenzo had 'a certain respect for Fra' Girolamo, whom he considered genuinely holy'.[17]

'Many people thought, and a few still think, that what happened to Fra' Bernardino could easily happen to me,' Savonarola wrote on 10 March to another member of the San Marco community, a close ally. This was Fra' Domenico Buonvicini da Pescia, who was away, preaching in Pisa. Alluding to the possibility of banishment, Girolamo admits, 'I've been in some danger.' However, he says he is not too worried about it and that Christ has been encouraging him through 'the voices of his spirits'.[18] He adds: 'The count continues in the way of the Lord and is often to be seen at my sermons.'

Pico was listening more and more to the Frate. He had developed a passion for Aquinas, whom he had previously criticised – now he called him 'the splendour of our theology' and believed he was closer to the truth than any other philosopher. Already, he had given his property in Mirandola to his nephew Gianfrancesco Pico, since he wanted to live a quiet life, devoted to study. Yet he constantly quoted a saying of Francis of Assisi, 'a man knows only as much as he puts into practice', and we know from Gianfrancesco's biography that for long his secret dream was to preach barefoot through the cities and villages of Italy. He thought of becoming a Dominican but found it hard to take the final step, despite Girolamo's urging. Meanwhile, he lived very simply.[19]

Pico found a new friend, another member of Lorenzo de' Medici's circle, who helped him give food and clothing to the poor. He addressed such affectionate sonnets to him that it has been implausibly suggested that their relationship was homosexual. This was the Florentine humanist and poet Girolamo Benivieni, who had been a pupil of Marsilio Ficino. A nervous, melancholy young man, he had been both terrified and reassured by the sermons of Savonarola to whom he grew devoted.[20] (His brother, Domenico Benivieni, a former professor of logic at Pisa and now a Canon of San Lorenzo, was also an admirer of the Frate and later wrote enthusiastically in praise of his prophetic gifts.)

The next sermon that Fra' Girolamo preached was on Wednesday in Holy Week, in the chapel of the Palazzo della Signoria to members of the Council. His opening words were that he was feeling very uneasy, as if on the stormy waters of Lake Tiberias, and that in the Signoria's presence he would have to be careful about what he said. He then added, somewhat tactlessly, that he felt rather like Christ in the pharisee's house. In the event, he was the reverse of careful. He told his astounded audience:

Everything bad and everything good in this city depends on that one man at the top, who's responsible for every single thing wrong with it, since if he acted as he ought, then the whole city would be purified. But tyrants never change their ways because they are arrogant and live on flattery, and don't want to give back what they've stolen. . . . They leave everything to crooked ministers whose flattery they swallow and only worry about the rich. They expect the poor and the peasants to sweat for them without proper wages and let their ministers take this attitude for granted. They bribe voters, farm out taxes, appoint criminal tax-collectors and debase the coinage, which all helps to make the burden on the poor even more unbearable.[21]

This latest sermon was the most blistering criticism of Lorenzo ever heard in public – all knew whom Fra' Girolamo meant when he spoke of 'tyrants'. But instead of banishing him, Lorenzo asked Mariano da Genazzano to demolish him by superior eloquence. Only too ready to oblige, Fra' Mariano announced that on Ascension Day he would preach in the priory church of San Gallo (built for him by his patron). Hearing Mariano was about to attack him, Savonarola observed, 'I shall wax and he shall wane.'

Fra' Mariano's text was 'It is not for us to know the time nor the hour.' However, carried away by enthusiasm, he lost his temper. After claiming that Savonarola was a false prophet who spread scandal and rebellion among the lower orders, he tried to parody his gestures and began to insult him. He was a worm, a cockroach, a snake, a wolf in sheep's clothing, a clown who did not know his Bible and could not even read his Latin office, shouted Mariano, who then began yelling obscenities from the pulpit. But he only succeeded in shocking the Florentines.[22]

On the following Sunday, Fra' Girolamo preached a sermon in the Duomo on the same text, which he delivered with deliberate mildness. He reminded Fra' Mariano that when only a few days before his outburst at San Gallo the Augustinian had visited him at San Marco, he had complimented him on both his learning and his preaching. 'Who suggested you should attack me? And why did you change your mind?' he enquired, in the gentlest way, neatly implicating Lorenzo.[23] Shortly after, with his reputation in tatters, Mariano da Genazzano left Florence for Rome. Girolamo had made an implacable enemy.

Lorenzo then arranged for a Franciscan, Francesco d'Aragona, to hold forth against Savonarola at Santa Croce, but Fra' Francesco soon found that he was doing well if he drew an audience of ten. Lorenzo nevertheless refrained from banishing Savonarola. He might well have done so in July 1491 when the friars elected him prior of San Marco. His election was peculiarly awkward for the Medici because of the family's links with the priory, as everybody in Florence realised. Not only had the Medici rebuilt it, but they had been its main benefactors ever since. A custom had grown up that each new prior, after his election, paid Lorenzo a courtesy call, since San Marco was only a few hundred yards away from the Palazzo Medici, but Fra' Girolamo refused when the friars reminded him of it, saying, 'Who made me Prior? God or Lorenzo?'[24]

Lorenzo the Magnificent was losing his grip, because of ill health – he suffered from an agonising form of gout that grew worse every day. Leaving Savonarola undisturbed in the priory, he tried to bring him to heel with surprisingly half-hearted stratagems. He went to Mass at San Marco, afterwards walking in the garden, in the hope of meeting and charming him into submission. However, when told of his presence Girolamo stayed in the house, observing, 'He can walk where he likes.' He sent presents that were returned, Girolamo's comment being, 'A good watch dog doesn't stop barking in defence of his master just because somebody throws him a bone.'[25] Next, Lorenzo made his chancellor drop a large quantity of gold coins into the priory alms box, which was the friars' main source of income. But Fra' Girolamo gave them to the Fraternity of San Martino for distribution among the city's poor, observing that silver and copper coins were good enough for friars.

Finally, Lorenzo sent five of the most important men in Florence to San Marco, to remonstrate with Savonarola. The meeting took place in the sacristy. They warned him that his sermons were putting both himself and his friars in danger of expulsion. 'I know very well you've been sent by Lorenzo,' he replied. 'You can tell him to do penance for his sins, because the Lord is no respecter of persons and doesn't spare even princes.' The five repeated their warning that he ran the risk of being banished from Florence. 'Only people like you, with families, are frightened of exile,' was Girolamo's response. 'I'm not frightened, because if I did have to leave, your city would be no more than a speck of dust to me, compared to the rest of the wide world. No, I'm not worried. He can do what he wants, but he ought to realize this. Yes, I'm here as a stranger and he's certainly the most important man in the city, yet I will remain and he will depart – I'm staying and he's going to go.'[26] They realised he was predicting Lorenzo's death. He ended by telling them that all sorts of changes were coming to Italy, that as well as Lorenzo, Pope Innocent and King Ferrante of Naples would soon be dead. Many people heard him make this prophecy in the sacristy, reports of it spreading all over Florence.

It is important to appreciate, however, that his sermons had more to do with the next world than fifteenth-century Italy. His fundamental message was an unmistakably Thomist one: 'The life of a man is knowledge, just as the life of a bird is song,' he told his audience in one of these sermons of 1491:

> Earthly life is not only deceptive but can never be enjoyed in its entirety because it lacks unity. If you love riches, you must renounce the senses, if you abandon yourself to the senses you must renounce knowledge – and if you really want knowledge, you can't hold high office. But the pleasures of heavenly life can all be enjoyed, through the vision of God, the ultimate felicity.[27]

The 'joust' between Lorenzo de' Medici and Savonarola came to a close at the end of 1491, when Lorenzo's health finally collapsed.

Girolamo must have known he had been risking not merely exile but his life. Yet even at this date he was aware that his real enemies were in Rome.

At the start of his Lenten sermons, before the confrontation in the sacristy with Lorenzo's men, he had compared the 'great prelates' (by which he meant the Roman cardinals) to Leviathan, reminding his hearers of their terrifying power. 'Imagine the sort of persecution that would take place and how savage it would be, if a man who preached the truth fell into their hands,' he told them.[28] 'Who on earth will believe him after he's been excommunicated? After he's been arrested, after the mob has been misled with lies and false doctrine, after the mighty of the Church have made their public pretence of being holy?' In the words of Ridolfi, one of Fra' Girolamo's most understanding biographers, this accurate forecast of how he would end was 'a true and really astonishing prophecy'.[29]

EIGHT

The Sword of the Lord

The pope and prelates – Flemish, 1517

Behold the sword of the Lord over the earth.

Savonarola, 5 April 1492

Savonarola continued to denounce Lorenzo's leadership to the congregations that packed the church of San Lorenzo during his Lenten sermons for 1492. 'Perhaps I should start with princes and great men, but I'm not going to, for two reasons,' he declared. 'First, they seldom if ever attend sermons. Second, if they do attend, they insist on hearing things that won't upset them.'[1] He attacked 'great men' who forced citizens to vote the way they wanted, together with poets and 'learned men' (humanists) who flattered princes.

Great men, as if unaware they are no different from anyone else, want to be praised and blessed by everybody. . . . But the true preacher is incapable of flattering them and attacks their vices instead, and because he refuses to treat them as other people do, they won't tolerate him. So he has to expect hostility and persecution from them, either open or secret.

As Lent went by, he grew fiercer and fiercer in his denunciations, telling the Florentines that frightful punishment would come upon them, but that then a new way of life would emerge in the city.

On the night of 5 April the lantern on top of the great dome by Brunelleschi that crowns the cathedral of Santa Maria del Fiore was struck by lightning and demolished, smoking slabs of charred marble hurtling down through the dome into the nave. The lions in the city's lion-house were driven mad with fright by the storm, and tried to kill each other. During the same night, apparently unaware of the thunderbolt, Girolamo suddenly woke, to find himself speaking the words, '*Ecce gladius Domini super terram, cito et velociter*' ('Behold the sword of the Lord over the earth, swiftly and speedily').[2] Next morning he repeated them when telling his deeply alarmed hearers at San Lorenzo that the lightning was an omen of the evils he been forecasting. In the devastated cathedral, another Dominican preacher, Domenico da Ponzo, assured the congregation that, however disbelieving they might have been until now, a portent of this sort meant they must place their trust in Savonarola, who was a man of great sanctity, justified in predicting that a scourge was about to strike the people of Florence.

Lorenzo de' Medici was mortally ill, having been confined to his bed since February. His sense of the fleeting nature of life, voiced in his poetry, had caught up with him. The thunderbolt convinced him that his death could not be far off. He exclaimed, 'I see I'm going to die – it fell on the side facing my house.' He felt no better after swallowing a paste of pulverised pearls and other jewels, a medicine prepared by a doctor sent by the Duke of Milan. His disease seems to have been a rare and agonising form of feverish gout, by now racking every part of his body. Like every man of the Quattrocento, he combined the medieval with the Classical and for all his humanist affectations he had always remained a convinced Christian. Seeing that he was nearing his end, Pico advised him to prepare himself for death by sending for Savonarola. Lorenzo did so without hesitation, saying, 'I can think of no more honest friar.'

When he arrived, according to Villari,[3] Lorenzo told him that three sins lay heavily on his conscience. These were the massacre at Volterra, stealing the funds of the Monte delle Fanciulle and the reprisals after the Pazzi conspiracy. Girolamo replied that he must do three things. First, have complete faith in God's mercy and, second, give back what he had stolen. Lorenzo nodded his agreement. 'Savonarola then stood up, and whereas the dying prince lay cowering with fear in his bed, he seemed to soar above his real stature as he said: "Lastly, you must restore liberty to the people of Florence." His face was solemn, his voice almost terrible. . . .' Villari says that when Lorenzo refused, turning his face to the wall, Girolamo left without giving him absolution.

What really happened was described in a letter by Angelo Poliziano, who had been present.[4] Fra' Girolamo did indeed visit the deathbed, but without any reservation gave his blessing to the dying man, who appeared to be comforted. Only forty-three, Lorenzo died on 8 April – less than a year after Girolamo had foretold his death. Requiems and dirges were sung for his soul at San Marco.

The reason why Savonarola opposed Il Magnifico was that he saw the lack of morality behind the man and his regime. Ignoring Lorenzo's attractive qualities, Fra' Girolamo regarded him not merely as a tyrant, but as a near pagan who was deliberately corrupting the Florentines, giving them a soft and frivolous life to rule them more easily.

While preaching on Good Friday, five days after Lorenzo's death, Savonarola had a vision (later described in his *Compendium Revelationum*). He saw a huge black cross rising up from Rome into a pitch-black sky that was lit by flashes of lightning, to tower menacingly over the whole world – on it was written 'Crux irae Dei' ('the Cross of the wrath of God').[5] When it had filled the sky, a hailstorm blew and killed many. But the sky cleared. Then he saw a cross rise from the Heavenly City of Jerusalem, its rays bathing the earth in a golden light, while choruses of angels sang and every flower bloomed. On this second cross was written 'Crux Misericordiae Dei' ('the Cross of the Mercy of God'), and all the nations were coming to adore it.

He told his congregation what he had seen in his vision, without giving any clear explanation of what it might mean, but even the simplest realised the implications – that something very unpleasant was about to come out of Rome, which would be destroyed by an extremely angry God. On the same day as the vision, on 13 April, a Florentine nobleman wrote to a friend that Fra' Girolamo was now insisting daily that all men would soon feel the scourge of God, 'and I gather that this morning he announced that God has already passed judgement, and that nothing can save us'.[6]

The only hint as to what the scourge might be was in the Bible: 'And I looked, and behold a pale horse; and his name that sat on him was Death, and Hell followed with him,' said the Apocalypse. 'And power was given unto them over the fourth part of the earth, to kill with sword, and with hunger, and with death, and with the beasts of the earth.' There were those who feared the scourge might be the Last Judgement, while others suspected that antichrist had already been born. They were not majority views, however. Nor were they Fra' Girolamo's. Most people thought the scourge would be war: on hearing that Lorenzo had died, the comatose Innocent VIII muttered, 'This is the end of peace in Italy.' But who was the enemy?

'Antichrist had already been born.'
From *L'Antéchrist*, Lyons, *c.* 1490

There were plenty of potential foes, and another war like the War of Ferrara might break out at any moment. 'Deprived of Lorenzo de' Medici's advice, no one knew how to satisfy or keep in check the ambitions of Lodovico il Moro, guardian of the Duke of Milan,' Machiavelli recalled. 'In consequence, soon after Lorenzo's death the seed of terrible troubles took root, and these would ruin and keep on ruining Italy.'[7]

Then there were the Turks, who, in 1477, invading from the Balkans, had burst without warning into Friuli to kill and enslave, devastating the villas of the Venetian patricians, while in 1480 they had captured Otranto by surprise, building a pyramid of skulls with the heads of Christians who refused to convert to Islam. They continued to menace the entire Adriatic coast, refugees arriving every year from what had been the Byzantine Empire or from the Aegean islands, Greeks or Venetian colonists, with tales of mutilation and massacre. Not without reason, some feared an Ottoman conquest, and that St Peter's at Rome and the Duomo at Florence might find themselves transformed into mosques, just as Hagia Sophia had been transformed at Constantinople.

Yet during 1492 Lodovico Il Moro did not seem to be any sort of threat, while the sultan did not appear to have designs on Italy. So, what was the scourge? But Fra' Girolamo was convinced that one was coming, and coming soon, as he assured his hearers.

Lorenzo was succeeded by his son, Piero de' Medici. Twenty-one years old, good looking, showily athletic, a lazy, not very intelligent young man, he was bored by banking and statecraft. His mother and wife were Orsinis of the southern branch, from feudal Apulia, and, arrogant and overbearing, he followed his maternal forebears in despising merchants. Prone to wild rages, he was incapable of understanding, let alone running, the subtle political system that he had inherited. Inevitably, he fell out with his father's friends and Medici cousins, growing more unpopular by the day with Florentines of all classes. They began to compare him with Rehoboam, Solomon's feckless son, who had declared, 'My father hath chastised you with whips, but I will chastise you with scorpions.' However, Piero was amiability itself where Savonarola was concerned, perhaps because he was frightened of him.

Pope Innocent VIII died on 25 July. He had been in a coma for many weeks, so an enterprising Jewish doctor tried to revive him with an early form of blood transfusion, three boys being paid a ducat each to give some of their blood – sadly, they died during the operation from 'air entering their veins', while old Innocent finally expired. Fra' Girolamo was regarded with increasing awe – this was the second death of a ruler he had accurately forecast.

On 11 August 1492 the Cardinal of Valencia, Rodrigo Borgia, was elected pope by the Sacred College, having bought his fellow cardinals' votes with huge sums of money or promises of wealthy bishoprics and abbeys. (He sent four mules laden with coin to Cardinal Ascanio Sforza, the brother of Lodovico Il Moro.) Borgia's election was simony of the most bare-faced sort, and while simony had decided other papal elections in recent years it had never been seen on quite such a scale. His private life was equally scandalous. He had sired eight bastards on three different women, again not entirely without precedent for a pope in recent times, while although over sixty – a venerable age for the period – he kept an adored young mistress. This was Giulia Farnese, wife of Orsino Orsini, famous for her lovely face and magnificent figure, whom the Romans piously christened the 'Bride of Christ'.

Radiant with triumph, bursting with vitality despite his age, full of jokes and *bonhomie*, at his coronation Rodrigo Borgia received each cardinal's homage with a warmth that delighted the more naive spectators. A Monsignor with humanist tastes hung at the window of his house a placard with an inscription comparing Julius Caesar and the new pontiff: *'ille vire, iste deus'* ('that one was a man, this one is a god'). Not all those present shared his opinion: 'We're in the wolf's jaws and he's going to gobble us up,' the young Cardinal Medici muttered fearfully to another cardinal.

Alexander VI was impressively intelligent, with a flair for handling matters of state, enormous charm and a keen sense of humour. But, as Guicciardini tells us, these qualities were accompanied by insincerity, avarice, cruelty, a deplorable private life and relentless determination to enrich his bastards.[8] He adds that King Ferrante of Naples, a man who never wept when his children died, burst into tears on hearing of Borgia's election, telling his wife the new pope would bring misfortune on Italy and on Christendom. Historians are wrong, however, in attributing the deaths of so many of Alexander's enemies, even his own death, to poison. While His Holiness condoned one or two murders, he is unlikely to have been a poisoner since so few efficient poisons were available. (Aconite and belladonna were unreliable while arsenic was too easily detectable – from the agony it inflicts, like a rat gnawing the intestines, and the way it preserves the corpse.)

Nor had Alexander ever been a Jew, as enemies alleged. His aquiline profile may have looked semitic, but he was a believing Catholic. He introduced the ringing of the Angelus bell throughout Western Europe, tried to discover the fate of the lost Christians of Greenland and added to the list of books prohibited as a danger to faith and morals – complaining of the new printing presses that made them so easily available. There was an undeniable grandeur about the man who divided America between Spain and Portugal, who dominated his Rome like a colossus.

That said, any attempt at whitewashing Papa Borgia contradicts all the evidence. The argument that Guicciardini was told lies about him by his arch-enemy, Cardinal della Rovere, does not hold water, since Guicciardini had plenty of other sources. In any case, there are more witnesses than Guicciardini to His Holiness's depravity. According to the Papal Master of Ceremonies, Johan Burchard, Alexander enjoyed a party given by his son Cesare at the Vatican in 1500 during which fifty prostitutes danced naked and then crawled on their hands and knees to pick up chestnuts from the floor, before making love on the floor with some of the guests – the famous 'joust of the harlots'.[9] If this was only rumour, why did the normally discreet Burchard record it?

The new tyrant of Rome was without principle or scruple. 'Alexander VI did nothing but deceive men, and never thought of doing otherwise,' comments Machiavelli in *The Prince*.[10] 'No man ever gave his word more convincingly, made promises with such solemn oaths and kept them less. . . .' Contemporaries would have had no difficulty in recognising Guicciardini's portrait of him – nor would Savonarola.

During the election, the new pontiff's principal opponent had been Cardinal Giuliano della Rovere, often known as the Cardinal of San Pietro in Vincula. One of Sixtus IV's nephews, this big Ligurian[11] was no longer the lean and hungry young prelate painted by Melozzo da Forlì but a triple-jowled, bull-necked Prince of the Church, with a face ravaged by syphilis and a fixed, ferocious glare, so fond of jewels that he wore six rings at a time. Despite his gambling, he was virtuous by comparison with Papa Borgia, with only three acknowledged bastards. He was prone to violent rages in which he shouted and bellowed, thrashing his courtiers with his cane. As blunt as he was overbearing, he never concealed his humble origins, openly recalling his days on board a felucca.

Before the election, Della Rovere and Borgia had quarrelled fiercely at the dying Pope Innocent's bedside, yelling insults at each other. Now, the Cardinal stated publicly that Alexander was a simoniac who had bought the Chair of Peter and was occupying it illegally, that he was not even a Christian but a *marrano* or Spanish Jew who merely pretended to be Catholic. Prudently, Della Rovere then took refuge at Ostia, the nearest seaport to Rome. He had been bishop here since 1483 and its castle was his country home, where he spent his time fishing and hunting.

Receiving a honeyed invitation from His Holiness to visit him at Rome, he accepted; but did not go. On the day he was expected, his palace was ringed by 300 lancers and two squadrons of mounted crossbowmen – an observer wrote, 'If he had come, they would have taken him to the Castel Sant' Angelo before he had time to cry "God help me!"' Soon his castle was besieged by papal troops. Fleeing by boat to Liguria in April 1493, then going on to France – where, conveniently, he was Bishop of Avignon – Della Rovere made sure that his version of Borgia's election circulated widely. It would certainly have reached the Frate's ears, reported by alert friars.

Towards the end of 1492, during the night before his final sermon in Advent, Fra' Girolamo had another vision. He saw a hand in the sky brandishing a sword inscribed with the words that he had uttered on the night of the thunderbolt, '*Gladius Domini super terram, cito et velociter*'. He heard a tremendous voice roaring that it was the Lord who spoke. 'The time draws near when I shall unsheath my sword,' said the voice. 'Repent before my anger is unleashed, for when retribution comes you shall seek refuge and you shall find none.' Then angels descended, offering all men a white robe with a cross – those who declined it or urged others to do so were evil or lukewarm priests. Amid deafening thunder the hand turned downwards towards the earth, as if to smite it, and the air was filled with flames and fiery arrows, omens that war, famine and plague were about to engulf the world.[12]

Finally, Girolamo heard himself commanded to give an account of his vision to his flock, to fill them with the fear of God and make them pray He would send good shepherds who would try to save the lost sheep – they should realise that the sword he had seen, with war, famine and plague, signified the rule of irredeemably wicked priests, who would never enter the Kingdom of Heaven and would try to prevent anyone else from doing so. He, Girolamo, had been shown all this to make him realise that the activities of these evil priests were more damaging to the diseased Church than any persecution.

In the *Compendium* Savonarola explains that when he preached next day he dared not tell his congregation all he had seen because many would have found such marvels hard to credit. Yet he described a good deal, repeating a sentence he remembered hearing during the vision, 'The iniquity in my temple screams up to me from the earth.' Although it was only a few months since the election of the new pope, Fra' Girolamo was telling his hearers they ought to interpret the vision as an unequivocal expression of God's anger that so evil a man as Rodrigo Borgia should have become the head of His Church.

This 'vision of the sword' epitomised Fra' Girolamo's message to the Florentines. It so much impressed the della Robbia brothers at San Marco, Fra' Ambrogio and Fra' Mattia, that they struck two fine portrait medallions – the first of many medallions of him – showing on one side his cowled head in profile and on the other a hand grasping a sword poised menacingly above a city, presumably Florence. Both medallions bear his name, '*Hieronymus Savonarola Ferrarensis*', with the words he had seen written on the sword. The profile is undeniably impressive, a strong, deep-lined face with hooded eyes, one of the most convincing likenesses we have of him.

Although his words have not survived, it seems from the *Compendium* that in the sermon after the vision Girolamo predicted the coming from beyond the mountains of a conqueror like Cyrus, the King of the Persians – and, as his hearers knew from the Old Testament, Cyrus had freed the Israelites from their Babylonian captivity, enabling them to rebuild the Temple at Jerusalem. He added that because the conqueror would be guided by God, 'he shall take cities and fortresses with great ease'. In support of his prediction Girolamo cited a passage from Chapter 45 of the Book of Isaiah referring to Cyrus, which in view of what was going to happen in Italy is worth giving in full:

I will loose the loins of kings, to open before him the two-leaved gates; and the gates shall not be shut. I will go before thee, and make the crooked places straight: I will break in pieces the gates of brass, and cut in sunder the bars of iron. And I will give thee the treasures of darkness, and hidden riches of secret places.

Years afterwards, Fra' Benedetto, who had been present in the Duomo during the sermon, wrote a short doggerel poem, a 'Summary of prophecies the writer heard being made by the prophet Ieronimo [Girolamo] when preaching on the topic of Noah's ark in the days when no one was expecting any danger':

> Soon you will see each tyrant overthrown,
> All Italy you will see defeated,
> To her shame, disgrace and ruin.
> You, Rome, will soon be captured,
> I see the blade of wrath come down on you . . .[13]

Few of Savonarola's congregation, not even Benedetto, can have taken at face value what they heard him say on that morning in Advent. The handful who realised its implications no doubt thought they were listening to a madman. The friar in the pulpit was prophesying not only the dethronement of Pope Alexander, but the imminent invasion and conquest of Italy.

Yet when 1493 began there was still not the slightest sign of Savonarola's king from beyond the mountains. Despite his prediction that the King of Naples would die at the same time as Lorenzo and Pope Innocent, old Ferrante continued to reign – hale, hearty and baleful. Even so, Girolamo strengthened his position. Frightening and uncanny, his sermons went on packing the Duomo while his personality was winning him more and more friends. Clearly, he possessed enormous charm as well as an impressive manner.

He spent the Lent of 1493 at Bologna, preaching in the Dominican priory. His sermons here drew the same crowds that they did at Florence, but he avoided prophecy, and the Bolognesi (even at that date excessively sophisticated) declared that he was a simple man and a preacher for women. Among those who came to hear him, according to the Pseudo-Burlamacchi, was Ginevra Bentivoglio, consort of the Lord of Bologna, who made a point of arriving late with a large retinue. Savonarola told her, 'My lady, you would please God and myself if you could manage to come before the start of the sermon, and not disturb both me and the congregation.' It made no difference, so finally he shouted, 'Look, here comes the Devil, interrupting God's word!'[14] The same source tells us that Ginevra reacted by ordering her *Bravi* to cut him down in his pulpit, and that, when they did not dare, she sent more *Bravi* to the priory to kill him, but he frightened them so much that they ran away. Modern authorities question this story, but it is not unlikely. The lady was the wife and daughter of tyrants and Machiavelli relates how a few years earlier her own daughter had had her husband murdered in their bedroom by *Bravi*, 'because of either jealousy or ill treatment or sheer wickedness'.[15]

Savonarola's visit to Bologna was part of a campaign to gain support for his plans to reform San Marco. Since he had become prior the community had attracted increasing numbers of recruits. These included representatives of several of the greatest Florentine families and even a Jewish convert, who had taught Hebrew to Pico. To house them, the priory would have to be enlarged by taking over a nearby house or building a new monastery. He favoured the second solution, hoping that the community could exchange San Marco for a plainer priory better suited to the Dominican spirit. It would be a rough and ready, single-storeyed edifice with a low timber roof and wooden door-frames, tiny wattle-and-daub cells and a plain brick church without marble. A friend donated a site called Monte Cavo in the wild chestnut forests around Careggi, while younger friars were ready to build it with their own hands; but the project was vetoed by the Master General of the Dominicans and Piero de' Medici. Instead, the community took over the house of La Sapienza next door.

Girolamo believed that the Church's reform must start with the religious orders, which was why he wanted to move into the woods. 'We [at San Marco] are not living a new way of life,' he explained in a letter of 1493 to an abbess whom he knew at Pisa. 'Building a humble priory, wearing coarse old habits that are patched, eating and drinking sparingly the way the saints did, living in a poor cell without anything unnecessary, keeping silence and devoting oneself to contemplation and solitude, cut off from the world . . . that's not a new way of life.' What is new was 'friars building palaces with marble columns and living in cells fit for princes, owning possessions contrary to their oath . . . wearing fine cloth instead of serge, praying very little, roaming around fancying what poverty is like while lacking for nothing'.[16]

He warned his brethren that he had had a vision of the fate of the twenty-eight friars from San Marco who had died in recent years. No less than twenty-five were damned for all eternity because of their ineradicable love of *superfluità* (small luxuries), which had meant breaking their solemn vow of poverty.

As a first step he wanted to turn San Marco and a few other Tuscan priories into a new congregation, separate from that of Lombardy. Supported for reasons of prestige by the ruler of Milan, Lodovico il Moro, the Lombard Dominicans opposed the proposal and secured the backing of the Venetian, Bolognese and Neapolitan governments. On his side, Savonarola had every one of his friars, Cardinal Carafa (the order's Cardinal Protector), the Florentine Signoria and Piero de' Medici – who knew that if Girolamo sold off the estates given by the Medici he could buy them back cheaply. When the brief granting independence was placed before the Pope on 22 May 1493 he said he was too tired to do any more business, but Carafa laughingly dragged the signet ring off his finger and sealed it. A new Tuscan congregation came into being, consisting of San Marco with the priories at Fiesole, Prato and Bibbiena. Fra' Girolamo, who remained prior of San Marco, was made Provincial in charge. Now he had no meddling superiors to block his reforms.

Able at last to bring in the changes he wanted, Savonarola introduced manual labour not just for lay brothers but for those not engaged in theological studies. This was profitable as well as healthy, since among his friars were painters, illuminators, sculptors, architects, brass-founders and wood-carvers. Studies included Thomism and scripture, and also Hebrew, Syriac or Chaldean – which shows that he accepted Pico's view of philology as an essential tool for interpreting scripture. There was a renewed emphasis on preaching centred on the Bible. Life became still more austere, with longer hours of prayer and fasting, poorer clothing and furniture, with water replacing wine at meals.

Meanwhile, Piero was upsetting rich and poor alike, if for the moment there was only muttering and no open revolt. Increasingly tyrannical, he more or less abandoned the system his Medici forebears had operated so successfully for decades, never making the slightest pretext of consulting the *Grandi* as had always been done by his father, alienating Florentines every day by his bullying. However, he left San Marco in peace and did not try to meddle with Fra' Girolamo's preaching.

During Advent 1493 Savonarola delivered twenty-five sermons, which meant a sermon every twenty-four hours. While emphasising the value of faith in a way that Martin Luther would one day find admirable, in impeccably Catholic fashion he also stressed free will and the need for good works. As always, he spoke simply and directly. When explaining the real meaning of Christian charity, and no doubt recalling his grandfather, he told his hearers:

Think, for example, of a doctor who brings love and charity to the sick, because if he's genuinely good and kind as well as learned and skilful, then nobody could be better. . . . You can see how love is behind everything he does, ruling and directing the way he uses his medical knowledge. He ignores his own exhaustion and fatigue as irrelevant, ponders over the symptoms, then writes out his prescriptions and sees they're properly prepared, never leaving the sick man. But if he's only interested in money, then he doesn't take enough care of the patient and his skill fails him.[17]

At the same time Fra' Girolamo dwelt on the shortcomings of the worldly, especially the clergy:

They enjoy tickling men's ears with all their talk of Aristotle and Plato, Virgil and Petrarch, and aren't the slightest bit interested in saving men's souls. . . . Why don't they concentrate on the one Book? . . .[18]

As for Italy's rulers:

Such wicked princes must have been sent as a punishment for the sins of their subjects. Their courts and palaces provide dens for all the beasts and monsters of the earth, since they house the vicious and the criminal. . . . There you can see the false counsellors who are always thinking up new burdens and fresh taxes to suck the people's blood. There you can see fawning philosophers and poets who with every sort of lie and fable pretend to trace the family trees of these miserable princes back to [pagan] gods. But worst of all are the priests who use the same sort of tricks. This, my brethren, is the city of Babylon, the city of the foolish and unbelieving, the city that is going to be destroyed by God.

He continued: 'The Devil has summoned his followers and they have struck fearsome blows at the very gates of the Temple' – a reference to the Rome of Alexander VI and his cardinals. 'They have not only pulled down God's Church, but built another to their own design . . . constructed of sticks, of Christians who are as dry as tinder for the fires of Hell.'[19]

> Go to Rome, go anywhere in Christendom, and in the palaces of all the great prelates and the great lords [the cardinals] you'll find that people are only interested in poetry and fine speeches. If you look carefully, you'll see that they are all holding books of the Classics in their hands, telling each other how they can guide men's souls with Virgil, Horace or Cicero. And you don't need to know just how much the Church is in the hands of the astrologers. Every prelate and great lord [cardinal] relies on some astrologer, who decides the exact time when he ought to go on a journey or do business.
>
> There you'll see great prelates with mitres of gold and precious stones on their heads, silver crosiers in their hands. They stand in front of the altar, dressed in fine brocade copes and stoles, chanting those beautiful vespers and masses, very slowly and with such magnificent ceremonies and so many organs and choristers that you are struck dumb and think that all these priests must be really good and holy men. You can't believe they could ever possibly be wrong, but feel everything they do and say has to be obeyed just as if it were the Gospel. . . .

'In the Early Church,' he continued, 'chalices were made of wood and prelates of gold. Today's Church has golden chalices and wooden prelates.'[20]

Savonarola blamed all the ills of Italy on these 'great prelates' – the cardinals. 'We've become the most despised of nations. The Turks have taken Constantinople, we've lost Asia, we've lost Greece, we've started paying tribute to the Infidel. . . . The only hope left for us is that God's sword will strike the earth soon.'[21]

NINE

'The Devil has summoned his followers'

Ludovico Il Moro – *Istoria di Cremona*, 1645

*The Devil has summoned his followers together and they have
struck fearsome blows at the very gate of the Temple.*
Savonarola, *Prediche sul Salmo Quam Bonus*

The key to Italy's future was the paranoia of Lodovico Sforza,
known as 'Il Moro' – from his badge of a Moor's head rather
than his swarthy complexion – who was uncle of the youthful Gian
Galeazzo II of Milan and the duchy's regent. When Gian Galeazzo
came of age, Lodovico refused to relinquish the regency, striking

coins with his head on one side and his nephew's on the other, although aware that the Milanese hated him for his harsh taxation. Notorious for treachery, Il Moro was the most dangerous of the peninsula's rulers, not excepting Ferrante of Naples.

Interested only in hunting and the pleasures of the table, Gian Galeazzo did not contest his disinheritance or being under house arrest at Pavia. In any case he was in poor health, unlikely to live long, while there were rumours that he was being poisoned. His young wife, Isabella d'Aragona, begged her grandfather King Ferrante to intervene, but Ferrante merely muttered a few threats. Inanely, her husband then told Lodovico what she had done, convincing Il Moro that Isabella's father, the future King Alfonso II, meant to attack him as soon as he became king.

Piero de' Medici was the catalyst in this explosive situation. Eager to placate Ferrante, Lodovico had suggested that Milan, Naples and Florence should send a joint embassy to Rome, but Piero, eager to lead an embassy of his own, persuaded Ferrante to decline. Glad of the opportunity to snub Il Moro, Ferrante informed him he had done so at Piero's request. Lodovico immediately suspected there had been a secret agreement between Naples and Florence, that their rulers were planning to march on Milan to overthrow him and reinstate Gian Galeazzo. Full of foreboding, he negotiated alliances with the Pope and with Venice. Even then he did not feel safe. As a last resort, he sent secret agents to France, who pestered the 22-year-old Charles VIII to make good the claim to the throne of Naples he had inherited from his Anjou kinsmen.

Il Moro was encouraged by his father-in-law, Ercole d'Este. Ferrara had a tradition of friendship with France, and a recent French king had given Duke Borso the rare privilege of quartering the fleur-de-lys in his coat of arms. Now that Ercole's Neapolitan duchess was dead, he was not particularly worried about what might happen to her unpleasant relations at Naples, while the French could make useful allies against his mortal enemies, the Venetians. Later, Pope Alexander VI would blame the Duke of Ferrara almost as bitterly as Lodovico for letting the French loose on Italy.

King Ferrante died in January 1494, fulfilling Savonarola's prophecy. Terrified by the widely reported hostility of Ferrante's son, Alfonso II, Lodovico began to beg the French openly to overthrow him. His envoys argued that Charles had a far better claim to the crown of Naples than King Alfonso, that the Neapolitans would rise in support of the French and that the country would provide a perfect base from which to wage a holy war on the infidel Turks – they had learned that the French king, obsessed with chivalry, was eager to go on crusade.

It is likely Savonarola knew of Charles's claim to Naples, an awareness that may have inspired his prophecy of another Cyrus. He was always well informed about public affairs – the French were to be amazed by his detailed knowledge of Venetian politics – since the Dominicans had priories all over Europe and friars from France regularly visited San Marco en route for Rome. They would have told him how, since 1486, when Ferrante succeeded in murdering most of his barons after arresting them at a wedding banquet, Neapolitan political exiles at the French court had been urging Charles to rescue their fellow countrymen.

A lack of reliably informed visitors explains Girolamo's silence about the New Cyrus during most of 1493. In the meantime, everybody in Florence remembered his prophecy of how Italy's three main rulers would die in the near future, and the death of King Ferrante, the last of the three, made them even more eager than usual to hear what he had to say in his Lenten addresses for 1494; they would not be disappointed. He built these Lenten sermons around the text from Genesis about Noah's ark, telling the congregation that instead of a flood there would come an army from whom the Florentines must take refuge in a spiritual ark. Other cities and strongholds would be incapable of resistance, opening their gates without trying to defend themselves as soon as the enemy appeared before their walls. He predicted, with uncanny accuracy, that Florence's ruler, badly advised, 'would do the opposite of what he ought', a barely disguised criticism of the fatuous Piero. As always, in the course of almost every sermon he complained of Italy's loose living, of her evil prelates and astrologers.

Meanwhile, if we are to believe what Guicciardini says in the *Storia d'Italia*,[1] Charles had become convinced that he really was the rightful King of Naples, a belief he had acquired when a child as if by instinct, and which was strengthened by encouragement from people whom he trusted. The same people told him that once he had occupied Naples, it would be easy to conquer the Turks. One of these advisers was the 'holy man' at the French court, the strange St Francesco di Paola,[2] an illiterate Calabrian hermit who had been more or less kidnapped by Charles's father on account of his therapeutic powers and whom the king had known since his early boyhood. A shrewd peasant from the Regno, who knew just how much Alfonso was detested by his subjects, Francesco urged Charles to claim the throne that was his by right and save the Neapolitans from oppression. He also told him to see himself as God's instrument for the renewal of Christendom. Charles took his advice seriously because the 'holy man' was regarded as a prophet. But when he received Lodovico's invitation to cross the Alps only two other advisers encouraged him, Guillaume Briçonnet and the Seneschal de Beaucaire, both self-made and therefore highly unpopular. Most of his court argued against it, pointing out that Alfonso was an experienced soldier who had defeated the Turks at Otranto. They reminded the King that his own father, the wily Louis XI, had never bothered about the claim to Naples because 'sending armies over the mountains was seeking disaster, buying danger with vast amounts of French blood and treasure'.[3]

King Charles vacillated for months, and until the late summer no one expected him to lead the expedition in person. Even after assembling an army at the foot of the Alps he had doubts. His mind was finally made up by Cardinal della Rovere, who marched into Lyons in June 1494 escorted by 200 Ligurian infantrymen and made a rousing speech 'that stirred him to the soul'. In the words of Philippe de Commines, who was with the King, the expeditions 'lacked money, tents and everything else necessary'.[4] But on 2 September 1494 King Charles crossed Monte Ginevra with 24,000 horse and 22,000 foot. A week later, he was welcomed at Asti by Lodovico.

According to Fra' Girolamo, some Florentines had been saying 'He's coming', and others 'He's not going to come' or 'He hasn't any horses and it will be winter soon'. However, Girolamo never wavered in his conviction that the invasion would take place. During Lent he had told his congregation that God was about to cross the Alps into Italy at the King of France's side, leading his horse by the bridle. Lack of confidence in Piero de' Medici's ability to handle the situation made the Florentines even more fearful. Many remembered Savonarola's prediction, based on a shrewd appreciation of Piero's character and the political situation, that he would do the opposite of what he ought. When haranguing King Charles at Lyons, Della

Rovere had assured him Piero would be panic-stricken by the approach of his army, 'because he knows that the city of Florence, always well disposed towards the kings of France, is panting to regain the liberty he has stolen from them'.

The French had already formed a poor opinion of Piero. 'A man of very little ability,' says Commines,[5] adding that people thought the Medici were 'in a declining condition'. Piero had sent two embassies to Charles while he was still in France, claiming that his father, Louis XI, had told Florence to ally with Naples and that it would be unfair to end the alliance. Should His Majesty of France enter Florentine territory, however, then of course he would do his best to be of service. But when he sent this message Piero had been convinced the king would never come in person. Commines recalls:

In both embassies there was an enemy of the Medici, notably Piero Capponi in the second, who often told us what was being done to turn the city of Florence against Piero de' Medici, making him out to be worse than he really was, besides advising us to deport all Florentines from France. . . . I mention this so that you will able to understand what was going to happen later on, since the king had taken a great dislike [*grande inimitié*] to the said Piero.[6]

From Florence opponents such as Capponi made sure the French were kept informed of everything that happened in the city. Yet Piero never suspected that Capponi was his enemy.

On St Matthew's Day, 21 September, Fra' Girolamo delivered a sermon at San Lorenzo, everyone in the city trying to push their way into the building to hear him. His text was from the sixth chapter of Genesis, 'And behold, I, even I, do bring a flood of waters upon the earth'. Those among the congregation familiar with the Bible knew that the next words were, 'to destroy all flesh . . . and everything that is in the earth shall die'. When Fra' Girolamo spoke these words in his terrible new voice, his friend Pico della Mirandola's hair stood on end, as he later confided to him. The Frate continued:

Behold, the sword has descended. The scourge has come at last, the prophecies are finally fulfilled. Behold, it is the Lord God himself who leads these armies . . . not I but God foretold this. And now it is coming. Indeed, it has already arrived.

People in the cathedral began to weep and howl, screaming to God to have mercy on them.[7]

The French advance was delayed briefly when Charles fell ill at Asti with chickenpox. He recovered after a month. On the march south, at Pavia he visited a gravely ill Duke Gian Galeazzo, pitying the young man whom he and his courtiers suspected was being murdered by his uncle. When the Duke died a rumour circulated, spread by Lodovico, that the cause was 'immoderate coitus', but many believed he had been poisoned – Guicciardini was convinced of it. However he may have died, by now King Charles had no illusions left about Il Moro.

Slowly the French pushed south, shocking the Italians by their ferocity. In the wars of the *condottieri* little blood had been shed, the only casualties being those knocked off their horses – after which, unless held for ransom, they were stripped to their shirts and sent home. This was not the French way. When the Duke of Orleans routed a Neapolitan force at Rapallo and the Sieur d'Aubigny drove back another in the Romagna, they gave no quarter, while during the sack of Rapallo soldiers who had surrendered and non-combatants were slaughtered – some in their beds. Everywhere the French and their mercenaries killed, burned, raped and looted. Recalling the end of the Roman Empire, Italian humanists lamented that the barbarians had come again.

In mid-October King Charles recommenced his advance. Piero's cousins, Giovanni and Lorenzo de' Medici, arrived in the King's camp, telling him that the Florentines were ready to welcome him. With unexpected energy Piero hired mercenaries and reinforced garrisons. As the French grew nearer, however, there was panic in Florence, its citizens walking silently through unswept streets and past closed shops. Many fled. Among them was the young Michelangelo, despite his admiration for Savonarola.

Having stormed the key Tuscan castle of Fivizzano on 29 October, killing its garrison to a man, the French then laid siege to the equally important hill fortress of Sarzanello. 'Had the place been properly garrisoned, the king's army would have been destroyed because it is in barren country high up in the mountains where no food was available, while there was deep snow,' recalls Commines.[8] As it was, the besiegers made very little progress since the castle could be held by a handful of men and was flanked by two other strong fortresses.

A really determined attack by the Florentines might have ended the invasion.

Meanwhile, reports arrived of another French army advancing on Pisa. At the same time, 'The Florentines were inclined to ally with us because they disliked Piero de' Medici, who was playing the tyrant with them, much to the displeasure of his kinsmen and other leading families in the city,' says Commines. He adds that, in any case, 'the Florentines are most unwilling to fight against the French Crown, towards which they are always friendly and well disposed on account of all the business they do in France'.[9]

Losing his nerve, Piero suddenly changed sides in the most bare-faced way possible. Riding into Charles's camp at Santo Stefano he handed over Sarzanello together with the other fortresses, the city of Pisa, the port of Livorno and other towns and castles, besides anything else the King wanted, for as long as he cared to occupy them, arranging their immediate surrender. The French negotiators laughed when, afterwards, they told Commines how Piero gave up places they had scarcely liked to mention. He also offered the King 200,000 florins and his house in Florence. All this was done without consulting the Signoria although it sent messengers who tried in vain to stop him. Throwing away an excellent bargaining hand, Piero had parted with the Florentines' entire line of defence – all the strong towns and fortresses that their forebears had gained with such painful effort during the last hundred years.

On All Saints' Day, 1 November, while Piero was still with Charles, Girolamo embarked on a new series of sermons:

> Before there was any hint or whisper of these wars that have come upon us from beyond the mountains, I foretold great tribulation. You also know how only two years ago I warned you, 'The sword of the Lord is coming, swiftly and speedily.' God, not I, sent this warning and now it is coming true.

The punishment he had always foretold was smiting Italy because of the sins of her people. 'Because of your lust, Italy, because of your greed, your pride, your envy, your thieving, your extortion, you will suffer all kinds of affliction, with many scourges. . . . Oh Florence, because of your brutality, your greed, your lust, your envy, you are going to suffer countless trials and tribulations.' But the tempest had arisen principally because of the clergy's evil ways. 'Woe unto you that wear the tonsure!'[10]

He went on preaching for three days, days when the Florentines feared that the French might attack their city at any moment. 'Behold, these hosts are led by the Lord! Oh Florence, the time for singing and dancing is over – now is the time for you to weep floods of tears for your sins!' He told them to make ready with prayer and fasting: 'Oh Lord, spare the Florentines, a people which longs to be your people!' He used up so much energy in the pulpit that he thought he had given himself a heart attack. With his medical knowledge, he wondered, as he recalled in the *Compendium*, whether he had damaged his pectoral vein. He remained ill and faint for some days. Nevertheless, while as keen as anybody else to see Piero overthrown, he was determined to avoid a bloody revolution.

When Piero returned to Florence on 8 November already alarmed by its growing hostility, armed magistrates refused to let him into the Signoria. Next day, mobs carrying any weapons they could find gathered in the main squares while the Vacca, the Signoria's great bell, sounded the call to arms. Cries rang out, '*Abasse le palle*' ('Down with the balls!' – balls were the Medici emblem). Wearing armour, Piero tried to argue with the crowds, but there were catcalls and he was stoned – even children threw stones at him. He took shelter in his palace.

That night Piero fled secretly with his wife and children, his *Bravi* managing to keep open the San Gallo gate for just long enough to enable them to gallop through. His little party had ridden barely twelve paces when they heard it being slammed behind them. When he arrived at Bologna Giovanni Bentivoglio told him contemptuously, 'I would rather be cut to pieces than lose my principality in such a way!'[11] Eventually he found refuge in Venice. His brother, Cardinal Giuliano, also escaped, disguised as a friar and unrecognised despite his snub nose and goggle eyes. Meanwhile, the Signoria had offered a reward for their capture, dead or alive.

Savonarola was absent from the city during the coup, engaged on his own embassy to King Charles. Yet he made certain there would be little violence, apart from the looting of one or two houses which belonged to Medici supporters. He had been more than justified in predicting that Piero would do the wrong thing.

TEN

The New Cyrus

Charles VIII – *La Somme rurale de Boutheillier*, 1486

Make bright the arrows; gather the shields: the Lord hath raised up the spirit of the King of the Medes: for his device is against Babylon, to destroy it.

The Book of the Prophet Jeremiah 51: 11

None of Savonarola's biographers has done justice to Charles VIII. Yet despite his oddity he almost fulfilled the role chosen for him by Girolamo. The King was the Frate's hope – and the Frate's undoing.

'Don't forget to send Fra' Girolamo Savonarola as one of our ambassadors, since he has the people's love,' Piero Capponi advised the Florentines.[1] Instead of riding to Charles's headquarters, the Frate went on foot, accompanied by two of his friars.

Early in November, Girolamo was received in audience at Pisa by a gnome-like creature with spindly legs, a pigeon chest, crooked shoulders and a head too large for its body. (Guicciardini claims that Charles looked 'more like a monster than a man'.[2]) Behind the scrubby beard grown on campaign, his face was flabby, with a beak of a nose and thick lips, redeemed only by the dignity of his eyes, while he spoke as if he had too big a tongue. He wore splayed shoes to accommodate six toes on each foot. Although more or less literate, the King was obsessed by chivalrous romances – read to him by a court reader – and owned a collection of heroes' weapons that included the swords of Charlemagne and St Louis, the battle-axe of Bertrand du Guesclin and the armour of Joan of Arc. His ultimate ambition was to go on crusade, to liberate Greece and the Holy Land from the Infidels. In preparation, he had bought the title of 'Emperor of the East' from the nephew of the last emperor who had reigned at Constantinople.

Yet he was far from unintelligent.[3] This can be seen from his choice of advisers, men of the calibre of Guillaume Briçonnet or Philippe de Commines. Overcoming his handicaps and appearance, he knew how to command and make himself obeyed, even how to inspire devotion. 'He was only a little man in body and in mind, but so good natured that you couldn't possibly meet a better creature,' says the normally cynical Philippe de Commines. 'Besides, he was the most amiable and best tempered prince in the world. I don't believe he ever said anything that would upset anybody.'[4]

King Charles was accompanied on his Italian expedition by Commines, whose memoirs are history in the modern sense and not a mere chronicle of events. A professional statesman, he had been one of Louis XI's most trusted advisers. He was also immensely experienced – he had negotiated with Charles the Bold of Burgundy, Emperor Maximilian and Edward IV of England – and was a good judge of men. He was to meet Savonarola twice and record two long conversations.

Savonarola's first audience with Charles VIII at Pisa was a distinct success. He was warmly welcomed by Charles, who by now knew something about him. In the fashion of the time, the Frate delivered a formal oration in Latin. 'At last, Oh King, you have come.' He told Charles that he was an instrument in the hands of the Lord, who had sent him to heal all the many woes of Italy, 'as I have been foretelling for several years past', and also to reform the Church which now lay prostrate in the dust. But if the King was not just and merciful, if he failed to respect the city of Florence, its women, its citizens or its liberties, if he forgot the tasks with which God had entrusted him, then He would choose another to perform them and His hand would send down terrible punishments on him. In effect, Fra' Girolamo was telling Charles to march on Rome, arrest Alexander VI and summon a council of the Church, which would then depose him on the grounds of his illegal election, and elect a proper pope in his place, pledged to reform.

Savonarola was harking back to the conciliar movement, which at the Council of Constance earlier in the century had ended the Great Schism by deposing the rival pontiffs and electing a new pope. It had decreed that if a council of the Church was not summoned by the reigning pontiff every ten years, then the princes of Europe had the right to summon one. However, a council had not met since 1439. Girolamo knew, too (and if Charles did not know, his lawyers could tell him), that the Pragmatic Sanction, which embodied a decree of the Council of Basle asserting the supremacy of councils over popes, had actually been incorporated into French law. Although a Bull of Pius II had since condemned appeals from the Pope to a council, it was irrelevant in this case because Alexander had been illegally elected, while his scandalously unchristian life amounted to 'infidelity'. Understandably, French statesmen such as Commines were delighted by this revival of conciliarism, since in the long term it might enable France to control the papacy.

At the same time Savonarola did not forget for a moment that he had come to Pisa as an envoy for the people of Florence. He told the King that he must be merciful to those who had tried to oppose him, since they had not understood that he was sent by God: 'We welcome you with joyful hearts and cheerful faces,' he assured Charles on their behalf. 'Your arrival here has filled with joy everyone who serves Christ, and who is eager that justice should be done.' He ended his oration by promising that if the King did as he told him, then 'God will add to your kingdom in this world and see that everywhere your armies are victorious, and in the end He will bring you to the everlasting kingdom of heaven.'[5]

Charles listened courteously, then took him aside to talk in private. Presumably Fra' Girolamo seized the opportunity to explain at more length the task of reforming the Church and how essential it was to depose Alexander. According to Girolamo, during the audience the King became so moved that at one point he burst into tears, and it certainly looks as if Girolamo found a sympathetic ear.

In the words of the Catholic historian Eamon Duffy, 'Contemporaries viewed Renaissance Rome as we now view Nixon's Washington, a city of expense-account whores and political graft, where everything and everyone had a price, where nothing and nobody could be trusted.'[6] The French king can have been no exception. Nor had he forgotten how at Lyons Cardinal della Rovere urged him to depose the evil 'Spanish Jew' who had usurped the papacy. His army's banners were embroidered with such meaningful slogans as '*Voluntas Dei*' or '*Missus a Deo*' ('The Will of God' or 'Sent by God'). It certainly looked as if Charles was Savonarola's King Cyrus.

Fra' Girolamo also obtained firm assurances that the King was in no way hostile to the Florentines, although he could not deflect him from making a triumphal entry into their city. In consequence, Girolamo returned to Florence with a much more satisfactory answer than the one brought by her other ambassadors. Clearly, he had made a considerable impression on King Charles.

But as soon as he returned, he suffered two painful personal blows. The first was the sudden news, received on 15 November, that his mother Elena Savonarola had passed away at Ferrara. Some months later, he mentioned her in a sermon while he was describing how he had become a friar. 'My mother cried for many years, and I let her cry. Now she knows that she was wrong.'[7] Yet he had not quite lost all contact with his family, since his brother Marco joined the priory, taking the name in religion of 'Fra' Maurelio'.

The second blow was the death of his friend Giovanni Count Pico della Mirandola on 16 November, still only thirty-two years old. Recently Savonarola had been helping him with his latest book, another refutation of astrology – in which Pico pointed out that not only were astrologers incapable of predicting even the weather, but that they denied the freedom of the human will by worshipping the

planets instead of God. For years Savonarola had tried to persuade
him to become a Dominican, without success, but when he came to
say goodbye Pico asked to be received into the Order. He was buried
at San Marco in the Dominican habit. In his funeral oration
Girolamo said that had Pico lived longer, his books 'would have
surpassed everything written by any other man for eight centuries'.
He added that he had feared for his friend's salvation, but now knew
that, because of his almsgiving and the brethren's prayers, Pico
would only need to atone for his sins in Purgatory.[8] (Despite his
piety, almost until the end the Count had kept a concubine.)

All Italy was saddened by the news of Pico's death. When King
Charles had heard he was ill, he had sent two of his own physicians
to Florence to try to save him.[9] The life by his nephew, which
was published two years later, was an immediate success and
went into several editions – a testimony to Europe's respect. In 1510
Sir Thomas More published an English translation, *The lyfe of
Iohan Picus, Erle of Mirandula*.

'Perhaps no other human being has possessed so fine a mind,' Fra'
Girolamo had claimed in his oration.[10] Burckhardt called Pico's
speech on the dignity of man 'one of the noblest of that great age'.[11]
Pico had said:

> God gave man freedom to will and love by making him a being
> neither heavenly nor earthly, neither mortal nor immortal, free to
> overcome and form himself. 'You can sink into a beast and yet be
> born again in the divine likeness . . . to you alone is given growth
> and development depending on your own free will. You bear
> within you the germ of universal life.'[12]

This was part of Girolamo's own creed.

Pico's nephew, Gianfrancesco, who had been his pupil and almost
his son, and who eventually became Prince of Mirandola, was
already another of the Frate's loyal disciples, a regular attender at
his sermons. If unlike his uncle in appearance, an unimpressive little
figure with a pinched face and long, pointed nose, he too was
scholarly, if not so gifted. He would write a hagiographic life of Fra'
Girolamo, one of the first. Gianfrancesco's career was to be ruined
by bitter family quarrels, during which he lost his principality – and
ended in horror when he was an old man.

Giovanni Pico della Mirandola with his nephew – and biographer – Gianfrancesco. From *Johannes Picus Mirandula, Opera Omnia*, Siena, 1509

An old enemy, or at any rate the ally of an old enemy, died a week later. This was the poet Poliziano, once Lorenzo de' Medici's favourite, who had recently made himself an object of hatred because of his stubborn loyalty to his patron's son. If one may believe Paolo Giovio, writing in the next century, the homosexual Poliziano suffered a fatal stroke from 'love fever' while serenading a good-looking pupil. His last request was to be buried in the Dominican habit at San Marco and rest besides Pico, whom he had always admired despite a certain enmity. Girolamo saw no objection to this reconciliation in the grave.

With King Charles riding at its head, the French army marched into Florence early in the evening of 17 November. Charles was in gilded armour with a cloak of cloth of gold, his helmet crowned with a diadem, while his lance was resting on his hip – to leave no doubt that he came as a conqueror. Four mounted knights in armour bore a canopy over his head while his commanders and advisers rode at his side, Cardinal della Rovere immediately next to him. Crossing the Ponte Vecchio, they went straight to the Duomo so that

The best likeness of Girolamo Savonarola. Michelangelo, who had seen him with his own eyes, said that with it 'art reached its zenith and from now on could only decline'. Intaglio on cornelian by Giovanni delle Corniole. (*Museo degli Argenti, Florence: © Scala*)

A realistic portrait of Pope Alexander VI (Borgia), who stood for everything that Savonarola detested – and destroyed him. Medal. (*Bibliothèque nationale, Paris*)

Opposite: Borso d'Este, Duke of Ferrara, surrounded by his courtiers – his regime gave Savonarola a lifelong hatred of tyranny. Fresco (damaged) by Francesco del Cossa in the Sala dei Mesi. (*Palazzo Schifanoia. Commune di Ferrara, Civici Musei di Arte Antica/© Scala*)

Ercole d'Este, Duke of Ferrara – a *condottiere* and tyrant who, ironically, became Savonarola's most powerful supporter. Medal by Baldassare d'Este, 1472.

Opposite: Lorenzo de' Medici – Savonarola's first great enemy. This bust of 1825 by Ottavio Giovanozzi is more convincing than many contemporary portraits. (*Galleria degli Uffizi: © Scala*)

Opposite: Girolamo Savonarola (above), with his terrible vision of the sword of God of 1492 (below). Medal of *c.* 1493 by Ambrogio and Mattia della Robbia.

How the fifteenth century imagined evil men (including a cardinal) would react to their damnation. Detail from Fra' Angelico's *The Last Judgement.* (*Museo di San Marco, Florence*)

Portrait by Botticelli traditionally said to be of Piero de' Medici ('the Fatuous'), Lorenzo's arrogant son, who was driven out by the Florentines and schemed ineffectually against Savonarola. (*Galleria degli Uffizi, Florence*)

the King could give thanks. 'Everyone cheered him, rich and poor, old and young,' Luca Landucci tells us. 'But when he was seen on foot the people thought he looked much less imposing, because in reality he was a tiny little man.'[13]

On the other hand, the Florentines were awed by the army that marched behind the royal party, estimated at between ten and twelve thousand men (the remainder had been left behind in garrisons or were marching towards Rome with the bulk of the artillery train). They had never seen troops like these campaign-worn soldiers in faded red and yellow – the King's personal colours. They bore no resemblance to the swaggering amateurs led by *condottieri* to whom the citizens had been accustomed. Nor had they ever seen such guns as the Frenchmen's cannon.

At their head strode a gigantic swordsman carrying an enormous two-handed sword, who preceded four kettle-drummers and two bandsmen blowing fifes. Then came a hundred splendidly mounted archers of the royal bodyguard, then 200 dismounted men-at-arms, followed by the Swiss pikemen in striped doublets and the Gascon swordsmen who formed the infantry. The cavalry, the flower of the French nobility, came next, mounted men-at-arms in full armour with swords and ponderous lances, whose chargers had cropped ears, hogged manes and docked tails – the riders carried silken banners while despite their hardships many wore velvet cloaks and had gold chains round their necks. The most fearsome of Charles's soldiers, however, were his Scots bowmen, who in the opinion of one observer looked like animals (*'uomini bestiali'*).[14]

The King installed himself in the Medici palace, his troops in any house that took their fancy; many of them looted their billets. Throughout the army's stay there were ugly confrontations in the streets between Frenchmen and Florentines, and it was surprising that less than a dozen men were killed. At first, Charles somehow kept his men under restraint, if not entirely – as yet, he had not forgotten Fra' Girolamo's dire warnings.

But to the citizen's consternation, Charles then made it known that he wanted to restore Piero de' Medici as soon as possible. This was remarkable since privately he despised a man whose wife and mother-in-law could tearfully promise that he would be quite content to return as a puppet-ruler and 'share the government with the king'. Probably, Charles had only suggested Piero's restoration as a bargaining counter, since he was determined to extract as much money as he could from the city, to pay for his march on Naples. He demanded the enormous sum of 150,000 gold ducats, more than the city could possibly afford. When he met the Signoria on 25 November and they produced a treaty that promised him only 120,000, he shouted, 'We're going to have to sound our trumpets!' He was threatening to put the city to the sword.

In response, the white-haired Piero Capponi, red in the face with fury, seized the treaty, tore it to pieces and roared, 'If you blow your trumpets, then we'll ring our bells!' Knowing that the Florentines were well armed and that just before his arrival militiamen had been hidden in the more defendable *palazzi*, the King did not care for the prospect of a battle to the death in the streets. He tried to defuse the situation by making a weak joke and muttering, 'Capponi, Capponi, you're a fine capon'. Then he gave way, accepting the lesser sum. He also abandoned any suggestion of restoring the Medici.

Charles showed no sign of departing, despite the atmosphere in the city growing more tense every day. His troops were starting to rape and murder, breaking into houses at night, while an increasing number of them were being knifed in retaliation. As a last resort, the Signoria begged Savonarola to force the King to depart. Going to the Palazzo Medici, the Frate demanded to see Charles, pushing his way through the guards. He found him in full armour, about to sack the city. Greeted by Charles with respect, Savonarola brandished a brass crucifix in his face, saying:

> Instead of honouring me you ought to honour Him who is King of Kings and Lord of Lords, who gives victory to princes in accordance with His will and justice, but punishes unjust monarchs and is most certainly going to destroy you and all your army unless you stop your cruel treatment of our poor city, full of young girls, orphans and other harmless souls. Their prayers will strike you down if you're so ill advised as to try and take what doesn't belong to you. Be satisfied with winning their affection and don't let yourself be angered by people who only want to keep faith with you.[15]

Charles still delayed, so Fra' Girolamo paid him another visit, pointing out bluntly that by staying too long in Florence he was not only harming the city but weakening his chances of conquering Naples. 'Now listen to the voice of God's servant! Continue on your journey without any more delay. Don't try to ruin this city or you'll bring God's anger down on your head.'[16]

When at long last the King decided to leave, his chamberlain methodically looted Piero's palace on the pretext that the Medici bank in Lyons owed him a large sum of money. Among the many treasures amassed by Lorenzo which he stole were an entire unicorn's horn, prized for its supposed power of detecting poison and valued at 7,000 ducats. The Signoria had already confiscated most of Piero's jewels, together with a collection of antique cameos and 3,000 ancient gold and silver coins.

Charles and his army finally marched out of Florence on 28 November. Philippe de Commines smoothly observes that her citizens had been happy to make a treaty with his king, who made only a short stay. In reality, it had seemed an eternity to the Florentines, but at least Charles left without sacking their city. As they heard the sound of the French drums and fifes die away in the distance, they gave the credit for his departure to Fra' Girolamo.

The all-conquering French army went to Naples by way of Rome. But would the 'new Cyrus' fulfil his mission when he met Pope Alexander?

ELEVEN

The New Moses

Savonarola in his cell – *Della Simplicitate della Vita christiana*, 1496

I am not worthy to be compared to the prophet Moses.
Savonarola, *Prediche sopri i Salmi*

The fall of the Medici transformed Savonarola's message. Instead of doom and suffering, he promised the Florentines a future in which, if they responded to his call, they were going to be rewarded so wonderfully that all Christendom would follow their example. Their city was to grow 'more glorious, richer and more powerful than ever before', he told them. 'I'm not just preaching to Florence, but to all Italy. I've singled out Florence because she is the navel of Italy and God wants it like this – a voice here is heard throughout Italy, just as the body's vital functions go forth from the heart.'[1] Her people were God's Elect because of their intelligence and their new liberty, 'more to be prized than gold or silver'.

Yet Fra' Girolamo was in no sense a millenarian, as has sometimes been claimed. He was much too orthodox a Catholic. What he wanted was to use the Florentines as a means of renewing the Church. When he said 'riches', he meant spiritual riches. As must be perfectly clear by now, he despised worldly goods no less than had Francis of Assisi, and, if he did not say so openly, regarded their possession as harmful. His idea of an earthly paradise was a society in which men and women lived according to the Gospel. And the expansion of Florentine territory would be brought about by her neighbours' admiration, not by war.

Meanwhile, the political situation was extremely dangerous. Piero de' Medici had been chased out by a popular revolt set in motion by the *Grandi*, who hoped to keep the old system of government without the Medici; but, having tasted freedom, the ordinary citizens were determined not to relinquish it. Soon even the *Grandi* accepted that Florence must have a new political system, recognising that the regime operated by the Medici had vanished beyond recall. However, the citizens saw 'liberty' as the right to serve on one of the committees that ran the city, whose membership had been monopolised for the last sixty years by the Medici's men.

Soon after King Charles's departure the Florentines summoned what they called a *parliamento* to discuss reorganising their government.[2] This was a gathering of all the citizens, who assembled in the Piazza in front of the Palazzo della Signoria in order to debate motions put to them by the *Gonfaloniere*. This particular *parliamento* was comparatively small, with many *Grandi*, and the heated debates about a new constitution were long and angry.

Piero Capponi wanted a constitution modelled on that of Venice, run by patricians like himself. Paolantonio Soderini, a former ambassador to Venice, also favoured the Venetian model, but with a broadly based Grand Council. However, although Sodernini had some support, the *parliamento* was full of patricians who distrusted 'the multitude'. Their leader was a lawyer, Guidantonio Vespucci (a kinsman of the Amerigo Vespucci after whom America is named), who hoped to keep as much of the old system as was possible, since it would enable the *Grandi* to retain power. The new Florentine republic should on no account copy the Venetian constitution, especially its Grand Council, he argued, because Florence no longer possessed a nobility strong enough to control it.

Yet everybody knew that the old system was inadequate, manipulated by the Settanta (the Council of Seventy), introduced by Lorenzo. Meanwhile, no one group was able to dominate the *parliamento*. Deadlock ensued except for general agreement on replacing the Settanta by twenty *Accoppiatori*, who were to appoint the Signoria, the Tens and the Eights. The *Accoppiatori*'s appointment was no more than a temporary measure, however. It was essential to introduce a new system as quickly as possible. The situation was becoming explosive since the different political groupings had very different objectives in mind. Piero Parenti tells us in his chronicle that 'we were all expecting ruin or death or, at the very best, large-scale blood-letting and a civil war'.[3]

Florence turned to Savonarola for a solution. By now a large element of the population had acquired almost complete confidence in his seemingly well-attested gift of prophecy. They remembered that in the days when there had been no sign whatever of any threat to peace, he had foretold the arrival of foreign armies into Italy, against whom neither fortifications nor soldiers would provide any defence. They recalled his insistence that his foreknowledge of the invasion, and many other things that had happened, was because it had all been divinely revealed to him and not because he used some human science such as astrology. At the same time, most people had been deeply impressed by the skilful way in which he handled the French.

Fra' Girolamo himself foresaw that he was going to play a key role. 'The priory of San Marco will gain great reputation and honour in Florence, and all government and every dignity will depend on its advice,' he had told Fra' Roberto Ubaldini da Gagliano even before Lorenzo's death. In the circumstances, as Machiavelli points out (in his *Discorsi*), he saw himself as another Moses, even if in January 1495 he declared 'I am not worthy to be compared to the prophet Moses.'[4]

In the past he had condemned the *Grandi* for building luxurious palaces and villas while countless poor men were losing their houses and their shops. He had also complained of the way they forced younger sons into the Church in pursuit of fat livings. But after Piero's fall he stopped criticising, aware that their cooperation was essential if the new regime was to survive. The fact that men from among the *Grandi* joined his community was to be of the utmost value – they gained him the goodwill of the establishment and enabled him to learn what it was thinking.

Indeed, one of his strengths was the goodwill of so many leading citizens. In July 1495 Piero Capponi wrote to Francesco Valori stressing the need for their class to support the new regime: 'I am convinced that Florence can only be governed with the consent of the people, not by edicts but by tacit agreement, if twenty-five or thirty men of rank, forgetting all their personal interests, ambition or greed, take over the running of this poor city.'[5]

Fra' Girolamo began his sermons for Advent two days after Charles left, asking everyone to give thanks that Florence had escaped unscathed. The sermons were based on the Book of Haggai, an apt text in the days after the end of the Medici's tyranny, since Haggai had addressed Israel after her escape from the Babylonian captivity. Although Girolamo had been critical of Lorenzo, he had not attacked the Medici regime, but he denounced it now in his first sermon. Quoting the opinion of Lorenzo's grandfather, Cosimo, that 'a state cannot be governed by paternosters', he commented: 'That is the view of tyrants, of men who are enemies of God and the people, a rule for oppressors, not a precept for helping and liberating citizens.'[6] The first step must be a law that prevented anyone from making himself a dictator.

The view that Savonarola came to see himself as a new Moses is borne out by his confidence. In one sermon, he contrasted the errors of astrology, which he called contrary to both religion and science, with his own unerring revelations. 'Even when I was very young they came to me, but I only began to preach about them when I went to Brescia. Then the Lord sent me to Florence, the navel of Italy, from where to start the renewal.'[7] Again and again, he emphasised that his message was punishment and renovation. As so often, he spoke of the sword hanging over the earth, of the great crosses soaring above Rome and Jerusalem. Identifying antichrist with the Turks, he insisted that only renovation could provide the priests with which to convert them. 'Oh, Italy! Oh, princes! Oh, prelates of the Church!' he cried. 'The wrath of God is coming and there is no hope for you unless you turn to the Lord.'

Yet, in another sermon, he revealed an inner melancholy:

A young man left home and went fishing in a boat and while he was busy fishing the boat's skipper sailed out to sea, beyond sight of port, and the young man began to weep.

Florence, that young man who weeps is standing here in the pulpit. I left my home for the port of religion and went there aged twenty-three to seek the two things dearest to me, liberty and quiet. Then I looked on the waters of this world and through my preaching I began to win a few souls and, seeing that I was happy at such work, the Lord led me on board a ship and on to the open sea, where I'm buffeted by waves and the land seems very far away. That's the reason for my anguish. Storms and tempests constantly gather in front of my eyes. I've lost sight of the shore while the wind is carrying me still further out.

By trying to save a few souls, I've come to a place from where there is no way back to a peaceful life. Why have I been turned into a man who brings chaos and upheaval to all the world? Once I was free, but now I'm a slave. I can see war and discord coming at me from every side.[8]

Savonarola foresaw a violent death for himself – 'the sharpened blade appears before my eyes'.[9] Often, his audience wept in sympathy – the man taking down the sermon, Lorenzo Violi, says he sometimes had to stop because of his tears.

The sermons made such an impact that when he demanded in the last of them that Christ should be declared King of Florence, the Signoria ordered the striking of a coin with the Florentine lily on one side and a cross with the words '*Jesus Christus Rex Noster*' on the other. This was not an attempt to erect a theocracy, but a symbolical gesture repudiating the Medicean dictatorship of the last sixty years. A genuine republican, Savonarola would later tell the citizens that the Grand Council 'is your King, Florence, your Lord'.

We can see from Luca Landucci's diary what a significant role the 'Frate', as everybody called him, had by now come to play in the life of the city. On 6 December he records: 'Fra' Girolamo preached, and he ordered that alms should be given to the "*poveri vergognosi*" [the 'bashful poor'], by which he meant poor people who preferred to starve rather than beg. Such a lot was handed in that it was impossible to count, gold and silver, cloth and linen, silks and pearls, together with other valuables, everyone contributing lavishly out of sheer love and charity.' Two days later, the awestruck Landucci describes a procession to the Duomo to give thanks for these offerings, a procession that was memorable for the large number of distinguished men and women taking part. 'Such devotion was shown as may never be seen again.'[10]

On the day that Landucci penned this, Manfredo Manfredi, Duke Ercole of Ferrara's ambassador to Florence, reported, 'This friar of ours, Girolamo Savonarola, enjoys so much influence and has such a large following in this city that it is something to be marvelled at. He is worshipped and revered as a saint.' In a further report, Manfredi added that Savanarola 'wants nothing less than the good of everybody, and strives for unity and peace, since he is convinced that this is the only way which will enable the city to live in tranquillity'.[11]

The new constitution only came into being because the Frate brokered a compromise between the *Grandi* and the less privileged elements. Those who framed it consulted him at every step and in 1495 or 1496 he referred in a letter to this 'government introduced by me'. Looking back from the early sixteenth century the chronicler Cerretani says that the Frate had been the first to give Florentines any real idea of what liberty meant. According to Guicciardini, he 'had already mentioned more than once the problem of changing Florence's [type of] government'.[12] He also expressed dislike for the conservative system proposed by men like Vespucci, insisting that it was God's will that genuinely popular government should emerge, 'to make it impossible for a handful of citizens to tamper with the security or liberty of others'.[13]

'Fra' Girolamo tried his utmost when in the pulpit to persuade Florence to choose a more sensible form of government,' Landucci notes on 14 December,[14] observing that 'he always favoured the people' and 'was adamant that nobody should be put to death, but that other sorts of punishment should be used instead'. The Frate was not consistent, however, since later we find Landucci writing, with approval, that he strongly recommended that any man found guilty for a third time of 'unmentionable vice' (homosexuality) should be burned, a recommendation which became law.[15] It is only fair to add that the penalty does not seem to have been imposed very often, if at all.

This sermon attended by Landucci on the previous day (called the sermon of the Rinnovazione because it summarises Savonarola's ideas on the renovation of the Church) also includes his views on a constitution. It has been described by the historian Nicolai Rubinstein as 'his great political sermon'.[16]

Among northern nations where there is always force in abundance but not too much intelligence, and among southern nations where by contrast there is intelligence but not a lot of force, rule by an absolute monarch may sometimes be best. But in Italy, and above all in Florence, where both force and intelligence exist in large quantities, where men have sharp minds and restless natures, government by one man can only end in tyranny.

This was obvious from Italian history – look at what happened to ancient Rome, or in more recent times to many other Italian cities besides Florence. 'The one form of government that suits us is a civil, collective government.'[17]

However, the Frate insisted that the Florentines must set Italy's spiritual reformation in motion before introducing political reforms. They were at the beginning of the Fifth Age of the Church, an amazing time during which the Turks and every other sort of pagan were going to be converted to the true faith. But first, Florence should purify herself thoroughly, by expelling bad priests and monks, and by legislating against sodomy – for which, he said, the city had a terrible reputation throughout Italy – and against pornography, gambling, drunkenness and lascivious dressing. When they came to reforming the constitution, whatever they did, he repeated, they must avoid tyranny.

'May real misfortune strike you, Florence, if you choose a tyrant to crush and oppress everybody,' he continued. 'From tyrants come all the evils that bring ruin on cities.' Tyrants were sent by God to punish people for their sins, and when they had been sufficiently punished God mercifully removed the tyrants – a reference to the Medici. 'When you've purified your hearts and worked out what is right, then you can sit down and plan your government, first making a rough draft, after which you can amend it and go into the details,' he advised. In his opinion the citizens should establish a Grand Council on the Venetian model, to make certain that no man could be appointed to office without the assent of the people, who must always retain 'the sole right of creating magistrates and enacting the laws'.[18] He then asked his hearers to assemble under their local *gonfalonieri* and discuss their ideas for a new constitution. He repeated, 'I believe that the one which is going to be chosen will be based on the Venetian model.'

He did not limit himself to constitutional theory, however, insisting that immediate steps should be taken to help the poor. Food must be handed out to the indigent, shops reopened so that business could return to normal and provide employment. He proposed a radical reform of the city's unjust and inefficient system of taxation, which was crushing the poorer classes while failing to produce adequate revenue. Taxes must be reduced, except for those on the rich. 'Levy taxes on real property alone, abolish all loans and arbitrary assessments' was his advice. He also insisted that lasting reconciliation must be no witch hunt for Mediceans – 'Florence, forgive and make peace.'

Many citizens had been nervous about what might happen if no general agreement could be reached on the new form of government. 'If it had not been for him there would have been bloodshed,' recorded Landucci on 21 December.[19] In the end, the Florentines accepted his arguments and a new constitution was adopted before the month was over – after Girolamo had been several times to the Palazzo della Signoria to hear drafts read out for his approval.

It was more democratic than the Venetian constitution, with a Consiglio Maggiore of 3,200 citizens elected from among a total population of about 90,000, which was divided into three parts, each one holding office for a six-month period in turn. Members must be at least twenty-nine years old, with a father, grandfather or great-grandfather who had held one of the city's municipal offices, and be without any arrears of tax. This Grand Council appointed all officials and approved all laws. There was also a Council of Eighty, elected by the Grand Council every six months. In modern terms, the two bodies roughly corresponded to a national assembly and a senate. The administration remained in the hands of the Signoria, but its officials were now chosen by the Grand Council instead of by the Settanta – or, more recently, by *Accoppiatori*. Although the Signoria was obliged to refer to the Council of Eighty not less than once a week, there was no check on its executive power, the new constitution's one grave weakness which nobody, not even Fra' Girolamo, had anticipated. Nevertheless, if clumsy it was a genuinely representative government. But would it work?

'Everyone felt very distrustful, fearing [some sort of] trouble at the beginning of this new government,' Luca Landucci noted on 28 December.[20] Yet everything went off smoothly because of

Girolamo's exhortations from the pulpit, which were heard by vast audiences: Landucci tells us that it was normal for 13,000–14,000 people to attend his sermons. But by New Year's Day 1495 the chemist was full of optimism. He records 'The new Signoria entered into office, and it was a joy to see the whole Piazza filled with citizens, quite different from other times, as a new thing, thanking God who had given this impartial government to Florence and delivered us from subjection. All this had been done at the instigation of the Frate.'[21]

At the same time he aroused a good deal of hostility, as can be seen from an entry in Landucci's diary for 11 January 1495:

> Fra' Girolamo preached, and spoke much concerning the various reforms in the city; and exculpated himself from various accusations, saying that there were devils who disturbed the life of the commune; and that they wrote forged letters, which made it appear as if the Frate had been encouraging Piero de Medici's hopes of returning, in order to make the people turn against him. Nevertheless all this was untrue; he was entirely for the people's side and the common weal. He was calumniated by these foxes; but the truth would always prevail.[22]

A few days later, Landucci informs us that his attempts to keep the peace were making some citizens grumble that 'This little friar is going to bring us bad luck.'[23]

Even so, Machiavelli and the historians Guicciardini and Giannotti who all lived under Savonarola's system thought that no better form of government could have been found. Guicciardini, for example, admits what an enormous amount Florence owed to this humble friar, who had made the revolution at the best possible time, and who had managed to do it without spilling a single drop of blood. But for him, says Guicciardini, the Florentines would have begun with a government run solely by patricians, which would then have been replaced by too democratic a one that could easily have collapsed amid riots and bloodshed, culminating in an armed *coup d'état* and Piero de' Medici's restoration. Only the Frate had the wisdom to hold the reins loose at first, so that he would be able to use the curb at just the right moment.[24]

TWELVE

'Deposing the Pope'?

The pope and cardinals – *c.* 1495, French Book of Hours

With the king there were about eighteen cardinals . . . all eager
for a new election and deposing the pope.
Philippe de Commines, *Mémoires*

If we only read the *Diarium* of Johan Burchard, the infuriatingly
discreet Papal Master of Ceremonies, we should think that
Charles VIII merely went on a pilgrimage to Rome and never
threatened Alexander. Fortunately, Commines gives an account of

the King's occupation of the city.[1] Although he was away on an embassy to Venice, his friends and colleagues were there, and he grasped the political implications better than anyone.

Having paused at Siena for a few days, Charles resumed his march south, to be welcomed to the Orsini clan and their innumerable feudatories around Rome. He sent Cardinal della Rovere to seize Ostia, the city's only outlet to the sea. The Cardinal's brother, Giovanni, intercepted a papal envoy and a Turkish agent, with papers in their baggage that showed Alexander was offering to stop any crusade to recover Constantinople if Sultan Bayezid would pay him. He was already receiving 40,000 ducats a year for keeping Prince Cem (the Sultan's brother and rival) in safe confinement.

His Holiness had been badly shaken by the capture of his mistress Giulia Farnese by French raiders, although he managed to ransom her for 3,000 ducats. (He wore lay clothes to welcome Giulia home – a black jerkin with gold brocade and a richly embroidered Spanish belt from which hung a dagger.) For a moment he contemplated abandoning Rome. Finally he decided to stay and negotiate, telling his Neapolitan allies to leave the city. Visibly terrified, he took refuge in the Castel Sant' Angelo.

On the last day of 1494, his lance resting on his hip, King Charles rode through the gate of Santa Maria del Popolo at the head of his troops, to be greeted enthusiastically by the Romans. (At precisely the same moment, the Neapolitan army marched out through the gate of San Sebastiano on the far side of the city.) According to Guicciardini, many of the cardinals, led by Della Rovere and Ascanio Sforza, begged King Charles to let them elect a new pope,[2] telling Charles that he would rank in history with his ancestors Pepin and Charlemagne, who had rescued the Church from oppression. He could never trust Alexander, they warned. Treacherous by nature, he was filled with hatred for the French and, should he make peace, it would be from fear.

Philippe de Commines gives a similar account to that of Guicciardini.[3] He tells us the King was accompanied by eighteen cardinals, a majority of the Sacred College, who were all in favour of Alexander's deposition and a new election. On two occasions Charles had his heavy guns moved into position in front of the Castel Sant' Angelo, loaded and ready to fire at a moment's notice. The old castle – once the Emperor Hadrian's tomb – could not stand up to cannon fire. In any case, as if by divine intervention and without a shot being fired, a large section of the castle's outer wall collapsed within a week of the French army's arrival.

Referring to the two most influential cardinals, Della Rovere and Sforza, Commines writes:

I think both of them would have agreed to elect a new [Pope] had the King wanted it, even a Frenchman. I can't say whether the King did the right thing or not, yet I suspect he made the right decision since he was young and ill-suited for carrying out the huge task of reforming the Church even if he had the power, as he was well aware. I am sure that sensible, reasonable men would have seen it as a good, great and saintly achievement, but it would certainly have been a most difficult business.[4]

What Commines does not mention is the role played by his colleague Guillaume Briçonnet, Bishop of St Malo. Never wilier than when cornered, His Holiness had identified Charles's principal adviser as the key to the situation. Originally a small tradesman from Tours and a widower who had entered the Church late in life, with a financial acumen that made him indispensable, Bishop Briçonnet set more value on a cardinal's hat than on any scheme of reform. Burchard blandly pretends that the Bishop only received the hat because the King requested it for him, but he does not disguise the alacrity with which the pontiff sent for the red robes, clothing the man with them on the spot. In return, Briçonnet persuaded the King to negotiate with Alexander instead of arresting him. If Guicciardini can be believed, the Holy Father bought the goodwill of all Charles's other advisers, too, 'with presents' – including, no doubt, that of Commines. But it was the new 'Cardinal of Santa Pudenziana' who changed the King's mind.

Alexander agreed to a mutual defence pact guaranteed by a 'perpetual' alliance, promising to surrender any towns Charles might need for military purposes and to crown him King of Naples. He also handed over Prince Cem, whom Charles wanted to use as a bargaining counter with the Sultan. In addition, he swore to make peace with his cardinals. As a guarantee, he gave a hostage. This was his nineteen-year-old son, the Cardinal of Valencia, better known to history as Cesare Borgia.

In Commines's opinion, this agreement between Alexander and King Charles could not possibly last, because the concessions forced out of the Pope were excessive. Even so, as Guicciardini observes sardonically, Alexander put on a convincing display of sincerity and, besides dazzling the King with his winning manner and amusing wit, succeeded in overawing him.[5] After the agreement had been signed, as 'Eldest Son of the Church' – an ancient title of the kings of France – Charles was received with due pomp in the basilica of old St Peter's, where he was allowed to kiss the papal toe and the papal cheek. The Holy Father celebrated a Pontifical Mass in thanksgiving.

The King stayed in Rome for a month, methodically sending raiding parties over the Neapolitan frontier and encouraging Alfonso's subjects to rise against him. Then he marched out of the city for the final phase of his campaign, the invasion of Naples, 'apparently great friends with the Pope', according to Philippe de Commines, who adds, however, that eight cardinals left Rome in a fury.[6] They realised that Alexander had outwitted Charles and would turn on them all, just as he had turned on his ally King Alfonso. A few days after leaving Rome the papal hostage, Cesare Borgia, disappeared from the French camp. Despite his father's apologies it was believed that he had acted on his instructions.

Filtering back in rumours and then confirmed, the news must have come as a devastating blow for Savonarola. The 'new Cyrus' had missed his opportunity of deposing Alexander and saving the Church. Yet Girolamo never for a moment questioned his gift for prophecy. He was convinced that, whatever happened, the French King would carry out the mission given to him by God.

THIRTEEN

The French Leave Italy

A man-at-arms – Flemish, 1517

Remember the example of Saul, who, having been chosen by God, was afterwards rejected by Him.
        Savonarola to Charles VIII, letter of 26 May 1495

Charles met with little resistance as he marched south. The Neapolitans hated their royal family and entire regions rose in revolt. They had been bled white by tax gatherers, who were often foreigners – Catalans or Valencians like the Borgias – while their great nobles had been massacred by Ferrante and Alfonso. Haunted by the ghosts of the barons he had murdered, King Alfonso suddenly lost his nerve and abdicated, fleeing to a monastery in Sicily where he died shortly after. The new king, Alfonso's more likeable son Ferrante II (popularly known as 'Ferrando') tried to put up a fight, but his troops melted away and he took refuge on Ischia.

On 22 February the French entered the city of Naples, Cardinal della Rovere riding at the King's side, to be met by an ecstatic reception. Charles was speedily crowned, not only as King of Naples but as King of Jerusalem and Emperor of the East. An embassy arrived from the new Florence to congratulate him. It consisted of some of the republic's most important citizens, Paolo and Bernardo Rucellai, Lorenzo Morelli, Guidantonio Soderini and even a Medici – Piero's kinsman, Lorenzo. But Charles swiftly alienated his new subjects. Besides granting the greatest estates and the richest heiresses to his commanders at the expense of the local nobility, he allowed his troops to plunder and rape at will.

Early in April a letter reached the King from Philippe de Commines, who was still in Venice. Out of the blue, it warned him that an Italian League had been formed against the French by Lodovico il Moro, the Venetians and Pope Alexander, supported by the Emperor Maximilian and King Ferdinand of Spain, and that it was assembling an army with the intention of cutting off his retreat to France. The prime instigator was the ever fearful Il Moro, who feared that Milan would be overrun by the French if Naples was ruled by the King of France.

In the meantime, Commines met Savonarola. 'I forgot to mention that while at Florence on my way to join the King, I visited a friar preacher called Frère Jérôme [Girolamo] who is in a reformed priory and lives a very saintly life, so people say.'[1] This must have been during April 1495 when Commines was travelling north from Naples:

> The reason [I wanted to see him] was because he had always preached strongly in support of the king, and what he said stopped the Florentines from turning on us since no preacher ever had so much influence over a city. However much people may deny it, from the start he insisted that our king would come to Italy because he was sent by God to punish the tyranny of the princes, none of whom would be able to stand up to him. He also

predicted that [Charles] would come to Pisa and that on the day he entered it the government of Florence would fall, as in fact happened, Piero de' Medici being chased out the same day. In his sermons he has foretold many other events before they have taken place, such as the death of Lorenzo de' Medici, which he declared had been revealed to him. In addition, he has preached that the Church will be reformed by the sword. This has not yet occurred, but it very nearly did and he still maintains that it will. Some people disapprove strongly of his claiming that God has revealed such a thing, while others believe him. Personally I think he is a genuinely good man.

I asked him if our king could get back [to France] without danger, in view of the huge army the Venetians were assembling – about which he knew far more than I did, despite my having just returned from Venice. He told me there would certainly be fighting on the way back but that courage would bring the king through, even if he only had a hundred men with him, since God who brought him would be guiding him on the journey home.

On the other hand, because he had failed to help with the Church's reformation and had let his men pillage and rob so many people – including all the friendly Italians who opened their gates in welcome, as well as the hostile ones – God had pronounced a judgement on him and, in short, one day he would have to suffer a severe chastisement. However, if I told him to take pity and stop his men from committing any more crimes, and punish them if they did, as was his duty, then God would remit his sentence, or at least mitigate it, although it would not be enough for him to plead, 'I've done nothing wrong myself.' He said he was going to the king to say so. And indeed he did, besides demanding the return of Florence's towns.

It occurs to me now that he must have been thinking of the death of Monseigneur le Dauphin when he mentioned a 'sentence of God', because I can't imagine anything that could have hurt him more. I mention all this so people will be able to understand that the entire [Italian] expedition was a true mystery.[2]

As Sir Francis Bacon observes, Charles VIII 'conquered the realm of Naples, and lost it again, in a kind of a felicity of a dream'.[3] Even before receiving Commines's despatch, the King had made up his mind to go home. On 20 May he marched out from Naples, going north through the Apennines. He left behind him the Comte de Montpensier as Regent, with several thousand men, but within a few months Ferrante recovered the entire kingdom apart from a few isolated French garrisons.

King Charles had another ally besides Florence, whatever Guicciardini may say about all the Italian princes being frightened of enslavement by the French. Although Duke Ercole was Il Moro's father-in-law, he welcomed the prospect of a Franco–Neapolitan monarchy which might enhance his own position, while he had little love for the Milanese and hated the Venetians. Despite sending one of his sons with a force of Ferrarese men-at-arms to serve in the League's army he was determined not to join it – another son and another Ferrarese force were serving with the French. Ercole was even inclined to accept the Frate's view of Charles as the new Cyrus who had been entrusted by God with the reform of the Church.

Pope Alexander suspected that Ercole had joined Il Moro in persuading Charles to invade Italy. 'May God forgive the Lord Lodovico and the Duke of Ferrara,' he had told the humanist Pandolfo Collenuccio in November 1494, when Collenuccio obtained an audience by pretending to be Ercole's envoy. Pandolfo argued that the Duke had tried to stop it. 'I don't think so,' grumbled the Pope. 'He deserves a lot of the blame.'[4]

The Frate had acquired not just an ally but a disciple. 'We learn that the venerable Fra' Girolamo Savonarola, our Ferrarese subject who is in Florence, has been been giving his opinions publicly in his sermons, and continues to give them, on the present difficulties of Italy, while it very much sounds as if he is threatening the sovereigns of Italy,' Duke Ercole wrote on 13 May to his envoy Manfredo Manfredi. 'We want you to visit him and in our name ask him to tell you about the difficulties and what he thinks will happen, and about our own affairs. . . . We feel certain he will respond to our request, because of his loyalty to us and good nature, and also for the sake of his native land for which, surely, he must still feel some affection.'[5]

Manfredi saw Savonarola four days later, reporting that the Frate did indeed still see Ferrara as his native land. He was doing his best to keep the Florentines loyal to the French alliance 'by convincing them that the Most Christian King was certain to reform the Church and bound to win all his battles'.[6] He was also very willing to help the Duke, 'aware of how devout is His Excellency, who leads a holier life than any other sovereign in Italy'. Instead of commenting on Ferrarese affairs to a mere envoy, he would write personally to His Excellency. While his letter has not survived, we know from the Duke's reply that he was pleased with Girolamo's advice: 'your suggestions are full of prudence . . . we shall be very glad to receive the little book you say you are going to send us when you complete it' (that is, the *Compendium Revelationum*).[7]

Remembering how the Frate had detested the Este in his youth and what he had told the Florentines about tyrants, his enthusiasm for the ruler of Ferrara may come as a surprise. But since Lorenzo and King Ferrante had left the scene, and as Il Moro was by now regarded with contempt, Ercole had become the foremost Italian ruler, while it looked as if he would back Charles, who asked him to garrison Genoa. As the *Diario ferrarese* tells us proudly, 'the Duke of Ferrara was the best loved prince who supported the King in Italy and the King would do nothing unless the Duke of Ferrara wanted it'.[8] And both Fra' Girolamo and Florence needed allies. Above all, Girolamo was intrigued by a prince who, it seemed, might introduce Savonarolean reforms into his own territory. Soon the Frate was in touch with Ercole's Dominican confessor, a Fra' Tommaso.

Ercole had first approached the Frate in much the same way that he might have consulted an astrologer – to learn what he could see in the future. But soon the Duke began to fall under his spell. He may originally have heard of him from Pico della Mirandola, of whom he had been 'marvellously fond' – Pico loved Ferrara and had spent a lot of time there, in his villa outside the city.[9]

Fra' Girolamo wrote to Charles on 26 May, stressing three key points: he, Girolamo, was God's prophet, Charles was God's king and the Florentines were God's own people. His object was to make him play his appointed role and at the same time be grateful to Florence. 'From among all the princes of Christendom God has chosen you to fulfil this mystery of renewing the Church,' he told the King, continuing:

God has chosen this city, peopling her with his servants, and is going to magnify and exalt her. . . . I must remind you that it was God Himself who long ago explained to me why you were coming to Italy. If only you had acted in accordance with the words that I spoke to you just before you left Florence [that is, if only Charles had deposed Pope Alexander and summoned a Council] then people would now be shouting 'Blessed is he who comes in the name of the Lord.

Remember what I have already made abundantly clear to you by word of mouth and in writing, that the people of Florence are thoroughly loyal to you, save for a very small band who, despite the wishes of the majority, have tried to urge the contrary. Ignoring any attempts to turn them against you, they remain loyal, and this is mainly due to my preaching. . . . Remember, too, that although you have given no particular sign of any favour or love for the city, and that although others may have tried to bribe her into opposing you, she has stayed firm in her loyalty, and she will go on like this with the help of my sermons. . . . Once again, I warn you that if you don't do as I say, then God will visit you with such afflictions that you will be forced to obey.[10]

Fra' Girolamo hoped that on the way home Charles would pause at Rome to settle accounts with Alexander VI. However, understandably apprehensive and knowing that the King was in a hurry, the pontiff fled from the city on 1 June as soon as he heard that the French army was near, returning only when it was safely out of sight. Once more, Charles had failed to perform the task for which he had been chosen by God.

When the King reached Siena on 13 June the Florentines were outraged to learn that in spite of all his promises he had no intention of returning Pisa – which they had ruled since 1406 – or any other of the towns and fortresses whose possession was seen as essential for the republic's security. He even assured the Pisan envoys that they would never again be governed from Florence. What upset the Florentines still more was that he brought Piero de' Medici with him, accompanied by 2,000 mercenaries.

Fra' Girolamo caught up with the King at Poggibonsi a few days later. Despite Pisan hatred for Florence, he had to try to win back Pisa and the other towns and at the same time convince Charles that he must return to Italy at some future date. Guicciardini gives a sardonic account of what took place, recording that Charles was met by Savonarola, who, 'claiming in his usual way divine authority for everything he said', exhorted him to return the towns to the

Florentines. He went on to threaten that if Charles did not keep the promises he had sworn on the Gospels then the Lord would punish him swiftly and without mercy.

The King had been giving different replies on different days, here and at Castel Fiorentino, sometimes promising to return the towns when he arrived at Pisa, sometimes contradicting himself, saying that before he made his original promise to the Florentines he had assured the Pisans he would see that they stayed free. At the same time, he never stopped telling the Florentine ambassadors that they would get their lands back as soon as he reached Pisa.[11]

Fra' Girolamo did at least succeed in terrifying him. As before, he spoke as God's prophet: 'You have angered the Lord by breaking your word to the Florentines and abandoning the task of reforming the Church, with which the Lord has so often made you aware through me, and for which he has chosen you by such easily recognizable signs,' he told the King. 'You are going to escape from your present dangers, but if you fail to resume the task which the Lord is repeating to you through the voice of his poor servant, then I tell you that in his anger he will visit you with heavier misfortunes and someone else will take your place.'[12]

A cowed Charles asked Girolamo to come with him to Pisa. Luca Landucci reports approvingly on 17 June that the Frate had told the King at Poggibonsi that he should treat Florence well because she was his friend. 'So he really was of great assistance to Florence, and the king listened to him,' adds Landucci. 'At this time the Frate was held in such esteem and the people were so devoted to him, that there were many men and women who, if he had said, "*Entrate nel fuoco*" ['Go into the fire'] would actually have obeyed him.'[13]

After another meeting with Charles at Castel Fiorentino, Girolamo declined his invitation to accompany him to Pisa. He did not want to risk being taken prisoner by the Pisans and used as a hostage. When he returned home to Florence, according to Landucci he told his congregation that he had spoken to the King, who had promised a great deal that was excellent, and that he had warned him that if he did not keep his promises:

God would take his [royal] office away from him, so that he would no longer be God's representative, and that he would also lose the dearest thing he possessed. . . .[14]

Commines, who had rejoined Charles in Tuscany, was at both his meetings with Savonarola. He writes:

He always preached publicly that the king would return to Italy refreshed, in order to accomplish the mission that God had given him, which was to reform the Church with the sword and chase the tyrants out of Italy, and that if he did not, then God would punish him cruelly.[15]

He adds that the Frate had his sermons about this put on sale:

The said Frère Jérôme told me with his own mouth, when I spoke with him our way home through Italy, that a judgement had been given in heaven against [the king] should he not perform the task ordained for him by God and if he did not stop his men pillaging.

Just as Savonarola predicted, King Charles managed to fight his way back to France against daunting odds. The forces of the League failed to intercept him at Pontremoli, 'where Frère Jérôme's prophecy came true, which was that God would lead the King by the hand until he was out of danger', Philippe de Commines recalls. 'For it seemed that our enemies must have gone blind or lost their wits not to block this pass.' On 6 July, although outnumbered three to one Charles and his army cut their way through the League's army at Fornovo – it was during this battle that the Italians coined the famous phrase about the ferocity of the French as soldiers, '*la furia francese*'. 'God did what Frère Jérôme promised,' says Commines. 'Namely, ensuring that we won the day.'[16]

The encounter at Fornovo, vividly described in Commines's memoirs, had been very close, both sides suffering severe casualties. The League even claimed the victory after capturing the King's baggage. However, having experienced Italian civilisation and Italian luxury, the French were certain to return.

Nobody could have been more relieved by the news of Fornovo than Duke Ercole, who had finally allied with Charles. It looks as if he did so because of Savonarola's advice and the result confirmed his faith in the Frate. His decision was warmly approved by his Ferrarese subjects, who much preferred the French to the Venetians. But he earned the hatred of all the other Italian states except Florence.

On 8 September 1495 His Holiness sent a bullying letter to the Florentines, threatening them with excommunication if they went on helping the French – a letter which they ignored, but remembered with resentment. He also wrote to Charles, ordering him to leave Italy immediately or else to present himself at Rome. Charles wrote back, saying he had every intention of coming to Rome, but wanted a firm promise that the Pope would stay to receive him and not run away as he had done during the King's most recent visit.

At the end of October Charles re-crossed the Alps into France, just over a year after launching his invasion. In Guicciardini's words, for all his victories the King went home 'more like one who had been conquered than a conqueror'.[17] Yet he had passed through Italy like a hurricane and the peninsula would never be the same again. Unfortunately, he had omitted to reform the Church.

Charles's punishment came in December 1495 with the death of his only son, the three-year-old Dauphin Charles Orlando, which Commines recalls: 'it was the greatest loss that ever happened or could possibly have happened, to the king, since he never had another child that lived'.[18] Commines was sure that the boy's death had been predicted by the Frate. 'Concerning the king and the evils he said would come upon him, it all happened just as you have seen, first the death of the dauphin and then his own, and I have seen letters he wrote to the said Lord [King].'

Fra' Girolamo had convinced himself that Charles would one day return to Italy and fulfil his mission, sending the King letters (three have survived), which he insisted were written at God's command. The refrain in them is always the same: God brought Charles to Italy and then brought him safely home to France. Now that he has experienced the Frate's predictions and has seen how they come true, he does not need any other sign. The Frate is very sorry to hear of the King's misfortunes – a reference, presumably, to the death of the dauphin – but they have been ordained in heaven.

In these letters Savonarola claims unequivocally to be a prophet. King Charles's arrival in Italy had overcome any reservations about being able to see into the future; he could not accept that the French invasion had been coincidence. He explained to Charles that God tells the higher angels what he wants and that these then tell the lower. This process is paralleled among men. God enlightens the Church through his elect, just as he enlightens the lower angels

The battle of Fornovo, fought in a thunderstorm on 6 July 1495, when an outnumbered Charles VIII (right) cut his way through the Italians – as Savonarola had foretold. From *La Mer des Hystoires*, Paris, 1503

through the higher, and in the same way that lesser angels believe higher angels, men should believe those who are God's prophets. He always includes a warning that unless Charles comes back to Italy, God will assuredly withdraw his protection from him.

Charles did not answer any of these letters from Fra' Girolamo,[19] despite showing them to Commines. Even so, Girolamo was certain that the King was coming back to Italy at the head of a great army, and he had some reason for his optimism. Della Rovere was still at the French court, determined to overthrow Pope Alexander.

FOURTEEN

The Godly City

Savonarola and an astrologer – *Tratto contra li astrologi*, 1497

*God has chosen this city and filled her with his servants, and he
has chosen to glorify and exalt her, so that whosoever touches
her touches the apple of his eye.*
        Savonarola to King Charles VIII, letter of 26 May 1495

'The divine goodness has cast down all those tyrants and citizens
who tried to usurp authority over her,' Savonarola wrote of
Florence in his letter to King Charles of May 1495. 'This new,
popular government has been set up by God, not by man, and he is
determined it will prosper.'[1] Since Rome would not rid herself of

corruption and vice, Florence had taken her place as a city where men and women lived according to the Gospel. Until the French invasion Savonarola had predicted only the scourge; now he prophesied a new Christian era whose pioneers were the Florentines.

As has been seen, Fra' Girolamo had begun to preach this message in November 1494 in his sermons on Haggai, and he would continue to do so for the rest of his life. Yet he was never a millenarian revolutionary as some scholars claim. If he used apocalyptic imagery, his overriding aim was to reform and renew Catholic Christendom and he genuinely believed that he was transforming Florence into a state on the Thomist model.[2]

Many Florentines welcomed his message. After all, their legends promised them a glorious future. 'To the citizens of Florence their city was a living creature with a destiny shaped by God,' observes Donald Weinstein.[3] 'She was a favourite of the Lord . . . the centre of rebirth and Christian renewal.' Now she possessed a prophet to lead them towards such a rebirth, a prophet who had foretold the French invasion and saved them from destruction.

No doubt, Girolamo approved when during October 1495, by order of the Signoria, Donatello's *Judith cutting off Holofernes's Head*, which had formerly stood in the gardens of the Medici palace, was re-erected on the Ringhiera (the stone platform against the northern façade of the Palazzo della Signoria, near the main entrance, and the platform from where the members of the Signoria addressed the people). The statue bore an inscription implying that the subject of the statue – tyrannicide – should serve as an example for everybody who had the public good at heart.

According to Guicciardini, 'The veneration Savonarola now commanded, and the wishes of countless Florentines, swept aside any opposition.'[4] He adds that because the Frate was so powerful and since his followers, who included a large number of leading citizens, outnumbered the critics, public offices were monopolised by his supporters. The same chronicler explains why so many important people had joined his party, some from genuine idealism, some from ambition and some from fear.[5]

His followers – scornfully called *Piagnoni* (funeral waits or wailers) by their enemies – were intent on preserving the 'holy liberty' he had secured. Because the Frate said so, they refrained from reprisals against Mediceans. On the other hand, they had no time for the traditional opponents of Medici tyranny, the *Arrabbiati* (the 'Enraged'), members of the old wealthy class, the *Ottimati*, who had run Florence before the Medici and who looked back to the days before the Medici takeover in 1433. For the moment, they were all-powerful, although Polizzotto has estimated that at their strongest there can never have been more than about 400 of them[6] out of 3,500 Florentines who were eligible for the Grand Council, while they were split into three factions. These factions had very able leaders,[7] however, in Francesco Valori, Giovanbattista Ridolfi and Paolantonio Soderini. In August 1495 the *Piagnoni*-dominated council passed a law abolishing *parliamenti* so that 'no-one could emerge as a *capo* and declare himself a *capo*'. The law explained that *parliamenti* were no longer needed because 'government is in the hands of the people, who are the city's true and rightful lords'.[8]

Since he did not hold any formal office, Fra' Girolamo's position was not unlike that of a modern party boss without a seat in parliament. This meant that he could inspire and suggest policies – sometimes even dictate them – but that he was frequently unable to control his followers. Even the intellectuals were won over. Far from being out of harmony with the thought of the age, as historians such as Burckhardt supposed, Fra' Girolamo was very much in tune. 'The whole circle of literati, humanists and philosophers who [had] gathered round Lorenzo de' Medici seemed to have joined *en bloc* the Savonarolean movement'[9] comments Polizzoto. Girolamo captured them by his uncompromising clarity, his insistence on content rather than form and his stress on the primacy of truth.

Not all these admirers remained loyal but for a time he had some surprising allies. The Pseudo-Burlamacchi, for instance, tells us 'Ficino declared he had never met anyone with such sound ideas.'[10] This is confirmed in a letter of December 1494 by Ficino himself, who regularly attended the sermons at the Duomo. He says that the Frate is a man chosen by God. For four years he had warned the Florentines of the danger menacing their city, and they have escaped it only because of his call to do penance: everybody must listen very carefully to what he has to say about the future.[11]

Yet although Girolamo shared the great Platonist's conviction that the world was haunted by angels and demons, and no doubt welcomed his support, he continued to reject neo-paganism and astrology out of hand. With his own clear, Thomist mind, he had always seen that Ficino's '*pia philosophia*' would undermine the entire Christian revelation. It is scarcely surprising that within a year Ficino turned against the Frate, although during his lifetime he never dared to oppose him openly. After Fra' Girolamo's death, however, he published a formal apology to the College of Cardinals for having let himself be deceived by that 'Antichrist Hieronymus of Ferrara, greatest of hypocrites'.[12]

But there were plenty of other humanists who remained faithful, such as Girolamo Benivieni, a friend of the late Giovanni Pico; Gianfrancesco Pico, Pico's nephew; and Giovanni Nesi. Intellectuals of this sort believed that the Platonism of Ficino, astrology and the cabbala – if by now they largely rejected them – had foretold Savonarola's coming. They suspected that he was a man who understood the secrets of the universe, a miraculous seer whom Nesi called 'The Socrates of Ferrara'.

Once an enthusiastic Ficinean but now a fervent *Piagnone*, Benivieni wrote *canzoni* inspired by the Frate's prophecies. Extolling Florence as a New Jerusalem, these ballads were sung as hymns on feast day processions. In addition, he translated his devotional works and polemical letters into Italian, besides writing a species of introduction to his *Compendium Revelationum*.

Aged twenty-six in 1494 and full of youthful enthusiasm, Count Gianfrancesco Pico took every opportunity to promote the Frate. In his widely circulated life of his uncle, published in 1496, he rebukes those who accuse Girolamo of 'telling hypocritical lies, being deluded or misled by the trickery of demons'. People must place absolute trust in 'someone with so much erudition and authority, with such prudence and integrity, a man whose complete reliability has been proved by his studies of Aristotelean philosophy, sermons, inspired interpretation of Holy Scripture, predictions of what is going to happen – known throughout Italy to be fulfilled – and holy way of life'. Yet he retained his Ficinean vocabulary, claiming that his uncle had been capable of summoning up 'watery Thales, fiery Heraclitus and Democritus amid his atoms, together with Orpheus and Pythagoras . . .'.

Giovanni Nesi was yet another humanist supporter, despite retaining the vocabulary of Platonism. Influenced by books traditionally attributed to the mythical magus Hermes Trismegistus, in 1497 he published the *Oraculum de novo saeculo* ('An Oracle for the New Age'). Written as if recalling a dream, it insists that Ficino's theory that spiritual perfection can give a man godlike wisdom has been proved by Savonarola, who is a Hermetic oracle. Nesi uses Ficinean imagery – a goose turning into a swan, a worm becoming a phoenix or an eagle copulating with a phoenix – together with astrological symbolism. He meets a woodpecker (a *picus*), in fact Giovanni Pico's ghost, who tells him that not only does the Frate understand Plato and the cabbala and how to read the moon, but the secrets of the Bible. Nesi was far from alone in thinking that Savonarola had found hidden keys to the meaning of life.

Nesi stresses Fra' Girolamo's appeal to thinking men. 'A friend to everybody wherever they may come from, backstreets or crossroads, kings' palaces, great men's mansions or philosophers' lecture halls.' The Frate is in no way exclusive, insists Nesi. Above all, his language is impressively clear, just as the plain language of Socrates had attracted Alcibiades far more than the dazzling oratory of Pericles.[13] In fact, he is 'Socrates from Ferrara', but with more determination and a purer inspiration.

Girolamo was delighted by Nesi's *Oraculum*, not because he enjoyed flattery but because he recognised its value in winning over intellectuals. 'An elegantly written little book,' he observed. 'By a layman, yet a very knowledgeable one with unusual gifts.'[14]

Throughout, Savonarola reassured ordinary citizens that whatever might happen, and despite suffering severe chastisement, in the end Florence would prosper as never before. Luca Landucci recorded in his diary for 1 April 1495:

> Fra' Girolamo preached and said and testified that the Virgin Mary had revealed to him that, after going through much trouble, the city of Florence was to be the most glorious, the richest, and the most powerful city that had ever existed, and he promised this absolutely. . . . All these things he spoke as a prophet and the greater part of the people believed him, especially quiet people without political or party passions.[15]

Although the 14,000-strong congregation that Landucci notes in his diary on more than one occasion seems barely credible, it may have been near the truth. People swarmed in from the surrounding countryside, from noblemen to peasants, travelling by night so as to be in time to hear his sermon the next morning. 'There was no lack of rich citizens, full of charity, to supply them with food and drink,' recalls the Pseudo-Burlamacchi. 'And they gave lodging in their houses to twenty, thirty or forty at a time.'[16]

'The cathedral church of Santa Maria del Fiore, big and capacious as it is, was simply not big enough to hold the multitude of his hearers,' writes a Savonarola supporter, the Florentine Jacopo Nardi, in his *Storie di Firenze*:

> It was necessary to build all along the side of the walls, and within earshot of the pulpit, high tiers of wooden benches standing one above the other on which people could sit, rather like a theatre, with more tiers of the same sort in the area around the entrance to the choir, and also in that around the main door into the said church.

The Pseudo-Burlamacchi gives an eyewitness description of the congregation assembling:

> People got up in the middle of the night to make sure of finding seats for the sermon and, coming to the cathedral doors, waited outside till they were opened, ignoring any inconvenience, even the cold and the wind, or standing in winter with their feet on the marble; and among them were young and old, women and children of every sort, who came with such jubilation and rejoicing that it was really quite astonishing to hear them, coming to the sermon as though to a wedding.
>
> The silence in the church was profound, every one going [quietly] to his place, and those who could read held tapers in their hands so that they would be able to read the service and the prayers. And while many people were gathered together in this way, not a sound could be heard, not even a 'hush', until the children arrived to sing hymns with so much sweetness that heaven itself seemed to have opened.
>
> They waited for three or four hours until the Frate finally ascended the pulpit, and the attention of such a huge mass of people, all of whose eyes and ears were fastened on the preacher, was wonderful to see. Then they listened so intently that when the sermon ended, it seemed that it had only just begun.[17]

A woodcut in the *Compendium Revelationum* shows the Frate in his black and white Dominican habit, waving his arms as he vehemently preaches to a packed church. The congregation are crowding up the pulpit stairs. This crude little picture conveys the extraordinary rapport that existed between Girolamo and his followers. If frightened out of their wits, they were desperate to hear his promises of a wonderful future.

The most important of his sermons continued to be delivered during Lent and Advent. In 1495 they discussed a group of Psalms and the Book of Job; in 1496 the Books of Amos and Zechariah and those of Ruth and Micah. The surviving sermons were recorded in a primitive shorthand, whose writer admits that often he was shaking violently, which cannot have made for clarity. The haphazard jottings were translated into Latin, then rendered into Italian again, before reaching the press.

The admiring Landucci records:

All the said sermons have been written down and published by a young notary, whose name is Ser Lorenzo Vivioli [recte Violi], who has achieved a superhuman feat, as we may say, having written down everything that this Frate ever said in the pulpit, and [his] epistles and other things written and spoken during many years. You could not find anything more marvellous in the world and no other miracle can be required in this work than the fact of the very least word and act being inscribed exactly, without a single iota wanting, which may well seem impossible, but it was done by divine permission, as is thought by righteous men.[18]

In one of his sermons on the Psalms Fra' Girolamo denounces astrology as a means of knowing the future. It can't work since it is contrary to what our religion tells us and defies the principles of science, he says. Prophecy on the other hand, 'because of divine involvement is able to tell us the future, although the seer may not necessarily be a good man, like Barlaam in the Bible, for example, who was unquestionably a sinner if a prophet,' he explains with due humility. 'Visions came to me when I was very young, but I only began to expound them at Brescia,' he adds. 'Then God sent me to Florence, the heart of Italy, so that the reformation of all Italy might begin here.'[19]

Invariably, Savonarola dwells on the need for Florentines to live in harmony and unite, reforming their lives as well as their government. In his sermons on Job, for example, he says:

> God is essentially free and the just man is free in the same way as God – the only real liberty for us consists in wanting righteousness. . . . What freedom can there be in being ruled by our passions? In our own case, Florence, do you genuinely wish for liberty? Citizens, would you truly like to be free? First of all, love God, love your neighbour, love one another, love the welfare of all, and if you have love and union of this sort among you, then you'll have real liberty.[20]

The world was divided into two armies, the army of the Devil and the army of Christ. 'Christian life doesn't consist in ceremonies but in practising goodness, which means compassion.'[21]

Reading Savonarola's sermons, let alone a few short extracts, one cannot recapture their magic – one can only guess at it. Yet there is convincing testimony about what they achieved in Florence, where it really did seem as if the Early Church had returned. Ladies dressed plainly, sold their jewels and gave the money to charity, dissolute young men grew sober and studied theology, enemies became bosom friends, bankers and shopkeepers refunded unfair profits. Feasting and banqueting ceased, hymns were sung instead of *canti carnascialeschi*. Every day the churches were packed while in some houses people lived like friars, saying the monastic office and rising long before dawn to sing matins. Brothels closed their doors from lack of customers, as did gaming halls, while whores disappeared from the streets.

Almsgiving on such a scale had never been seen. Rich *Piagnoni* spent thousands of gold ducats buying grain cheaply in Sicily, then selling it to poor Florentines at cost price. An impressive amount was done to relieve poverty, encouraged by Fra' Girolamo, who told everybody to contribute generously and provide practical assistance. Members of the *Piagnoni* Compagnia della Carità visited the sick poor in their homes, nursing them during the night and taking them to hospital if necessary. *Piagnoni* funded hospitals out of their own pockets – for example the Ospedale del Ceppo – and even staffed them, besides providing dowries for penniless girls to find husbands or become nuns. Another confraternity engaged in helping the poor and taken over by the *Piagnoni* was the Buonomini di San Martino, which received funding from the Signoria in response to Girolamo's plea. As a modern historian comments, this charitable network was 'the best possible embodiment of Savonarola's teaching'.[22]

The Frate enlisted the *fanciulli*, the boys of Florence renowned for unruliness, to jeer every gambler or overdressed lady they saw. When anyone said, 'Here come the Frate's boys', even the toughest gambler took to his heels. They also went into the taverns to scold drunkards. During the days before the carnival, instead of throwing stones as in the old days, they collected alms and carried crucifixes or banners of the saints and the Virgin, while on the carnival they marched through the streets in procession bearing olive branches, accompanied by drums and pipers, and singing hymns. Every day during Lent, early in the morning they sang litanies in the Duomo.

Girolamo was trying to save them from prostitution, and he succeeded. 'Boys were so much respected that everyone avoided evil, and most of all the abominable vice,' comments Landucci.[23] It was impossible to speak highly enough of the improvement in their behaviour, Placido Cinozzi tells us. 'What they had been, how sunk in every kind of vice, anyone knows who has lived in this city . . . Florence had become another Sodom.'[24] At the Frate's urging, one of the regime's first measures was a new law against sodomy, passed by a big majority in December 1494. This insisted on a swift enforcement of the penalty, burning at the stake, the victims being strangled beforehand. (Other European countries were no kinder, hanging being the penalty in Tudor England.) The law was strengthened on four further occasions.[25]

Savonarola was in favour of harsh penalties. In March 1495 he spoke approvingly (in a sermon on Job) of how Moses put a man to death for gathering wood on the Sabbath. In July (in a sermon on the Psalms) he wanted to see three fires for malefactors burning in the Piazza, and grumbled at the Florentines' squeamishness. 'Oh, Frate, you are cruel!' they might say, to which he would answer, 'But it's you who are cruel by letting off some wretched man who puts the city in danger.'[26] He suggested that the lips of blasphemers be branded with a red-hot iron, a traditional penalty. For contemporaries this seemed admirable rather than repellent – the Frate was trying to stop men going down to the ghastly reality of an everlasting hell. Little if any burning or branding took place.

He toyed with a project for organising the women of Florence, proposing that groups should meet to discuss the city's problems. (The Dominican reform had been started by a woman, Catherine of Siena.) However, their outraged husbands forced him to abandon the idea. A Margarita di Martino wrote to him in 1496, complaining that after arousing women's hopes he had done nothing further and seemed interested only in the views of men and boys.[27]

Novices flocked to the friary. Between 1435 and 1489 the community had numbered about 35, but by 1498 this had risen to 240.[28] 'And Pandolfo Rucellai, who was already an old man, became a friar at San Marco,' noted Landucci in May 1495.[29] Very rich, one of the Council of Ten and the republic's envoy to King Charles, Rucellai gave up his money and resigned his offices to do so.[30] Two celebrated humanist scholars also joined, Antonio Vespucci (an uncle of Amerigo) and Zanobi Acciaiuoli. Intellectuals were well represented in the friary, by now an acknowledged centre of Florentine culture.

> There were constant visits by kindred spirits. Even after Pico's death the best and most scholarly Florentine minds continued to frequent the 'Academy of San Marco' and a few like Girolamo Benivieni were given keys to the friary so that they could go in and out whenever they chose. Among them, besides the scholars in the community, were Crinito, Fonzio, the Aristotelian Arduini, the Platonist Nesi (who may already have started on his *Oraculum de novo saeculo*, bursting with praise for the Frate) and the young Giovanfrancesco Pico . . . In consequence, it was a pleasant and learned company, and even pleasanter was the peace of the surroundings.[31]

Among the less distinguished recruits was Bettuccio Luschino, an illuminator by trade, who later wrote a short biography of Savonarola in which he gives an account of how he himself joined.[32] A foppish man of pleasure, poet and writer of songs, who had jeered at Fra' Girolamo when he saw him in the street, he tells us how he was persuaded by a woman friend to go to a sermon at the Duomo. When he heard Girolamo preach, he claimed 'I knew I was a dead man and not among the living.' He says that after selling his fine clothes, his scent and his lute, he went to San Marco and begged to join the community. Savonarola told him to try to lead a Christian life before taking such a step. After six months, during which he attended the services every day, he was admitted to the novitiate as Fra' Benedetto.

The community's phenomenal growth cannot have been due to Savonarola's preaching alone. The Frate was a natural religious superior and, as such, possessed a genius for human relationships, of which his friendship with Pico gives some hint. He must also have been a good psychologist, adept at identifying and encouraging personal gifts and aptitudes in very different people, at channelling their interests and energies so that they could find satisfaction in the Dominican way of life. The membership shows that he had a rapport with all classes, ranging from great patricians to the humblest plebeians. Both his brethren in the priory and his followers in the city outside were devoted to him, remembering him with deep affection long after he was dead. Despite his sternness, he had an unusually pleasant manner. Invariably polite, he never lost his temper, never raised his voice in anger – out of the pulpit at least – and he showed immense patience with enemies. Unlike so many 'holy men' of the period, he was scrupulously clean, his worn, patched habit always neatly pressed and without a speck of dirt.

Villari observes that many historians see Savonarola purely as a visionary, ignoring his practical side.[33] As he said over and over again, Christianity would never flourish if people were brutalised by poverty, and in February the Grand Council introduced a new system based on his ideas. It imposed a single tax of 10 per cent on all income from property, abolishing all loans, levies and arbitrary assessments, besides creating a new taxation office to ensure impartiality when valuing property. Even if the system could not produce enough revenue to pay for the ruinous war with Pisa, it was fairer than the old one and helped to reduce tension between rich and poor.[34]

Savonarola had less success securing the establishment of an effective court of appeal against sentences handed out by the tribunals – an appeal might only be made to the Grand Council, which could be manipulated by party factions.

The *Piagnoni*'s part in founding the Monte della Pietà has been justly called (by Lorenzo Polizzotto) 'the Savonaroleans' crowning achievement in social welfare'.[35] The Frate constantly encouraged people to assist it, for example during a sermon in Easter Week 1496, in which he showed himself at his most practical. 'Women in particular should endow it with anything they have left over from their needs. But everyone ought to contribute, by giving their [gold] ducats and not just their small change.' Financed by charitable donations, half municipal bank and half pawnshop, this institution enabled the poorer classes to use their possessions as security and borrow at low interest. Jewish money lenders, who until now had usually been their only source for a loan, always charged a standard 32.5 per cent with compound interest, so that after fifty years an initial loan of 100 florins would amount to nearly 50 million – what Savonarola called 'the whirlpool of usury'. It was alleged that when a Monte della Pietà had been proposed twenty years earlier, one of these money lenders blocked it by bribing Lorenzo de' Medici with 100,000 ducats.

The Monte della Pietà, which opened at Florence in 1496 and was run by *Piagnoni*, charged interest of between 5 and 7.5 per cent – extracting a solemn oath from its customers not to gamble with the money or blaspheme – and proved an enormous help to people who were starting small businesses such as shops, or to farmers needing to buy seed or improve their stock. All contracts with Jewish money lenders drawn up after its establishment were declared null and void. The money lenders were obliged to leave the city within twelve months, although the Frate seems to have intervened to stop their expulsion.[36]

Nor did Fra' Girolamo neglect the city's intellectual needs. The Medici possessions were still being sold off and in August 1495 Landucci recorded the auction of Piero's household goods – 'velvet counterpanes embroidered in gold, paintings, pictures, all kinds of beautiful things'.[37] It then began to look as though the Medici library would also be put up for sale, a priceless collection of Greek and Latin codices and illuminated manuscripts, since the republic needed money desperately. If bought by a Florentine it might not be available to scholars, or perhaps sold item by item. It might even be bought by a foreigner. Commines was demanding payment of 1,000 florins owed to the French and he had his eye on the collection. However, Girolamo hastily sold the only land still belonging to the friary and borrowed money – in October 1495 the friary bought possession of the library for a year for 2,000 florins, and by 1498 had succeeded in buying it outright, while the friars tried to recover borrowed or stolen works. The entire collection was housed in the library of San Marco, which was always open to the public. It remained here until the next century when it was moved to the Laurentian Library, built for it by Michelangelo next to the Medici parish church of San Lorenzo. Its survival is entirely thanks to the Frate.

Savonarola had become famous far beyond Florence, because of the wide circulation of his sermons, printed in a Latin which everybody could read. He received countless letters, some from as far off as England. (By the 1490s books ordered in London from Paris booksellers who stocked Italian publications arrived within a month.[38]) Even Sultan Bayezid at Constantinople ordered a translation of the sermons.[39]

The magnitude of Fra' Girolamo's transformation of the city is underlined by the nineteenth-century historian Ferdinand Gregorovius, who says that under the Medici it had been a place of 'heathen philosophers, voluptuaries, dilettanti, money lenders, traders, intriguing politicians and sharp-witted critics'.[40] This is how Villari sums up the change brought about by the Frate within a year of Piero de' Medici's overthrow:

> The liberty of Florence was established, the [ordinary] people authorised to carry arms, the system of taxation revised, usury extinguished by the Monte della Pietà, a general peace made, reorganized, *parliamenti* abolished for ever, and the Grand Council constituted, to which the Florentines showed a tenacious attachment that they had never displayed to any of their [previous] political institutions.[41]

One must never exaggerate the millenarian element in his message, as does Robert Weinstein, who claims that the Frate was a millenarian because of his 'view of the world as a battleground between good and evil forces, a chosen people, a vision of the ultimate redemption in an earthly paradise'. Obsessed by apocalyptic fantasies for years before he began his Florentine career, says Weinstein, Girolamo preached a divinely ordained revolt that would be rewarded by material prosperity. Weinstein also insists, unconvincingly, that he ceased to be fully Catholic in his concept of the Church.[42]

The Frate was credited with 'Joachite' views by some of his enemies, views influenced by the millenarian prophecies of a twelfth-century Calabrian abbot, Joachim of Fiore, that still enjoyed wide circulation: Joachim had divided history into three ages, prophesying how the third age, the Age of the Spirit, would be a time when all men became monks and spent their lives chanting the praises of God until the Last Judgement. Admittedly, in his 'Renewal' sermon of 1495 Fra' Girolamo cited 'the abbot Joachim and many others' as confirming his prophecy of a scourge. It is also true that one or two of his followers, such as the Franciscan Giorgio Benigno, thought he was ushering in a new millennium in which Christ would reign over the world for a thousand years, and that he echoed the abbot in predicting the conversion of Jews and Turks.

Yet Girolamo insisted that he knew little about Joachim and his ideas. Nor did he predict a new millennium and, although many of his hearers may have taken him literally when he promised riches, he meant spiritual riches: there was to be no revolt, no social upheaval of the sort that goes with milleniarism. His theological outlook remained impeccably Catholic. 'I declare and confess that the Catholic Church will endure to the day of judgement,' he told his congregation in February 1496, 'and while there may be different opinions on the exact definition of the Catholic Church, I myself rely on Christ and the decisions of the Church of Rome.'[43] Throughout, his object was not to establish a millenarian new order, but to make everybody live a Christian life. In the words of the Florentine chronicler Bartolomeo Cerretani, who as a young man had lived through the experiment, he was trying 'to bring back the early Church's simplicity'.[44]

It has also been suggested that the Frate was trying to build a theocracy modelled on that in the Book of Judges. But he had no wish to rule. He wanted influence, not power, so that he could turn Florence into a community of genuinely Christian men and women and use it to reform the Church. He was convinced that without living life according to the Gospel Christendom lacked any moral foundation and was bound to perish. This was why he was so certain of the coming of the 'scourge'.

'God be praised that I saw this short period of holiness,' wrote the *Piagnone* Landucci in retrospect. 'I pray Him that He may give us back that pure and holy life. To realize what a blessed time it was, you have only to remember the things that were done in those days.'[45]

FIFTEEN

The Arrabbiati

Critics – *Chronique de France*, 1492

. . . discord and division, the ancient malady of that city.
Francesco Guicciardini, *Storia d'Italia*

'A Dominican friar has so terrified the entire population of Florence that it is obsessed with piety,' the Mantuan ambassador reported in November 1494. 'For three days a week the people fast on bread and water, for two days more on bread and wine. All the girls and many married women have entered convents. You only see men, boys or old hags in the street.'[1] The ambassador's report is a caricature – Savonarola would never have flouted the Church's ban on married women taking the veil. Yet modern historians such as Ludwig von Pastor, the chronicler of the popes, give an equally distorted picture.

In reality, there was substantial opposition. No one puts it better than Burckhardt, however much he misunderstood Fra' Girolamo:

> That transformation of public and private life which the iron Calvin was but just able to effect at Geneva with the aid of a permanent state of siege necessarily proved impossible at Florence, and the attempt only served to drive the enemies of Savonarola to an implacable hostility.[2]

Many Florentines were angered by what they saw as puritan tyranny. If in practice extreme punishments seem to have been rarely inflicted, they help to explain why the Frate was so disliked by less religious elements, who called the followers not merely *Piagnoni* (wailers) or *Frateschi* (friars' men) but *Collitori* (neck-wringers). Their dislike was increased by people who climbed on the band-wagon – opportunists and hypocrites.

The Frate aroused deep hatred. Some thought he was a hypocrital fraud, others believed he was in league with the Devil and an evil spirit had taken possession of his body. Landucci records an attack on Girolamo on 24 June 1495 in the Via del Cocomora while he was walking home after giving a sermon,[3] when an attempt was made to break through his bodyguard and knife him.

The nucleus of the opposition was formed by the *Arrabbiati*. Besides being excluded from the new regime, they were infuriated by the Frate's insistence on pardoning Medici supporters. Allied to them were a group of about 300 dissolute young 'men of family', who bore the name of *Compagnacci* (companions, after banding together in a club). Led by a homosexual banker called Doffo Spini, they would stop at nothing to get rid of Savonarola, whom they hated for outlawing their pleasures – they tried to murder him more than once with poison or a stiletto.

The *Bigi* (the Greys) were supporters of the Medici, who would have been expelled from the city but for Fra' Girolamo. They hated him nonetheless, and hoped to restore Piero. Better organised than was at first realised, they were called Greys because they kept a low profile, plotting behind the scenes and recruiting. They worked with the *Arrabbiati*.

There was also a comparatively moderate and modern-sounding faction, who opposed Girolamo merely on the grounds that he was a friar – in their opinion friars should not meddle with politics. These secularists before their time were the *Bianchi* (the Whites). They too swelled the ranks of the *Arrabbiati*.

The *Arrabbiati* had other allies. The most effective were the *Tiepidi* (the Lukewarm), monks and priests who led lax lives and disliked any idea of reform. Many were highly influential. They spread defamatory rumours about Fra' Girolamo, accusing him of being a heretic or of being possessed by an evil spirit. What made the *Tiepidi* so dangerous were their contacts at Rome. 'You will have a much tougher battle with them than with any army,' Savonarola told his congregation. 'They are busy already, writing letters.'

There were many attempts to discredit the Frate. In January 1495 Filippo Corbizzi, *Gonfaloniere* and head of the Signoria, invited him to a debate at the Palazzo della Signoria. When he arrived he found himself among enemies, the most vociferous being a Dominican, Tommaso da Rieti and a Franciscan, Domenico da Ponzo. Many present remembered how in 1492 Fra' Domenico, an unstable figure with an unsavoury private life, had told everyone in the city that the Frate was a saint whose prophecies would come true. By now, however, he was proclaiming from the pulpit that God no longer made prophets and that Girolamo was a fraud.

Fra' Tommaso asked Savonarola to explain how he dared to interfere in matters of state, questioning his prophecies. Girolamo responded by inviting anyone in the room to cite any passage from the Bible that told men not to support a government for the sake of morals and religion, adding that his prophecies would be justified by coming true. He ended by quoting Christ's words, 'I spake openly to the world, and in secret have I said nothing.'[4] Then he walked out, after promising to answer the assembly's questions. He did so in his next two sermons, proposing there should be another debate, 'with good men who love the truth'. Yet in the second sermon he told the congregation he wanted to give up public affairs and become a real friar again.[5] He threatened to leave Florence and go to Lucca, 'which did not please the people', noted Landucci.[6]

Girolamo's most formidable critic was the Dominican Giovanni Caroli, former prior of Santa Maria Novella, a distinguished theologian and well-known author. A staunch Medicean, he attacked the Frate in a series of pamphlets that portrayed him as a rabble-rousing false prophet who was betraying his calling as a friar and ruining Florence – by arguing that the clergy was unfit to do its job, he was making men look for salvation outside the Church and destroying her.[7]

The Frate's position became stronger in mid-1495. The first meeting of the Grand Council took place in May, while a Signoria composed of men inspired by his ideals was installed in June. Over the years it would be followed by other Signorie who could be counted on to be loyal. Meanwhile, Landucci noted the building of a magnificent *Sala Grande* at the Palazzo della Signoria to house meetings of the Grand Council. Even for a great hall it was enormous, 177 feet long by 77 wide. Landucci says that 'the Frate encouraged the work'[8] – it was a symbol of everything he stood for politically. The Grand Council had their first meeting here in February the following year, although it was not yet complete. It is still there, now known as the *Salone dei Cinquecento*.

Even so, the Florentines were the reverse of tamely obedient. Landucci informs us that when at the end of 1495 the citizens learned that King Charles's agents had still failed to persuade the Pisans to return to Florentine rule, 'they turned against the Frate, venting their hatred by running round [the friary of] San Marco all night, shouting and yelling such insults as, "This pig of a little friar, we'll burn down his house over his head"'.[9]

In assessing the accusation raised against Savonarola – his support for the Florentine campaign to recapture Pisa, whose citizens were determined to remain independent – one has to take circumstances into account. Pisa had been ruled by Florence since 1416 and had only been lost when it seceded after Piero de' Medici surrendered it to the French in 1494. King Charles had promised on oath to give the city back, but as soon as he left Italy his governor sold it to the Pisans. Its recovery was a matter of life and death to the Florentines since it controlled the mouth of the River Arno and cut them off from the sea, at a time when communications with the north were blocked by enemies. Its loss threatened to ruin their trade.

The struggle to regain Pisa, fought on both sides by badly led militia and mercenaries, lasted until long after Fra' Girolamo was dead, draining Florence of blood and treasure. It was disfigured by atrocities on both sides. Landucci records how when the Pisans blinded two prisoners before killing them, Piero Capponi followed suit, putting out the eyes of Pisan captives.[10] Even so, Girolamo prophesied that the Florentines would regain Pisa – as indeed they did, but not until 1505. Throughout, this unpleasant war added to his difficulties.

SIXTEEN

The Duel Begins

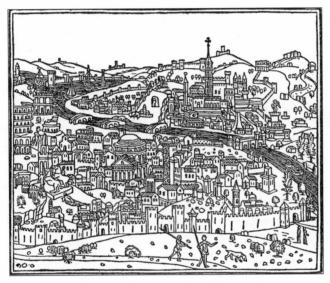

Rome – *Supplementum chronicarum*, 1486

For we wrestle not against flesh and blood, but against
principalities, against powers, against the rulers of the darkness
of this world, against spiritual wickedness in high places.

St Paul's Epistle to the Ephesians, 6: 12

Florence isolated herself by allying with King Charles. Every other major Italian state except Ferrara had joined the Holy League against the French, and Guicciardini says the Florentines ran a real risk of being attacked by their neighbours. However, they were encouraged by Cardinal della Rovere, who was eager for Charles to return. At the end of 1495 he tried to seize Genoa with his own troops, leading them in person, and made another attempt early the following year. He also wrote to Savonarola, promising him that a group of cardinals was coming to Florence to hold a council.

Lodovico il Moro, one of the architects of the League, did his best to stir up Florence against Fra' Girolamo through his ambassador, Paolo Sommenzi, who was a skilled *agent provocateur*. Even before the proclamation of the League Sommenzi had written to the Duke, 'I'm doing everything here that I can to turn the people into his enemies', and on 8 February, 'what is being done against the Friar is going well'. Sommenzi – whom Ridolfi describes as a 'devilish instrument of a devilish master' – had been plotting with the *Arrabbiati* and the *Tiepidi*.[1]

Fearful that Charles VIII would reoccupy Rome, Pope Alexander was worried by Florence's alliance with him. When His Holiness's agents told him that it was inspired by Savonarola, at first he thought the Frate was acting purely from a wish to regain Pisa. Alexander knew that Charles had promised to restore the city to the Florentines, who hoped he would give them all Tuscany as well.

But before King Charles had left Naples, the Pope began to receive a steady flow of letters from the *Tiepidi* at Florence, which alerted him to precisely what Savonarola was saying, that the Church must be reformed by the sword and he, Alexander, must go. Girolamo's implacable opponent, Fra' Mariano da Genazzano, who as General of the Augustinians had access to the Pope, corroborated such accusations, referring to the Frate as 'the Devil's Instrument'.

Letters like those of the *Tiepidi* arrived from clergy at Milan, prompted by Il Moro. The Duke's brother, Cardinal Ascanio Sforza, was at Rome to tell Alexander that the Frate was a threat to his papacy. In July 1495 these warnings were confirmed by the publication of Savonarola's letter of 26 May to Charles VIII, insisting that the King had a divine mission to renew the Church. Nothing could have been more calculated to alarm the Pope. Fra' Girolamo's enemies attacked the letter in a pamphlet published at Bologna and in a sermon at the end of the month he expressed regret that the letter had appeared in print, complaining that it was done without his knowledge.

Alexander was aware that the King of France had the power to summon a General Council and depose him. Three popes had been dismissed at the beginning of the century and he may have recalled the trial of Pope John XXIII (Cossa, not Roncalli) who spent the rest of his life in prison – as Gibbon famously puts it, 'the most scandalous charges were suppressed; the vicar of Christ was only accused of piracy, murder, rape, sodomy and incest'. As a papal nuncio in the 1480s, the Holy Father had watched King Ferrante and King Mathias Corvinus of Hungary try to summon a council to depose Innocent VIII. They had been unable to muster enough support from the cardinals, but nowadays a majority of the Sacred College would be delighted to get rid of Alexander.

While the Pope had identified Savonarola as an enemy, he did not know how to deal with him because of his following at Florence. However, the Frate could not do much harm unless King Charles re-occupied Rome again and so there was no need for haste. But when it became clear that the French were leaving Italy, even before they had gone home over the Alps he made his first move. A Florentine, Bishop Soderini was sent to Florence to investigate, where he rebuked the Signoria formally, saying it was unworthy of a great republic to let itself be ruled by a mere friar. He also sent disturbing reports to Rome of what Fra' Girolamo was preaching and advised that he should be summoned to Rome – nothing could be done with the Florentines while the Frate remained in the city.

Realising that trouble was brewing, Savonarola tried to pre-empt it by sending a letter to Rome, describing the reformation he had achieved in Florence and offering to submit his sermons 'for correction by the Holy Roman Church'. His letter, which has not survived, elicited a bland response from Pope Alexander in the form of a papal brief dated 25 July 1495:

> To our well beloved son, greeting and apostolic benediction. We have heard that of all the workers in the Lord's vineyard, you are the most zealous; at which we greatly rejoice and give thanks to Almighty God. We have likewise heard that you claim your predictions of the future proceed not from yourself but from God and for this reason we desire, as befits our pastoral office, to have speech with you concerning these matters so that, being by your help better informed of God's will, we may be better able to fulfil it. Therefore, relying on your vow of holy obedience [as a religious], we order you to come to us without delay, and will welcome you with loving kindness.[2]

'Come into my parlour', said the spider to the fly! In reality, this amiably phrased letter was a death sentence. If Girolamo survived the journey to the Eternal City, during which he could easily be murdered by the hatchet men of Piero de' Medici or Lodovico il Moro, he would end up in the Tiber or disappear into the Castel Sant' Angelo. Burchard's *Diarium*, describing the fate of a bishop who had forged papal briefs, gives us some idea of what might have happened to Girolamo. The bishop was

> taken to Emperor Hadrian's sepulchre [Castel Sant' Angelo], to a dungeon called 'Sammarocco' for perpetual imprisonment; where a plank bed was ready, with a tester at its head to keep out the damp from the walls, a straw mattress on it and two cloaks, besides a breviary, a Bible and a copy of the Epistle of St. Peter. There was also a jug of water, three loaves of bread, a flask of oil and a lamp.[3]

Burchard tells us that he died within a few months.

Before answering the Pope's brief, Savonarola delivered another fearsome sermon, in the presence of the new Signoria, who, although well disposed towards him, were not spared his criticism. He attacked evils still existing in Florence – gamblers, blasphemers and homosexuals. Florence should arrest one and put him to death as an example. 'I tell you, Almighty God wants justice. . . . Now is the time to weep, not to make merry.' He told the Signoria to root out opposition: 'Put an end to those names of *Bigi*, *Bianchi* and *Arrabbiati*, who are ruining the city.'[4] With his practical streak, he also advised them to make arrangements in case of an epidemic: 'the pestilence is certain to come'.[5]

He suffered from an intestinal problem, which was probably dysentery contracted after excessive fasting, so severe that he suspected it might be fatal.[6] 'I've got to get better,' he told the Duomo. 'Then I'll preach to you again – if I'm still alive.'[7] It delayed his reply to the Pope's brief, which was sent on 31 July: 'Most Holy Father, my ardent desire is to see the shrines of the Apostles Peter and Paul so I can pray at the altars of these great saints, and I am still more eager when the Holy Father deigns to summon his humble servant. But I have barely recovered from a serious illness which prevents my preaching or studying, and still threatens my life.'[8]

Excusing himself, he gives vivid details:

Because the Lord, working through me, has saved this city from bloodshed and placed it under good, holy laws, there are enemies inside and outside the city who, after trying to enslave it and being thwarted, are seeking my blood and frequently try to kill me with steel and poison. In consequence, I can't leave here without obvious danger, while I can't even walk through the city without an armed escort. Also, this newly reformed government that the Lord, through me, has been pleased to give Florence, is not yet firmly established and will clearly be in danger without [my] continued help.

Alexander sent back a gracious message, accepting Fra' Girolamo's excuses. But two months later, on 8 September, he issued a new brief, addressed to the friars of Santa Maria Novella at Florence, a community of unreformed Dominicans, who were no friends to those of San Marco. Abandoning the earlier bland tone, it denounced:

A certain Fra' Girolamo, a seeker after novelty and disseminator of false doctrines. . . . This man's wits have been so muddled by the upheavals in the affairs of Italy that he is trying to make people believe he has a mission from God and talks to God, although he is unable to prove it either by miracles or direct evidence from the Holy Scriptures, as Canon Law prescribes. . . . We have been very patient, hoping he would repent and make up for his sins by submitting to us, and putting an end to that scandalous secession from the Lombard congregation to which our consent was extorted by the plausible wiles of certain friars.

The brief ended by ordering Fra' Girolamo to accept the authority of the Lombard congregation without delay, to go immediately to wherever he was summoned, and to cease at once from any sort of preaching, whether in public or in private.[9] Disobedience would mean instant excommunication.

At the same time, Alexander sent an angry letter to the Signoria, saying he would excommunicate them too if they went on helping the King of France. He also gave money to Piero de' Medici, who hired several thousand mercenaries. Piero's plan was to force his way into Florence, where he hoped the *Bigi* would rise in his support.

The friars of Santa Maria Novella passed the brief to the friars of San Marco, no doubt with a certain satisfaction. Savonarola had been away in the country, restoring his health, but swiftly returned to Florence. On 29 September he sent a long letter to the Pope, impassioned but closely reasoned, in which he dealt with the accusations one by one. He claimed that His Holiness had been misinformed by enemies, who were slandering him. 'As for my doctrines, I have always been submissive to the Church.' He insisted that he was impeccably orthodox:

> As for prophecy, I have never quite claimed to be a prophet, although it would not be heretical if I did, but I have certainly foretold a number of things, some of which have already come to pass while others will come true at some future date.

He pointed out that he was far from being the first member of the fifteenth-century Church to prophesy – a reference to Catherine of Siena and Vincent Ferrer, both of them Dominicans and canonised saints. He reminded Alexander that the separation of the Dominican congregations had not been just the work of a few friars but had involved several Cardinals. 'For us to rejoin the Lombard brethren would only deepen the ill-feeling, which unhappily exists between the two congregations, and result in further disputes and scandal.'[10] He also wrote a letter to a senior Dominican at Rome, probably the Order's Procurator, with a request that he should defend him against the people who were filling His Holiness's ears with slanders: 'I know exactly who is behind these attacks and realize that they are the work of evil citizens hoping to re-establish a tyranny in Florence.'[11]

While waiting for Alexander's answer, Fra' Girolamo climbed into the Duomo's pulpit on 11 October, for the first time since July. Part of his sermon dealt with how the *Arrabbiati* must have plotted against him and he made a convincing guess at the way they had been slandering him. 'We're going to tell so many wicked lies about this man to the Holy Father that we should be able to force him to leave his lair, but if he refuses to budge, then we'll accuse him of being disobedient – we can catch him either way.'[12]

He also advised his listeners on how to defend themselves against Piero de' Medici's coup, which they had been warned was imminent. Brandishing a crucifix, he told them not to have any qualms about crushing Piero's followers. Anybody who tried to restore despotism in Florence should unhesitatingly be put to death, just as the Romans had dealt with the supporters of Tarquinius: 'Cut off his head, although he may be the head of his family, cut off his head!'[13] In addition, said the Frate, they ought to bring in a new law that would make anyone found guilty of speaking ill of the government liable for a fine of fifty ducats.

In the meantime, the Pope had realised Piero's coup would fail and that Savonarola and his friars could not be overawed by threats. So long as Charles VIII stayed in France the Frate was not a danger, while extracting him from Florence would antagonise its citizens. Alexander decided that, for the moment, silencing him should be enough. On 16 October he sent yet another brief:

We explained to you in earlier letters how we regret the disturbed state of affairs in Florence, which is due to your sermons. Instead of preaching against vice and concentrating on virtue, you predict the future, something that would stir up trouble even among peaceful people, let alone among Florentines who are so prone to discontent and faction. That is why we summoned you. But since we realize from your letters and the testimony of many cardinals of the Holy Roman Church that you are ready to submit yourself to the Church's judgement, as befits a Christian and a religious, we are happier about you and feel that you have not preached like this from evil intent but out of simplicity and misplaced zeal for the Lord's vineyard. However, we would be wrong if we did not command you by your vow of obedience to cease preaching, in public or in private, until it is possible for you to present yourself to us – and not protected by an armed guard, as is your usual way of going about. . . .[14]

For the moment, Fra' Girolamo could see no choice but to comply and wait for better times. Encouragingly, by the time he received the brief the Medici coup had collapsed in abject failure, Piero fleeing back to Rome, penniless and discredited. No doubt, too, by looking into the future yet again, Girolamo still further strengthened his conviction that King Charles was going to return very soon and depose Alexander. Moreover, if the Frate was forbidden to preach, at least people could read his book.

SEVENTEEN

The Compendium of Revelations

Savonarola meets the Devil – *Compendium Revelationum*, 1495

*But he that prophesieth, speaketh unto men to edification, and
exhortation and comfort.*

St Paul's First Epistle to the Corinthians, 14: 3

In his first letter to Pope Alexander, Savonarola stated:

Should your Holiness wish for any more information on what I
have publicly predicted about the coming chastisement of Italy
and about the renewal of the Church, you can find it all set out in
a book of mine that will shortly be published. . . . I am anxious to
have these predictions made available in print so that, should they
not be fulfilled, then the world will be able to know I have been a
false prophet. There are, however, other things of a peculiarly

secret nature which must remain under a veil, as for the moment I am not allowed to reveal them to any living creature.[1]

Yet there was nothing more likely to alarm and infuriate the Pope than the book's predictions.

It was not the first time the Frate had appeared in print, however – he had been publishing tracts and sermons since 1491. The tracts, each about a dozen pages long, were devotional, such as *Della orazione mentale* ('On Mental Prayer') which was in the classical tradition of Western mysticism, while another was a manual on how priests should hear confession. The first sermon to appear in print was *Predica della Rinnovazione* ('On the Renewal of the Church'), which came out in January 1495. Since it tells the story of his prophetic preaching, it may already have upset Alexander.

The colophon on the final page of the *Compendium Revelationum*, by 'the useless servant of Jesus Christ Father Hieronymus of Ferrara of the Order of Preachers', informs us it was printed at Florence in October 1495 by Ser Francesco Bonaccorsi. This is the revised version in Latin for scholars since an Italian edition, *Compendio di rivelazioni*, had been published by Bonaccorsi on 18 August, to be reprinted by another publisher twelve days later – with the woodcut of the author preaching in the Duomo. There were five editions in six weeks and another four during the following year, one printed at Ulm and another at Paris. Clearly the book was an immediate best-seller.

Ercole d'Este of Ferrara was so eager to read this book that he instructed his ambassador to commission a copy of the manuscript should it take a long time to reach the printing-press, promising that until it was published, 'we will keep it a secret for as long as he wants and not show it to anyone'. But within a few days Fra' Girolamo sent the Duke a copy of the first Italian edition, hot from the press and printed on special paper; and he refused to accept any payment. Later, he sent Ercole a copy of the Latin edition. On both occasions the Duke wrote a warm letter of thanks to the man whom everybody now regarded as Ferrara's most famous son, asking him to pray for 'our native land'. He did not say what he thought of the book's contents; perhaps he was disappointed that there was no mention of what might happen in Ferrara.

Yet those who bought the *Compendium* got their money's worth. Spiritual journeys to the next world were the fifteenth-century equivalent of space travel, and the slim little volume,[2] barely more than a hundred pages in length, cannot have disappointed the most avid reader. The author not only lists his principal visions, such as the sword of God raised to smite the earth and the black cross rising from Rome, but gives an account of a visit to paradise. Contemporaries saw nothing too unusual in all this – Martin Luther would describe a visit from the Devil at midnight.

Fra' Girolamo begins somewhat aggressively, quoting Christ on the foolishness of casting pearls before swine. He says that he includes his best-known predictions, in case they have been wrongly reported. By now he has no hesitation in calling himself a prophet, quoting Amos ('God does nothing without revealing his secret to his servants the prophets') when explaining why the coming of the French was revealed to him, and mentioning the 'supernatural light' by which a prophet can tell that his 'symbolical visions' come from God or that the words he hears are spoken by angels. He then stresses that the wickedness of Italy and above all of her rulers, clergy and princes, has angered God beyond endurance, to such an extent that He has decided to purify the Church. He has chosen Florence as a base from which prophecies will spread through Italy. After this, Girolamo gives summaries of his most important prophetic sermons.

He describes how his methods developed:

> At first I predicted future events by citing the Scriptures, by reasoning and by parables, because people were not ready. Then I started to reveal that I knew about the future from a source other than Scripture. Finally, I admitted openly that what I was saying came from divine inspiration.

He emphasises the divine role given to the King of the French, stressing how accurate he himself has been in predicting the invasion. Describing his embassy to Charles, he recalls explaining that God had appointed the King as His 'minister of justice'. He had told Charles that he knew the French were coming long before, but God would not let him speak the King's name. And he had asked Charles to forgive the Florentines for their initial hostility since they did not realise he had been sent by God.

The second part of the *Compendium* tells of a Dante-like pilgrimage to heaven as Florence's ambassador to the Virgin Mary, taking four companions, Faith, Simplicity, Prayer and Patience. As soon as he starts, he is waylaid by a hermit who tries to shake his confidence. The 'Tempter', as Fra' Girolamo calls him, begins by ascribing his visions and prophecies to melancholy or too much imagination. 'But instead of melancholy I'm full of joy and I can see beyond the natural order,' answers Girolamo. When the Tempter says they may be due to the conjunction of the stars at his birth, Girolamo dismisses this as 'a silly objection because astrology is foolishness'. The hermit asks: 'Could they be the work of the Devil?' Girolamo replies that he has seen all his prophecies come true and never been deceived in a single detail. The Tempter claims that the Lord has not spoken like this to any mortal since the Ascension, which Girolamo denies. Have his prophecies come from St Bridget or Abbot Joachim? 'I have not read Bridget's revelations and almost nothing by Joachim' is his response.

The questioner tries to frighten him. 'Surely it would be wiser for you to stay silent? You're too well known, not only in Florence but all over Italy.' 'But my job is to please God, not men.' The Tempter brings up the problems of San Marco's dispute with other Dominican congregations. Finally, he rebukes Girolamo for meddling in politics. Girolamo insists: 'My prophecies have helped to reform morals.' Laughing, his four companions now tell him that he has been talking to the Devil.

The description of his meeting with the Virgin Mary may have been unconsciously derived from that between Boetius and the majestic woman who embodies Philosophy in *De Consolatione Philosophiae*, a book still widely read in the fifteenth century. However, Boetius had not gone into such detail as the jewels on the Virgin's throne, which Fra' Girolamo included, possibly inspired by memories of constant meditations on the Coronation of the Virgin – one of the Mysteries of the Rosary, a devotion that was especially popular among Dominicans.

'The city of Florence shall be more glorious, powerful and prosperous than she ever was in the past, and her frontiers will stretch far further, wider than anyone expects,' Mary reassured him:

Anything she has lost, anything she may still lose, is going to be restored, together with new gains. Woe to those who rebel against

her, because they shall be punished severely. Four years have gone
by since the time when among your predictions you foretold how
the Pisans would try to regain their freedom during Florence's
times of tribulation, which beyond question would end in their
ruin. . . . You have foretold the renewal of the Church, which will
take place very quickly. Through the light of the Holy Spirit you
also foretell that the infidels will be converted, Turks, Moors and
all the others, and this too will happen, soon enough for to be seen
by many who are alive today. But, as you have said, the Church's
renewal and growth cannot take place without tribulations. So it
should not seem strange for Florence to have her share, although
she shall suffer less than anybody else. . . .

The Virgin handed Fra' Girolamo's angel a map of Italy, showing
great cities suffering horrors which, he says, 'I am not allowed to
reveal.' Then she produced another map, one of Florence, covered in
lilies reaching far beyond the city walls. 'Joyfully, I cried, "My Lady,
it looks to me as if all these little lilies go very well with the big lilies
[of France], that have also begun to bloom further afield." . . .' She
told Girolamo to assure everybody that God's promises to the
Florentines would be fulfilled. Evil men could do nothing to stop
them. In the meantime, the city would be punished if it did not drive
out blasphemers, homosexuals and gamblers. After repeating that
everything he had already foretold would happen within ten years if
not sooner, she sent him back to earth.

He warns those who may scoff that they will suffer 'sevenfold' more
than anybody else. They should read Old Testament Prophets such as
Ezekiel, Daniel or Zechariah, in which they will find just as many
strange and mysterious details, while not even the Gospels and the
Lord's teaching had been immune from questioning. He ends with a
sermon from Christ Himself, intended for the Florentines, which insists
that they must believe what Fra' Girolamo tells them. He anticipated
incredulity. Having first described his journey in May 1495 (in a
sermon on Ascension Day), he now complains that if critics listened to
him carefully, 'they would know I did not mean to say my mortal body
had been in Paradise, but that I saw it in a mental vision. Of course,
trees, streams, stairs, doors and chairs don't exist in Paradise, and if
these critics weren't blinded by malice, they would realize that the
scenes were put into my mind by angels.'

Outpourings such as those in the *Compendium* discredit their author in modern eyes as much as they impressed contemporaries. Fra' Girolamo seems to cross the border between intuition and hallucination. Biographers like Schnitzer or Ridolfi, who venerated him as a saint, spend as little time as possible discussing them. Yet, as Villari observes, a little harshly, 'the puerility of the visions may be taken as a strong proof of Savonarola's sincerity'.[3]

Soon the Frate's fiercest critic, Giovanni Caroli, was circulating a manuscript dialogue between himself and truth, modelled on Girolamo's dialogue with the Tempter, in which Truth says that Savonarola is just an opportunistic charlatan.[4] In *De modo discernendi falsum prophetam* ('How to Identify a False Prophet'), printed at Milan, the Franciscan friar Samuele Cascini claimed that such prophecies contradicted Scripture and accused him of being a heretic and trying to found a new Church.[5] Gianfrancesco Pico sprang to the Frate's defence, rejecting Cascini's arguments in a book which insisted that because the Bible is often unclear it has to be interpreted by prophets.[6]

While Alexander VI may have recognised the author's sincerity, he can hardly have been expected to welcome his prophecies. Nothing was better calculated to frighten the Pope more than Fra' Girolamo's insistence that King Charles was coming back.

EIGHTEEN

A Cardinal's Hat?

The Viper of Milan – Italian, sixteenth century

. . . death, a crimson hat, a hat of blood, that's what I want.
Savonarola, *Prediche delle Feste*

Just how shaken Alexander VI had been by Savonarola was shown during the late summer of 1496. His Holiness would offer the Frate a cardinal's hat, the ultimate papal bribe and the culmination of over a year's attempts to silence him.

After receiving the papal brief of October 1495, Fra' Girolamo ceased to preach for several months, in accordance with the brief. While despising Alexander as a man, he revered his office – even when outraged by the harm that so evil a pope was doing to the Church, he retained an instinctive obedience to the Vicar of Christ. Another reason for obeying was the need to recover his health.

Instead of preaching, he wrote. His most important publication during this period was the *Epistola a un amico*, which appeared shortly before Christmas and was swiftly reprinted. In this 'Letter to a Friend', he vigorously defended himself against the accusations in Alexander's brief. The *Arrabbiati* riposted with a scurrilously abusive *Epistola responsiva a frate Ieronimo*.

When Pandolfo Collenuccio came to see him in October 1495 and asked what he thought of the peace between the League and the French, the Frate gave his opinion unhesitatingly – no doubt because he knew it would be reported to Ferrara:

> Messer Pandolfo, I answer in the words of the Prophet Ezekiel: 'And you shall know that I am the Lord God. Because they have deceived my people, saying: Peace, peace; and there is no peace; and one built up a wall, and others daubed it with untempered mortar. Say unto them that daub without tempering, that it shall fall.'[1]

Despite repeated pleas from the Signoria, the Pope refused to lift the ban on his preaching. Fra' Domenico da Pescia tried to fill his place as far as possible. Eventually, after the Signoria had persuaded Cardinal Carafa to intercede, Alexander gave limited consent for Girolamo to preach during the Lent of 1496, but technically, the brief remained in force.

Girolamo made certain the carnival would be different from what it had been in former years. After Vespers on Shrove Tuesday, 16 February, 10,000 boys carrying olive branches marched through Florence behind banners of the cross, the Virgin and the saints, accompanied by drums and bagpipes. They sang hymns specially written by Fra' Girolamo and Girolamo Benivieni. Luca Landucci says he was delighted to see his sons 'among those blessed and clean-minded troops of boys'.[2] From the context, it is obvious that the diarist's satisfaction was due to more than sentimentality. Because of the moral climate created by the Frate, the boys of Florence no longer prostituted themselves to sodomites, mugged citizens in the streets or tried to kill each other by hurling rocks – the 'mad and bestial game of stones'.

Months of frustration found an outlet in Fra' Girolamo's Lenten sermons on Amos and Zechariah, which he began on Ash

Wednesday, 17 February. He made the first a dialogue: 'What's been happening?' he asks himself on behalf of the congregation. 'Frate, you're keeping us all in unbearable suspense.' At first, he avoids any hint of conflict with Pope Alexander. No excommunication had arrived, he insists, and if it did it wouldn't make a jot of difference. 'The Pope can't make me do something contrary to charity or the Gospel and I don't believe the Pope wants me to do any such thing.'[3]

He had stayed silent for so long, he explained, to look for errors in his previous sermons, but had not found one. 'I have always believed, and I believe now, everything taught by the Roman Church. I've always submitted to her authority and still do.' He adds:

> I've written to Rome to say that if by accident I have preached or written anything heretical . . . then I'm ready to make amends and retract in public what I may have said. I'm always willing to give way and obey the Church of Rome, and I solemnly declare that whosoever obeys her will never be damned . . . while there may be different views on what exactly is the Church, I myself rely entirely on Christ and on what the Roman Church decides.[4]

But Girolamo went on to argue that while the Church is infallible where dogma is concerned, no one is bound to obey a command from the Pope which he knows to be wrong. Although a perfectly orthodox view, impeccably Thomist, by expressing it he left himself open to misinterpretation.

He also spoke of his reluctance to preach again:

> I've set out in the centre of a raging tempest, buffeted on all sides by contrary winds. I long to reach harbour but don't know the way, I long to take my rest but I can't find a resting place, I long to keep quiet and stay silent, but I can't. . . .[5]

He complained that his enemies had been sending all sorts of lies about him to Rome. He put his trust in young people rather than the old. 'In you, young men, lies my hope and the Lord's hope,' he declared:

> You're going to rule the city of Florence properly because you're different from your fathers who didn't know how to throw off

tyranny or how to appreciate God's gift of liberty to his people. But as for you, old men, you spend your whole time talking evil in your clubs and work places or sending letters from Florence which are full of lies. Because of you many are saying that I've plunged Italy into chaos. Oh you fools, why do you take such pleasure in lying? Where are the armies and vast amounts of money with which I'm supposed to create an upheaval like this? I'm not plunging Italy into chaos, but I can safely predict there will be chaos. I foresee the scourge being set in motion by your sins. . . . Unless you live in the fear of God and unless you learn to love free government the Lord will bring down sorrow on you and only for your children will he fulfil his promises of happiness in Florence.[6]

Within a week he was once again attacking the 'great prelates of Rome'. In Florence, 'we persuade men to live simply and women to live decently. You, by contrast, lead them down the road to lust and luxury and pride, because you've ruined the world, corrupting men with lustfulness and women with indecency, while you make children turn to sodomy and filthiness and become prostitutes . . . at night you go to your concubine and next morning you go to the Sacraments.'[7] Most of his congregation must have heard the well-founded rumours that this was Pope Alexander's normal custom.

On the fourth Sunday Savonarola warned:

Be prepared, I tell you, Rome, to suffer dreadful punishments. You're going to be bound in iron chains, you're going to be put to the sword, fire and flame are going to eat you up. . . . Rome, you've caught a mortal disease, you're sick unto death. If you want to be healed, give up feasting, give up pride, ambition, lust and greed since it's food like this that's made you ill.[8]

Because the whole of Italy was so full of evil, so full of whores and pimps, 'I shall overwhelm her with the scum of the earth, overthrow her princes and trample on the pride of Rome,' he promised.

Conquerors shall seize her holy places and defile her churches because they have been made dens of vice, and I shall turn them into stalls for horses and hogs, which will upset God much less than seeing them used by prostitutes. . . . Countless troubles shall strike you, Italy, trouble of war after famine, trouble of plague after war, trouble on every side. There will be rumour upon rumour, rumours of barbarians here, of barbarians there. . . . Men shall consult astrology, to no avail. The laws justifying priesthood shall disappear and priests be stripped of their orders, princes shall wear sackcloth, ordinary folk shall be crushed by suffering. All men shall lose courage.[9]

In another sermon he prophesied: 'Behold, the sky shall be darkened, behold, it shall rain down fire and flame, stones and rocks. Fly from Rome [which is Babylon] because Babylon means confusion, and Rome has confused all the scriptures, all the vices, everything.'[10]

In a further sermon the Frate touched on the city's political problems, giving a wonderfully lurid portrait of a Renaissance tyrant and what it was like to be the subject of such a ruler:

The word 'tyrant' means a man of utterly evil life, of much deeper wickedness than most men, a usurper of other men's rights, a murderer of his own soul and of the souls of others. The tyrant is proud, lustful and greedy and, since those three vices contain the seeds of all the other vices, he has within him the seeds of literally every vice of which a man is capable. All his senses are perverted, his eyes from watching debauchery, his ears from being flattered and listening to slander, his palate by the very worst sort of gluttony. He corrupts magistrates, robs widows and orphans, oppresses the poor and patronizes men who encourage him to swindle them. Eaten up by suspicion, he has his spies everywhere, determined that everybody shall be terrified and become his slaves. Where there's a tyrant, no one can be free or speak freely – people are afraid, virtue vanishes, vice prevails.[11]

In his last sermon in the series, Fra' Girolamo declared that no pope or religious superior could order him to do what was wrong. 'You're in error,' he would tell them. 'You're not the Roman Church, you're a man and you're a sinner.' He also mentioned his own fate. 'If you want to know how it's all going to end for me, I can tell you that it will end in death and in my being cut to pieces.' He then described yet another terrible vision which finished with darkness covering the earth, lit up by fire and lightning.[12]

These Lenten sermons on Amos and Zechariah were reported to Rome with relish by the *Arrabbiati*, and soon highly coloured versions of them were circulating all over Italy and in other countries as well. Their contents were bound to infuriate the Pope.

Piero Capponi was worried by Fra' Girolamo's lack of restraint. On 10 March, as tactfully as possible, he told a Pratica summoned to advise the Signoria that while it was beyond question that Savonarola's sermons had done Florence a very great deal of good, care must be taken to avoid provoking Pope Alexander. The Frate should certainly continue to preach, Capponi fully agreed, provided that the pontiff was prepared to give his permission. It would be no bad idea if the city's lawyers were to hold a meeting with Fra' Girolamo and discuss how he could preach without angering Rome.

'Render therefore unto Caesar the things which are Caesar's, and unto God the things that are God's,' observed Capponi, who knew he risked antagonising Girolamo and his followers.[13] Even so, he reminded his hearers that hostile measures taken by former popes against the city, such as placing her under interdict, had done serious damage, particularly to her trade and business interests abroad. An interdict prohibited priests from giving the sacraments of the Church to the people of the country or city concerned, from absolving them and giving them communion, from Christening, marrying or burying them. They became pariahs, other Christians being forbidden to have dealings with them. Capponi was not the only Florentine to worry about an interdict – rumours were running through the city that one was coming before Easter and that it would be wise to go to the sacraments while they were still available.

Capponi failed to grasp that Savonarola could not stop his attacks on Rome. They were an indispensable part of his message: he believed they were inspired by God, who would protect Florence under all circumstances. In a sermon during the last week of March, in which he promised that God was about to send 'a saintly pope' dedicated to reform, he cited chastity as a virtue necessary for a pope. Everyone in the Duomo knew it was a virtue unknown to Alexander Borgia.

Even so, Fra' Girolamo did at least omit from these ferocious sermons for Lent 1496 any reference to Alexander's election as pope, despite his conviction that it had been invalid, or to his belief that a reforming council should be summoned urgently. During the final sermon in the series on 10 April he became almost diplomatic, possibly because he knew that a commission of fourteen Dominican theologians had met in Alexander's presence to investigate accusations which had been made against him.

'Now I shall talk about the Pope,' he announced:

> It has been reported to His Holiness, by word of mouth and by letter, that I've spoken ill of him, which is not true. It is written in Holy Scripture, '*Principi populi tui non maledices*' ['you must not curse your people's ruler']. I've never done anything of the sort, and certainly I've never referred from this pulpit to anyone by name.[14]

The claim was scarcely convincing since it was only too easy to guess that whenever he spoke of Rome or 'great prelates' he had Alexander VI in mind.

The Pope was well aware of this. On 26 March Ricciardo Becchi, the Florentine envoy in Rome, reported to the Ten (responsible for foreign affairs) that Alexander and the cardinals had declared Florence was dishonouring and imperilling herself by permitting the Frate, the boys and the common people to behave as they did. Instead of Girolamo, they were now complaining of the government that let him go on preaching despite the Pope's wishes, let him speak ill of the pontiff, the cardinals and the entire court of Rome, let him claim he was a prophet who talked to God, let him encourage children and the rabble. It was a disgrace that a city should allow herself to be ruled by a friar and a mob of children. Such a government could only end in disaster.[15] 'In short,' ended Becchi, 'you are accused of losing your heads and the Pope is grumbling about all this in conversations with both the League's envoys and your defenders here.' On 30 March he reported that he had heard that the pontiff had now committed Savonarola's case to two cardinals and two bishops, besides ordering Torriani, Master General of the Dominicans, to start a legal process.

In response, the Ten, *Piagnoni* to a man, wrote defiantly to their envoy that the accusations he mentioned in his report were untrue. In any case, since Lent was over, there could be no further point in asking the Pope for permission for Fra' Girolamo to preach.

On 5 April Becchi had sent another report to Florence, informing the Ten that Alexander had told the commission of theologians that he wanted to punish Savonarola as 'a heretic, a schismatic, a man disobedient to the Holy See, and superstitious'. Only one of the theologians, a young friar, had been brave enough to defend the Frate, 'to the Pope's grave displeasure'. It is clear that enemies had been at work since 'either the Pope or one of the theologians declared that Fra' Hyeronimo [sic] was the cause of all the misfortunes of Piero [de Medici]'. Even so, says Becchi, some cardinals present had somehow dissuaded the Pope from taking action.[16]

A week later, Becchi wrote to the Ten, suggesting that the Signoria should send a tactfully phrased letter to Alexander, telling him they had asked Savonarola to obey His Holiness and strongly urged that in future he should always speak with restraint of the Pope, the cardinals and Rome. Accordingly, on 16 April the Signoria sent a letter to Becchi for him to show Alexander. It insisted, not very convincingly, that Fra' Girolamo had always spoken with perfect respect about His Holiness, adding that it was quite wrong to allege that he controlled Florence – he had never tried to do any such thing and to claim that he had was a calumny.[17]

Alexander was not the only Italian prince to be angered by Savonarola's sermons. Early in April Duke Lodovico wrote from Milan to his brother Cardinal Ascanio, saying that the Pope should send a Franciscan vicar-general to Florence to deal with the Frate. In a flattering reply, Alexander told Lodovico somewhat unrealistically that, if the Duke thought it was a good idea, Savonarola would be summoned to Rome.

In the meantime, Fra' Girolamo wrote to Il Moro that he had heard the Duke was complaining about his sermons, but this must be because enemies had falsely described him 'as being hostile to His Highness', which was untrue. In reality, he loved the Duke, he loved every prince in Italy, he loved all mankind, and he was ready to die for their salvation. The scourge was drawing near, but if Lodovico did penance for his sins, then God would surely pardon him and make him prosperous. Otherwise his affairs would end in ruin. 'One day you will see that my advice was better than any other given to you,' the Frate told the Duke. 'For these words of mine, I expect no reward other than disgrace,' he added. 'And persecution and in the end death, to which I genuinely look forward . . . since to someone like me dying for Christ is riches.'[18]

Another who complained about the sermons was Galeotto, Prince of Mirandola. A brutal man in no way resembling his brother Giovanni, he kept his mother and another brother chained in a dungeon. After replying that he had attacked no one and was only calling men to repentance to avert the coming scourge, Fra' Girolamo sent the Prince another letter, very different from the one he had written to Il Moro. Unless he changed his ways, he told Galeotto, harsh punishment lay in store – his goods, his body and his family would suffer. 'I can also tell you your life is nearing its end and if you don't do what I've said, then you'll go to hell.'[19]

Gianfrancesco Pico remembered, 'My father was at that time in the best of health and strength and seemed likely to have a long life. Yet he only lived for another two years after [receiving] this truly prophetic letter, and from that moment on the history of our family has been one long, blood-stained tragedy.'[20]

In contrast, Duke Ercole took the Lenten sermons very much to heart, as Savonarola was informed by the Duke's Dominican confessor, Fra' Tommaso. He and his court had already been fasting since January, to fend off the scourge. During the same month the Frate had sent him a copy of his latest book, with the message, 'I hope I shall soon see the land of my birth bear spiritual fruit because of Your Excellency.'[21] He had told the Duke to put sacred matters first in view of the tribulations drawing ever nearer, and to replace wicked ministers by men of probity since they were angering God. On Maundy Thursday Ercole gave his customary annual dinner for the poor – 154 this time – washing their feet and giving them new clothes as usual, so the *Diario ferrarese* tells us. Then, on the morning of Easter Sunday, it was announced from the balcony of the Palazzo del Ragione that by command of the Duke and on pain of dire punishment, no person should dare to blaspheme God, the Virgin Mary or the saints, gamble, commit sodomy, keep a concubine or let houses to whores or their pimps, while shops and stalls were not to do business on Sundays. Despite his former benevolence towards the city's Jewish community, from now on every 'Hebrew or Marrano' must wear a yellow 'O' sewn on to his coat, besides attending a sermon on Low Sunday in the Duomo.

In a letter to the Duke of 27 April, Fra' Girolamo expressed his satisfaction with these measures. He reminded the Duke that he must keep a sharp eye on his ministers. 'They are apt to undermine the mercifulness, the kind intentions and the good name of a sovereign with their own selfishly inspired measures and their wicked, unjust extortions, using insincere flattery [to get their way]. Men like these should be treated as enemies by Your Excellency.'[22] It appears that the Frate had been watching the city closely and had heard some unpleasant stories.

In the event, Duke Ercole's Easter proclamation does not appear to have had much effect, while the Low Sunday sermon failed to convert a single Jew. But one afternoon only two months after Fra' Girolamo's letter about officials angering God, a corrupt magistrate was disembowelled at his house with a dagger by irate victims, a deed hailed with delight by the Ferraresi. Remembering the Frate's warning, the Duke made no attempt to catch the assassins.

The book Girolamo had sent to Duke Ercole was *De simplicitate Christianae vitae*, probably the translation into Italian by Girolamo Benivieni. This was a straightforward explanation of what Catholic Christians believed, stressing the vital importance of God's grace, accompanied by advice on living a good life – the author insists in simplicity in everything, even in manners and clothes. However, his real object was to demonstrate that he could not possibly be accused of heretical or schismatic views.

After finishing his Lenten preaching, Savonarola went to Prato to give a course of sermons, attended by many people from Florence and the country round about. He delivered an impressive sermon to members of the University of Pisa who had taken refuge at Prato. Marsilio Ficino, who was present, supposedly expressed warm admiration for the sermon while, according to Cinozzi, the reaction of Oliviero Arduini, a distinguished theologian and authority on Aristotle, was, 'Let us throw away our books and follow this man, although we are scarcely worthy of doing even that.'[23]

Savonarola returned from Prato to Florence where he found a strangely altered situation. On 23 April Becchi reported from Rome to the Ten that Alexander had expressed himself as 'well satisfied' (*'assai ben soddisfatto'*) with Savonarola and what he was doing, and for some time there would be no more threats from Rome.

A charming letter arrived from the Duke of Milan, dated 30 April, in which Il Moro thanked Fra' Girolamo for writing to him so very frankly. Explaining that he had been misled by false stories of how the Frate had slandered him and disobeyed Pope Alexander, stories which he now saw were clearly untrue, the Duke promised that in future he would never believe such calumnies. 'If we have perhaps offended you or displeased you in any way, then we are extremely sorry and from this moment on we will never do so again,' protested Lodovico. 'You can rest assured that we shall always value your advice and your opinions.' He added that he prided himself on being as good a Christian as any other man, unaware of any sins for which he ought to atone. But if Girolamo should see fit to give him a penance, then of course he would certainly perform it.[24]

Alexander and Lodovico's benevolence was due to reports from papal and Milanese agents in France that Charles VIII was preparing another invasion, and after the League and Fornovo, both men had every reason to fear him. They needed a friend at court. The reports were confirmed when ambassadors from France arrived in Florence at the end of April, bearing the glad tidings that King Charles was returning. The Signoria elected in May reflected even stronger support for the Frate.

Girolamo's sermons in May show renewed confidence. 'I'm still here, instead of having run away as some people were predicting,' he told his followers in the Duomo:

The reason for my coming back is to refute the slanders spread by enemies. I also realize that, because of lack of encouragement from the pulpit, our numbers are decreasing. I even admit that I can't live without preaching. Above all, I am here to obey Him who is the prelate of prelates and Pope of Popes.

Later, he described how the Holy Spirit came down on the priesthood through the saints, to enter the Christian people. 'Nowadays, however, the corruption of clergy and Church prevents the Spirit from reaching believers,' he explained. 'We must pray to God to help us and hasten the coming of the scourge so that the reform of the Church will re-open the channels for grace and the Spirit.' This is the language of the Counter-Reformation, half a century before its time.

His attacks on the Church were as unrestrained as ever. 'You, you prelate who buys benefices, you're a thief!' he cried. 'You, you father who buys them for your children, you're a thief.' The reference to Pope Alexander, who was busily heaping the goods of the Church on his children and the entire Borgia clan, was unmistakable:

Prelates, lords of Italy, step forward! . . . Strip them of their possessions, O Lord, take away everything they have. The sword, the sword, that's the only cure! I warn you, Italy, I warn you, Rome, you can only be saved by Christ!

There would be bloodshed and cruelty on a staggering scale. God was going to trample on Rome – priests, bishops, cardinals, they would be trodden down. The sacred relics in the city would not save her. Rome was the source and origin of all sin throughout the world – queen of all wickedness, queen of all pride, queen of all luxury, queen of all vice, cause of every sin committed by priests and those who might otherwise have been good Christians.

Fra' Girolamo continued like this throughout the summer of 1496.[25] Reports of his sermons reached Rome, brought by *Arrabbiati*, who made them sound even worse. But because of the invasion scare, Alexander dared not move against him.

Yet it was not an easy period for Girolamo. As in the previous year, unending rain and storms and then floods destroyed the harvest, bringing hunger and sickness to Florence. In May Landucci noted bitterly, 'the downpour has lasted for about eleven months and not a week has gone by without rain'.[26] There were further outbreaks of plague and of a disease known as 'French boils'. The Florentine government was chronically short of money, everything being spent on the war to recover Pisa. Meanwhile, there was still no sign of King Charles and the 'scourge' – Landucci suspected that the French were making fools of the Florentines.

Even so, Alexander remained fearful and in the late summer he decided to buy the Frate with a cardinal's hat. The Pseudo-Burlamacchi says the offer was brought to San Marco by a Dominican. This was Lodovico da Ferrara the Order's Procurator, who, according to Fra' Girolamo himself, had been sent from Rome by Alexander to ask Girolamo's advice on how to win over the Florentines. All he had to do in return for the hat, explained Fra' Lodovico, was to stop attacking the pontiff.

In May the chronicler Parenti had recorded that Alexander sent one of his sons to the priory – the son being presumably Cesare Borgia, at that date still a cardinal – to find out from Savonarola whether there was some way in which his father could persuade Charles VIII to let him stay on as pope. If implausible, it is significant that such a story was credited by the level-headed Parenti. Clearly, the offer of a hat had been expected long before it took place. 'Come to my next sermon and you'll hear my reply,' Girolamo told Fra' Lodovico.

This was the sermon he gave to the Signoria at their invitation on 20 August, in the hall of the Grand Council, very different from his usual sermons. He showed the utmost diplomacy, especially about his pro-French policy. He had been accused of causing Florence's ruin, he declared, but why? Yes, it was true he had encouraged setting up the Great Council and abolishing the *parliamenti*, but everything would have broken down under any other government, because of the strife that was tearing the city apart. He had been accused of making laws, yet why complain if they were good laws? He had been accused of opposing the League when he had never even mentioned it in public – he had merely spoken of 'Lilies and Lilies'. Yes, of course he had written to the King of France, but only to warn him of what might happen if he did not do his duty. If there was famine, the poor had no grounds for grumbling since he had done all he could to raise funds to feed them.

He ceased to be subtle when he spoke of the Pope's offer:

People are saying the Frate wants money, the Frate has secret dealings, the Frate would like a cardinal's hat. Well, I can tell everybody that if I coveted such things I wouldn't be wearing a ragged habit. I just want to be glorified in You, my God. I don't have any desire for a hat or for a mitre, whether it's a big one or a little one, but only for the gift that you give to your saints – death, a crimson hat, a hat of blood, that's what I want.[27]

What would have happened, one may ask, had Girolamo Savonarola accepted the red hat? The possibilities are fascinating. Admittedly, he might have gone to Rome to put on the 'Sacred Purple' and join the College of Cardinals, only to vanish into one of the Borgia's dungeons. On the other hand, it is not entirely inconceivable that he would have succeeded Alexander as pope, elected with French support. If so, Christendom might have avoided the Protestant Reformation.

NINETEEN

The Burning of the Vanities

Savonarola gives a book to nuns – *Operetta sopra i dieci commandamenti*, 1497

. . . she saw something monstrous and many-coloured, in the shape of a pyramid, or, rather, like a huge fir-tree . . .

George Eliot, *Romola*

Savonarola is, of course, best known for his 'burning of the vanities' – his *'bruciamente della vanità'* – during Lent 1497 and Lent 1498, which supposedly involved the destruction of hundreds of works of art by great artists. In *The Waning of the Middle Ages* Johan Huizinga writes of an 'irreparable loss'. Before making such a claim, however, one should first try to discover what perished, and be aware of the context.

Although Pope Alexander, fearful of what revenge King Charles VIII might wreak when he came back to Italy, did not mount a campaign against Fra' Girolamo for some time after he had spurned the red hat, and while the *Piagnoni* remained in control of the city, the months that followed were difficult and dangerous for the Frate and the Florentine Republic. On 23 August Il Moro summoned the Florentine and Ferrarese envoys in Milan to an audience, and with deep indignation read out two letters, apparently written by Fra' Girolamo, which, so the Duke claimed, had been discovered en route for France. One of the letters, addressed to a mysterious 'Messer Niccolò', alleged that the French ambassador in Florence, the Archbishop of Aix, was a secret supporter of the Duke of Orleans (heir to the French throne) and lukewarm in his loyalty to King Charles, and detested Savonarola. The other letter, to a 'Fra' Clemente', was supposedly meant for the King himself, urging him to invade Italy as soon as possible.

In fact, both letters were forgeries, as the Duke must have known – he may even have had them forged himself – yet so plausible that they convinced many people. He sent copies to every Italian ruler, with an outraged note. He also sent copies to the Archbishop of Aix. At the same time, he wrote to the Signoria, complaining of Girolamo's pretended invitation to Charles, and declaring that he could not put up any longer with intrigues of this sort. His letter was read out publicly, in the presence of the Grand Council.

Relations between the Archbishop of Aix and Fra' Girolamo were bad enough already, as the Duke would have been informed by the indefatigable Sommenzi. The Archbishop had come to Florence in May with another of his King's demands for money, to finance the new French invasion, but Savonarola refused to listen to him, aware that the city was practically bankrupt. When the Archbishop read what had been said about him in the letter supposedly intercepted in Milan, he lost his head, blaming Girolamo and telling the Signoria that the Frate was ruining Florence – although Girolamo was France's greatest friend in the city. However, when the ambassador said he was going to denounce him in a sermon, the Signoria warned him that he would be lynched.

Ironically, no reaction came from Pope Alexander. Even so, the Frate was so worried that he publicly denied having written the letters, on 2 September, 'He had so many enemies, poor man,' commented Luca Landucci, that faithful if timid follower.[1]

On 26 September the little pharmacist recorded in his diary how news had come from the camp at Pisa that Piero Capponi – 'Piero of the Bells' as he was known, from his defiance of King Charles – had been killed by an arquebus,[2] and that his body was being brought back for burial. Attempting to retake the castle of Soiana, captured by the Pisans, he was in the trenches helping to lay a gun when he was hit by a bullet. He had foreseen his death, writing about it only the day before to his confessor at San Marco, Fra' Silvestro Maruffi, after his biggest bombard had blown up. His troops were so horrified that they fled. Piero was taken home along the Arno by barge to be given a state funeral attended by the Signoria and the Grand Council. He was a grave loss and not merely because he had been Florence's finest soldier. A staunch if occasionally critical supporter of the Frate, he had given him sound advice on political matters and would have defended him to the death.

Il Moro decided to involve the Emperor. Maximilian I (1449–1519) liked the idea of being crowned at Rome as Holy Roman Emperor – in theory he was only the King of the Romans until this took place – and asserting his role as the 'Temporal Sword of Christendom' although an imperial army had not been seen in Italy for two centuries. Conjuring up prospects of an imperial coronation, Lodovico persuaded him to lead an expedition against the Florentines, ignoring his dismal reputation as a general. Venice and the Pope supplied the penniless Emperor with funds.

'Maximilian arrived in Italy with very few troops, spreading a rumour that the large army he had given his word to bring would follow,' says Guicciardini drily.[3]

> 'Caesar' sent two ambassadors to Florence to say that because of the great campaign against the infidels he was contemplating, he had decided to come to Italy and settle matters there, and in consequence was asking the Florentines to promise to join all the other allies [the League] in defending Italy.

He also told them he intended to settle the quarrel with Pisa. Realising that Il Moro was hoping to use Maximilian to acquire Pisa for himself, the Venetians deflected the Emperor by sending an army to support the Pisans. Even so, they agreed with Milan that Maximilian should besiege Livorno, the key to Florence.

Although a seemingly sturdy child, the three-year-old Dauphin died in October – the chastisement Savonarola had predicted – and a grief-stricken King Charles postponed his invasion of Italy. The news could not have come at a worse time. No longer afraid of French anger, Alexander immediately sent papal and Sienese troops to attack the Florentines from the south. Although these were repulsed, a Venetian fleet blockaded the port of Livorno while Maximilian, joined by Pisan troops, invested it by land. Luckily for Florence, the League was hampered by the mutual rivalry of Venetians, Milanese and Emperor, all plotting to gain possession of Pisa.

There was no one in Italy who could help the Florentines, while despatches from France confirmed that King Charles had no plans to come and save them. Isolated, demoralised by the casualties in the Pisan campaign and the famine, as well as sporadic outbreaks of plague, by now they were terrified. Their terror was compounded by the prospect of losing Livorno, the only outlet for their trade overseas and the only port through which rescue could reach them. The news that a grain fleet from Marseilles, bound for Livorno with badly needed supplies, had been driven back seemed to be the final blow. There was uproar. 'Now at last we're seeing how the Frate has tricked us,' shouted Fra' Girolamo's enemies. 'Here is the good fortune he prophesied for Florence!' A desperate Signoria asked the Frate to restore the city's courage.

In response, he preached in the Duomo on 28 October, the day of Simon and Jude. He informed the citizens that their troubles came from not enough repentance – there was still too much blasphemy and gambling. Even so, the wonderful things promised for Florence were certainly going to come true, he reassured his anxious congregation, 'while the wicked will have their hell in this world and the next':

After you've made up your minds to unite and stop quarrelling, then you'll be able to listen to what I have to say. I should deserve to lose even my habit if we don't succeed in beating off these enemies. When you decide to follow my advice, I shall lead the attack myself, in front, with a crucifix in my hand, and our enemies will flee for their lives, to Pisa – probably further. Florence, have faith in what I'm saying!

Don't you remember how two years ago you were all in tears in this very church and how the revolution happened on the same day and suddenly you were free? How I persuaded King Charles to leave your city . . . how when he came back I went to him while you prayed; and God arranged for him to go away without doing us any harm? So have faith in what I'm saying now and put all your trust in the Lord. Whatever happens, I have no fear of the outcome, provided you keep close to the Lord, stay united and do what you can.[4]

He went on to rebuke opponents of the regime, of which there were three sorts, he said. First, there were the returned exiles, banished in the days of the Medici, who should be more grateful for being allowed home and ought to keep quiet. Then there were the Medici supporters, reprieved from the scaffold 'with the halter round their necks'. He told this second sort, 'You're all plotting and I know just what you're planning.' Last were the lukewarm office holders who did not enforce the laws so that the city was 'full of gambling, blasphemy, lust and fornication'. He warned the latter, 'If you don't maintain justice, then the scourge will certainly smite you.'

'Finally, let me tell everybody here, and I'm speaking in the name of the Lord, that anyone who wants to bring a tyrant back will assuredly come to a very bad end indeed.'[5]

He may have said this because he had heard plausible reports of yet another plot to restore Piero. His sermon contained a passage that later aroused awed comment:

Don't be afraid of anything, because when the real peril comes, '*transferentur montes in cor maris*' ['the mountains shall be moved into the depths of the sea']. The sea signifies the armies, which will be driven by the storm, in the same way the sea is driven by the storm. So, when danger threatens, God is going to pick up the mountains and move them into the sea.[6]

Two days later, the veiled painting of the Madonna dell' Impruneta was brought from her shrine in the hills and carried through the streets, the entire city imploring her intercession. For over a hundred and fifty years she had saved the Florentines from plague and famine, from flood and war. The huge procession had not yet reached the Duomo when a messenger rode up with news that the French ships from Marseilles had run the blockade and reached Livorno with corn and soldiers. Fra' Girolamo did not let himself be carried away. The following day, 1 November, was All Saints', and he preached again, warning people to stay patient without expecting an immediate victory. 'It's wrong to let yourselves be moved too easily by joy or sorrow. Don't forget to do everything humanly possible, and be readier than ever for war.'[7]

The day after being All Souls' Day, he preached on the 'art of dying', how real Christians never forget death. He warned that the moment of death is when the Devil makes his last attempt to destroy us. 'It's as if he plays a constant game of chess with mankind and is always waiting for the onset of death to checkmate us,' he explained. 'The man who wins at that moment wins the battle of life.'[8] This sermon, *Predica dell'arte del ben morire*, was so popular that it was reprinted several times. Early editions contain some fine woodcuts suggested by Fra' Girolamo, which shows a 'good death' and a 'bad death' – in affluent Florentine bedrooms with tiled floors. (Villari believed that these cuts were the work of Botticelli but spoiled by poor engraving.)

Despite the Frate's caution, the Florentines did not have to remain patient for long: on 16 November a gale blew up, driving the Venetian fleet ashore and sinking the admiral's flagship, which went down with all hands. Hundreds of sailors surrendered to the people of Livorno, more than a few of whom grew rich on ransoms and salvage. While storms are common in the Mediterranean at this time of year, people remembered Girolamo's prophecy that God would move mountains into the sea.

A rumour circulated that while this was happening the Frate comforted a despondent friar at San Marco, Fra' Sacramoro Malatesta, telling him, 'At this very moment the Emperor has been defeated and is fleeing, as you will hear this morning by the first despatches that reach the Signoria.'[9] If he really did say so, he was quite right. Emperor Maximilian, who had left the admiral's galley only moments before she sank, raised the siege at once, allegedly exclaiming he 'could not fight God as well as man', and beat an undignified retreat back to the Tyrol. He cursed Il Moro, the Venetians and the Pope for involving him in such humiliation.

Savonarola now faced a fresh onslaught on his congregation's independence. On 7 November the Pope had sent a brief to all its friaries, ordering them to join a new Tuscan–Roman congregation, whose vicar would be appointed by the order's Cardinal Protector and by its Master General. Officially, the reason was to ensure a stricter observance of the Dominican rule, but the real aim was to isolate Fra' Girolamo – whose name was of course not mentioned in the brief. Once under the authority of the vicar of the new

Savonarola's basic question to everybody: 'Up there? Or down there?' From his *Predica dell'arte del ben morire*, Florence, 1496

congregation, Savonarola could be told to go to another friary, even to one in Rome where Alexander could deal with him.[10] The scheme was the brainchild of the order's new procurator, the Florentine Fra' Francesco Mei, with the support of the Cardinal Protector, Oliviero Carafa, and the Master General, Giovacchino Torriani. This brief, too, turned out to be a dead letter. Every friar at San Marco joined in writing to Rome that it was irregular and that they did not want to abandon a strict observance to the rule for a more relaxed approach. The community's objections were later encapsulated by Fra' Girolamo in a pamphlet *Apologeticum fratrum Congregationis Sancti Marci* (1497), in which he argues that the order's superiors cannot make demands which go against the Dominican rule and are bad for friars' souls. 'Two hundred and fifty other friars have written to the Pope in protest and I can't oppose their decision, nor do I want to, since I consider it to be both an honest and a just one,' he stated, adding, 'We must never let ourselves be cowed by threats or [the menace of] excommunication, but be prepared to face death rather than yield to what would be poison and perdition for our souls.' The Roman bureaucracy were forced to let the matter drop, so angry that they tore up the entire dossier and trampled on the pieces.

Duke Ercole was having his own troubles with Rome. Since 1494 Alexander had been trying to appoint his nephew, Cardinal Juan Borgia, to the archbishopric of Ferrara, while the Duke wanted to give the see to his son, Cardinal Ippolito d'Este. Because of Ercole's refusal, the Pope put Ferrara under an interdict in September 1496, forcing the Duke to submit within a few months.

Fra' Girolamo was back in the pulpit for Advent 1496, with a series of sermons on texts from the Prophet Ezekiel. They included a passionate defence of his own position, with advice on how to run Florence. He grumbled that the Signoria was growing lax about disaffection. 'You're becoming like the rook on the steeple that at the first chime of the church bell is terrified out of its wits, but then grows used to the bell and perches there calmly, however loud it rings,' he admonished them on 13 December. There were plotters everywhere, 'holding secret meetings inside and outside the walls – attended by priests and friars – giving fine supper-parties and banquets, at which all they talk about is the Frate'. The aim of these gatherings was to destroy Florence's liberty, since the diners were

Medici supporters. The law must be enforced and guards, sword in hand, should break up their meetings. Two or three hundred armed men must be held in readiness and if that was not enough, then enlist the people.

'This poor friar has to fight the whole world single-handed,' Savonarola cried, meaning he was being threatened by the Pope as well as the Medici. 'Call doctors [of divinity], call prelates, call whoever you like. I'm ready to fight them all. But I can tell you that the Order of St Dominic has never produced a heretic.'[11]

Although the threat to Livorno was over, there was terrible misery in Florence during the winter of 1496/7 that continued throughout the spring and into the summer. Manfredo Manfredi reported on 25 February how country people were flocking into the city, crying for bread. This was because of disastrous harvests after prolonged bad weather in two successive years. Luca Landucci – who had hoarded food for himself and his family – noted on 6 February that women were crushed to death in the crowd in the Piazza del Grano (the corn market) when free grain was handed out. 'This may seem incredible,' says Luca, 'but I saw it myself.' The same thing happened four days later, when a man and a woman were killed in the Piazza. On 19 February he writes of a grain store being stormed. On 19 March he records, 'More than one child was found dead of hunger in Florence', and ten days later, 'men and women were falling down [in the street] exhausted by hunger, and some died of it, and many more were dying at the hospital because they were weak from starvation.'[12]

This was the background when the carnival ended on 7 February. On Shrove Tuesday few felt inclined to drink and dance, or chase girls. Fra' Girolamo knew how to catch their bleak mood at the giant bonfire that always marked the day.

The Pseudo-Burlamacchi tells us that an eight-sided wooden pyramid[13] with fourteen tiers of shelves was erected in the Piazza della Signoria, 60 feet high and tapering from a base 230 feet in circumference. (Another source says it had seven tiers, symbolising the deadly sins.) The structure was adapted from the wooden towers with statues of the saints, on carts drawn by oxen, that had always been a feature of the carnival. On each tier were sacks of straw, firewood and bags of gunpowder, while the pyramid was crowned by a wooden gargoyle. 'Vanities' collected by the Frate's boys were piled on each tier. We learn from the Pseudo-Burlamacchi and Landucci[14] that among them were obscene books, pictures and statues, lewd songbooks and musical instruments, dice, cards and gaming-tables, mirrors, scent-bottles, cosmetics and 'dead hair' (wigs).

The books included every copy of a new edition of Boccaccio's *Decameron* and works by Pulci. The pictures and statues seem to have been nude representations of ancient Greece and Rome's more lustful gods and goddesses, or portraits of the city's most frequented whores. There was a statue by Donatello, no doubt identified as homoerotic by boys who had been prostitutes. ('What fire would burn a marble statue?' asks Villari, but we know that Donatello carved in wood.) The Pseudo-Burlamacchi relates how a Venetian merchant tried to buy the collection for 20,000 ducats, an offer that was scornfully rejected, his own portrait being placed on top of the pyre.[15]

A choir of children on the Rhingiera outside the Palazzo della Signoria sang hymns and songs deriding worldly vanity, composed for the occasion by Girolamo Benivieni. Then the pyramid was set alight[16] and as the flames soared the Palazzo's trumpets sounded, the Vacca and the bells of all the churches pealed, and there were roars of applause from the great crowd filling the square. It was a willing sacrifice by men and women at the end of their endurance.

As soon as Lent began, Fra' Girolamo embarked on a series of sermons, on further texts from Ezekiel, during which he denounced priests for whom 'religion consists of spending the night with whores, the day gossiping in choir', and savaged the Pope even if he did not mention his name:

> Friars have a proverb, 'He comes from Rome, so don't trust him!' Now, you wicked Church, you listen to me! At the court [of Rome] men are losing their souls – they are lost. Miserable wretches! I don't say it's true of everybody there, but very few manage to stay sound. If you meet people who like being in Rome, you can be pretty sure they're cooked. Well, he's cooked all right. Do you understand?[17]

He was saying that the Vicar of Christ was destined for hell. He continued:

Once you felt some sort of shame for your sins, but now you're shameless. In the old days consecrated priests used to call their [bastard] sons 'nephews', but now they've stopped speaking of nephews and, on every possible occasion, they speak of their 'sons'. [Alexander VI was the first person to do so, and it is likely that Girolamo had been told of the recent birth of the 66-year-old Pope's latest bastard.] Oh prostitute Church, you display your foulness to the whole world, and you stink to heaven. . . . You multiply your fornications. . . . I tell you, this [whited] sepulchre is going to be burst asunder, because Christ will revive his Church.

TWENTY

Savonarola and the Artists

Savonarola's crucifix – *Operetta . . . della Orazione mentale, c. 1495*

the seraphic Fra' Girolamo
Michelangelo, letter of 14 March 1498 to Fra' Leonardo
Buonarroti

The burning of the vanities has earned Savonarola the reputation
of being a crude philistine and his behaviour may well seem to
confirm this view. We have seen how he wanted to exchange San
Marco for a shack in the woods, abandoning Fra' Angelico's
frescoes while he forbade his friars to use the beautiful psalters
illuminated by Angelico. In many sermons he criticised the 'great
prelates at Rome' for the excessive elegance of their vestments and
music. Yet his attitude was more complex than straightforward
philistinism.

Occasionally he used analogies from art to convey a spiritual message, and there are indications that he knew something about the theory of art, or at least of art as it was before Raphael's arrival in Florence. 'When a painter gives a carved [wooden] grape the colour of a living grape, try fastening it on a trellis visited by birds,' he suggested to his congregation during Lent 1497. 'To which grape will the birds go? They'll go to a real grape, not the painted one, because even if art reaches the highest possible point of perfection it can never imitate nature completely. There's something alive in nature, an indefinable quality that art cannot reproduce.'[1]

Some comments give the impression that he thought a good deal about artists. 'Ask painters which gives them most satisfaction, a picture revealing the work that went into it or a natural looking one that appears to be effortless,' he said in 1496. 'They'll tell you the second is best.'[2] In 1497 he remarked:

Every painter paints himself. . . . Of course he isn't doing a self-portrait when he's making pictures of lions or horses, or of [other] men and women, yet even so he's painting himself because he is a painter and expresses what's in his mind. However varied his subjects, his work bears the stamp of what he's thinking.[3]

The burning had been inspired by revivalism rather than philistinism, and had precedents in France and Hungary as well as Italy. Fifty years earlier, Bernardino of Siena had called bonfires like this 'burning the Devil's castle', when referring to the activities of his fellow Franciscan, John of Capistrano, who went from city to city telling everyone to burn frivolous paintings, playing cards and cosmetics. Parenti records that as recently as the summer of 1493 another Franciscan, the half-crazy Bernardino da Feltre, had organised a small-scale burning of the vanities in Florence.[4]

Next to eroticism, what the Frate most disliked was pagan imagery in Christian religious art, as he made plain in one of his sermons on Amos during Lent 1495 when complaining of the way Florentine ladies dressed daughters on their wedding day:

They put them on show, and dress them up to look like [pagan] nymphs. . . . And these are the sort of idols you're placing in my sanctuary! The old gods' images are just the same as the images and likenesses in the pictures you commission for churches, where young men point to this or that picture and say, 'There's the Magdalene' or 'There's St John'. The paintings you like seeing in the churches are portraits of some woman or other, which is quite wrong and shows a complete contempt for what God wants.

You painters, you're responsible for doing an evil thing and if, as I can, you were able to realize just how much harm you're causing, then you wouldn't do it. Because you're putting every kind of vanity into the churches. Do you really think the Virgin Mary dressed in the way you paint her? I can tell you that she dressed very plainly and wore a veil, being a woman who didn't want her face to be seen, and that St. Elizabeth dressed in the same simple way. You would do a very good action indeed if you could persuade yourselves to destroy all the figures painted in such a shameful fashion, since you're making the Virgin Mary look as if she clothed herself like a prostitute.[5]

Herbert Horne, an historian of Botticelli, contrasts the richly clad saints of Ghirlandaio's frescoes with the absence of portraiture and costume one notices in pictures by the Frate's disciple, Fra' Bartolomeo. He comments that Bartolomeo's influence on Raphael or Andrea del' Sarto 'shows how far reaching were the puritanical tenets of the friar'.[6]

Just how much Girolamo influenced art in Florence can be seen from the account in Vasari's life of 'Il Cronaca', Simone dell' Pollaiuolo, of how the new hall for Florence's Grand Council came to be built:

Advice on the problem was sought from Leonardo da Vinci, Michelangelo Buonarroti . . . Giuliano da San Gallo, Baccio D'Agnolo and Simone dell' Pollaiuolo, who was a devoted friend and follower of Savonarola. After much discussion and argument, these masters reached agreement and decided the hall should be built in the form it has kept down to our own day . . . the entire business was entrusted to Il Cronaca, not because he was considered an able artist, but as the friend of the above named Fra' Girolamo.

Vasari adds that 'Il Cronaca' became so obsessed with the Frate that he spoke of nothing else.[7] This was surprising in view of the fact that his nickname came from his giving long-winded accounts of the antiquities he had seen at Rome.

There were plenty of artists among Fra' Girolamo's admirers. The greatest was Michelangelo, who was profoundly moved by his sermons. There is even a possibility that some of Michelangelo's early work was influenced by him. While the life-sized crucifix of painted wood[8] which he made in 1493 for the high altar of Santo Spirito owes much to his experiments in dissection, it may also owe something to Girolamo's pamphlet the *Trattato dell' amore di Jesu Cristo* published in May the previous year, in which the author had told his readers to think of Christ as having a body 'nobly built, delicate, and very sensitive'. A small limewood crucifix tentatively attributed to the young Michelangelo, is of the sort and size – 'two palms high' – recommended by Savonarola in his sermons as an aid to meditation and a protection against the Devil.

There are examples in the Savonarola medallion by Mattia della Robbia and in a woodcut in the Frate's pamphlet of 1496, *Libro della semplicita della vita Christiana*, where he is seen writing in his cell among his books, with a crucifix of this sort standing on his desk. It was because of Fra' Girolamo's advice that during the 1490s crucifixes replaced the statues or paintings of the Madonna which until then had held pride of place in every Florentine household.

In March 1498, in a letter to his brother Leonardo Buonarroti, Michelangelo referred to 'the seraphic Fra' Girolamo', and he venerated him for the rest of his long life.[9] During the 1520s he was to be a committed supporter of the restored Savonarolean regime at Florence, playing a key role in the defence of the city against the papal army. Moreover, in 1554 his close friend Ascanio Condivi stated in his *Vita di Michelagnolo* [sic] *Buonarrotti* that Michelangelo 'read with the deepest study and attention the Old and the New Testaments, and also [the works] of those who explain them, such as writings by Savonarola, for whom he always kept great affection, never forgetting the memory of his living voice'.[10] Vasari echoes this statement in his *Lives of the Artists*, stating that Michelangelo 'had a great veneration for the writings of Savonarola, having heard his voice in the pulpit'.[11] While we have no information about Fra' Girolamo's opinion of the young artist's crucifixes, if he ever saw them, it is clear that Michelangelo found nothing in the Frate's Christianity to discourage him.

'Botticelli was a supporter of Savonarola's, which was why he gave up painting and then fell into grave distress because he had no other income,' Vasari misinforms us in his *Lives*. 'Even so, he stayed a stubborn member of his sect, becoming one of the *Piagnoni*, the snivellers, as they called them.' He lived in Via Nuova with his brother Simone Filipepi. A bookish man, a lover of Dante, Simone wrote a short chronicle of his times, which opens with an account of the Frate's sermons at Florence in 1489 and ends with Alexander VI's death in 1503. A fanatical *Piagnone*, Simone believed blindly in Savonarola's prophecies and political programme. In his rambling journal he takes particular delight in describing the fate of those among the Frate's opponents who came to an evil end.[12]

'With his own hands, the great Florentine artist Sandro Botticelli burned his own "pagan" pictures,' says the distinguished historian Professor Eamon Duffy (1997),[13] yet there is no record of canvases by Botticelli perishing with the vanities, let alone of his placing them on the bonfire. Admittedly, studies of naked women which were said to be more beautiful than any of his other works have disappeared, and it is not entirely inconceivable that these were among what Landucci noted as *'figure ignude'* on the bonfire.[14] The fact remains, however, that despite Savonarola's disapproval of nudes, Botticelli continued to paint them – for example, the handsome if decidedly unerotic girl in his *Calumny* of 1497.

On the other hand, his paintings became more spiritual, notably the *Virgin and Child with Three Angels* of about 1493 and the *Rest on the Flight into Egypt* of 1495–1500. According to Vasari, Botticelli had a woodcut made of a drawing he had executed as an illustration for Girolamo's *Triumphis Crucis*. No copy survives, and it seems more likely that it was used as a print by itself, for devotional purposes.[15]

Two of Botticelli's late works definitely show Savonarola's influence, although art historians differ as to their interpretation. But the message of his *Mystic Crucifixion* of 1500[16] can only be the great scourge prophesied by the Frate. While the picture does not embody any identifiable passage from his prophecies, it certainly reflects his prediction of approaching doom. Flames and dark clouds loom menacingly behind the cross, symbolising the tribulations that God is sending, a beautiful blonde Magdalene lies prostrate at the foot of the cross, and an angel stands at its right – whipping a small

A repentant
death. From
*Predica dell'arte
del ben morire*,
Florence, 1496

lion that he is holding by the leg. The Magdalene personifies Florence while the lion is the *Marzocco*, another city emblem.

The second painting is the *Mystic Nativity*, which he finished in January 1501, another mysterious picture (in the National Gallery in London), that echoed an Advent sermon preached by Fra' Girolamo in 1491. The artist wrote above it in Greek the words:

I, Sandro, painted this picture at the close of the year 1500 during the troubles of Italy in the half time after the time stated in the Eleventh of St John in the Second Woe of the Apocalypse in the loosing for three and a half years of the Devil who will be chained in the Twelfth when we shall clearly see . . .[17]

The remaining words are illegible.

An undatable *Adoration of the Magi* in the Uffizi in Florence contains a portrait of a friar, who might be the Frate. However, there is doubt as to whether it really is by Botticelli.

Although Vasari implies that Botticelli was illiterate, earlier paintings by him give a distinct impression of his having once been a disciple of Marsilio Ficino and a Platonist – and this is the view of modern scholars. His conversion to Fra' Girolamo's uncompromising Christianity, which unlike Ficino's thin-blooded Platonism held a message of hope, gave his art a new dimension.

Throughout the nineteenth and twentieth centuries, admirers of Savonarola, such as the Dominican Fra' Vincenzo Marchese, evolved a theory that the Frate had founded a school of painting at San Marco inspired by a purified Catholicism, a theory given substance by art historians. They claimed that the school had profoundly influenced artists who were not even Dominicans – for example Botticelli – and cited the painters whom Vasari named as among Fra' Girolamo's followers to make up a list of members.

The 'school of San Marco' theory was largely demolished in 1979 by Steinberg, in his study of the Frate's relationship with Florentine art,[18] which showed that while there had always been a Dominican tradition of art, this had concentrated on illuminating manuscripts rather than painting. No doubt there were miniaturists and wood-carvers among the friars, the latter presumably turning out the crucifixes recommended by Savonarola, but they scarcely amounted to a school.[19] As for the only sculptor, Pier Francesco della Robbia – in religion Fra' Ambrogio – apart from two portrait medallions, his output was limited to medicine jars and a coat-of-arms. None of the community's four mediocre painters produced works of any interest.[20]

On the other hand, we are told by Vasari that two artists of real distinction found themselves so moved by Savonarola's preaching that they contributed to the burning of the vanities. 'Baccio della Porta brought all the studies and drawings of the nude he had drawn to the pyre, where they perished in the flames. His example was followed by Lorenzo di Credi and many others.' Vasari does not name the others – perhaps because they were too obscure.[21]

According to Vasari, 'inspired by affection for Fra' Girolamo', Baccio painted a well-known portrait of him (which is almost certainly a bad likeness). On top of it, he wrote 'the effigy of a prophet sent by God'. He did not join the priory of San Marco until 1500, two years after the Frate's death, when he took the name of Fra' Bartolomeo. Probably due to his well-known association with the Frate, in 1510 he was commissioned by the Signoria to paint an altarpiece, a *Madonna and Child with St Anne and Other Saints*, for the great hall of the Grand Council (the picture still survives). Clearly Fra' Bartolomeo's art had never been discouraged by Savonarola, to whom his attachment is beyond doubt – he was so upset by the Frate's martyrdom that for a time he was unable to paint. A genuinely important artist, he ranks among the great Italian masters.

Fra' Bartolomeo can even be said to have founded a 'scuola di San Marco', but outside the priory. His most important follower was Paolino del Signoraccio, to whom he left his drawings, and who in one of his own paintings gave the Frate's features to St Dominic. Modern Tuscan academics have even devised a species of 'Savonarola trail',[22] an itinerary of visits to priories, such as those at Pistoia or Fiesole, whose churches contain paintings inspired by the Frate's cult. They include not only works by Fra' Bartolomeo and Fra' Paolino, but by lesser-known artists, such as Gerino Gerini, Bernardino Detti, Lo Scalabrino and Zanobi Poggini. Intent on preserving Savonarola's message, his disciples adopted the example of Fra' Angelico as a pivot around which to base their theories.

Lorenzo di Credi is perhaps best known for his haunting portrait of a young beauty, *La dama dei gelsomi*. He had been a pupil of Verrocchio at the same time as Leonardo da Vinci, although unlike Leonardo his painting owed everything to what Verrocchio had taught him. Vasari's statement that Lorenzo consigned his nudes to the flames is confirmed by the Pseudo-Burlamacchi. (However, Michael Levey comments, 'an early full-length Venus by him survives in the Uffizzi and does not make one greatly regret whatever he burnt'.[23]) Vasari makes it clear that sending his paintings to the bonfire was not just a momentary impulse: 'Lorenzo was a devoted adherent of the sect of Fra' Girolamo Savonarola, and steadfastly lived the life of an upright, honourable man.'[24]

The Pseudo-Burlamacchi (although not Vasari) mentions a further artist of some distinction who became a follower of the Frate.[25] This was the sculptor Baccio da Montelupo. Working in wood as well as stone, he was famous for his fine crucifixes, one of which he gave to the priory church of San Marco. He, too, never lost his reverence for Fra' Girolamo, and the Pseudo-Burlamacchi relates how after his death Baccio da Montelupo was miraculously cured of a deadly fever after praying to him.

Clearly Savonarola did not object to sitting for his portrait. He also sat for Giovanni delle Corniole ('Giovanni of the Cornelians') who engraved what is probably the best likeness of him, an intaglio on a cornelian, in which he seems to be surrounded by divine light or, as his enemies might have said, by hellfire. When Michelangelo saw the intaglio, he commented that art had reached its zenith and from now on could only decline – and Michelangelo had seen the Frate in the flesh.

Girolamo Savonarola cannot be called a philistine in the normal sense of the word. He certainly did not disapprove of art or artists; but he insisted that painting and sculpture must always serve a specific purpose – which was to spread his message. Botticelli's *Mystic Nativity* is the supreme example.

TWENTY-ONE

Excommunication

The Pope enthroned – French, sixteenth century

All people are forbidden to help him, speak to him or approve of anything that he does or says, since he is an excommunicated person who is suspected of heresy.

Alexander VI

On 25 February 1497 Charles VIII concluded a truce with King Ferdinand of Spain, promising not to enter Italy. Another French invasion had been averted. Cardinal della Rovere, incapacitated by secondary syphilis, gave in and asked the Pope to let him come home. No longer frightened of France, Alexander was free to deal with Savonarola.

The Frate's position in Florence was deteriorating. The *Gonfaloniere* who led the Signoria during January and February, Francesco Valori, was a committed *Piagnone*, although an ex-henchman of Lorenzo de' Medici.

But while honest and courageous, a handsome man despite his baldness and with a distinguished presence, the 'Florentine Cato' was overbearing. According to Guicciardini he 'imposed his views, regardless of what other people thought, bullying and abusing anyone who disagreed'.[1] Later, Fra' Girolamo admitted he was a person 'who frightened away his friends'.

Ignoring the Frate's warnings, Valori reduced the age qualification for election to the Grand Council from thirty to twenty-four. It was a disastrous step, opening the Council to pleasure-loving young men who hated Savonarola. Valori also used his powers to silence a group of Franciscan friars who had criticised the Frate from the pulpit, depriving them of their licences to preach.

In reaction to Valori, an openly hostile *Gonfaloniere* was elected for March and April. This was Bernardo del Nero, a prominent Medici supporter who owed his life and those of his family to Fra' Girolamo's protection in 1494. A canny survivor from Il Magnifico's regime – he had been a close friend of Lorenzo – although a leader of the *Bigi*, the Medicean party, he put little trust in Piero and realised that an early return to the former system was out of the question. Even so, he detested both the new form of government and Girolamo, regardless of the fact that the Frate had saved his life. Able and dignified, all the more dangerous because of his moderation, Bernardo del Nero represented the most formidable elements in the opposition.

Despite del Nero's pessimism the *Bigi* began to hope for Piero's restoration. There were rumours of a coup. On 7 March Becchi reported from Rome that Piero and his brother had been delighted to learn that shouts of '*Palle! Palle!*' had recently been heard in Florence and hoped to return within two months. Suspicions of a plot were recorded by Landucci later in March, but proved to be unfounded.

At the beginning of March Sommenzi reported to Il Moro in Milan that the Duke of Ferrara had visited Florence in disguise to hear Fra' Girolamo preach. In reality, it was Ercole's bastard son, Giulio d'Este. However, the Duke was increasing alarmed by the political situation and during Giulio's visit Manfredo Manfredi called at San Marco early one morning to discuss matters. Savonarola told him how grateful he was for Ferrara's support and that he knew the Duke was a deeply spiritual man who lived like a Christian and a Catholic. He would pray to God for an answer that would help Ercole. Next day he summoned Manfredi to the priory and gave him a letter for the Duke, in which he showed that he was well aware of how dangerous the situation was becoming. Referring to King Charles as 'the friend', he says the King is being led astray by bad advisers. It would be a good idea to use a little cunning and send an eloquent secret envoy to Charles, 'some reliable person, who would give him sound advice and open his eyes', someone devout and intelligent, in order to persuade him to return to Italy. As for matters at home, the Frate told Manfredi he suspected the new *Gonfaloniere* of planning to change the system of government, and that there would be serious trouble if he tried. The Frate was doing his best to control events, reported Manfredi, but powerful opponents were now emerging, without bothering to hide their hostility. The Frate had denounced anyone who wanted to destroy the Grand Council, which was God's work.[2]

Ercole d'Este cannot have derived much comfort from Savonarola's letter. He had said nothing about what was going to happen, despite his claims to be a prophet. At the same time, he was telling the Duke to persuade the French to invade. But if Ercole did so and was found out, he would risk being attacked by the armies of the League. He began to lose confidence in the Frate.

Fortunately for Savonarola, the Ten in charge of foreign affairs were supporters, and because of the unwieldy constitution could afford to ignore the *Gonfaloniere*. They did their best to protect the Frate when negotiating with Pope Alexander. On 14 March Alessandro Bracci (a new envoy to Rome, not to be confused with Becchi) sent a report to the Ten of a conversation with His Holiness. After hearing yet another Florentine plea for help in recovering Pisa, the Pope told Bracci with his usual playful *bonhomie* that the Signori had sent him a fat ambassador with a thin brief, adding that if only the Florentines would be 'good Italians' and join the League, they would get Pisa back at once.[3]

On the following day, Bracci reported another conversation with Alexander, who marvelled at the Ten's optimism.[4] The Holy Father joked with dangerous amiability that it must be due to the prophecies of Savonarola, whom he called 'that [walking] parable of yours'. If only he could talk to the Florentines himself, he added, he would free them from the blindness into which the Frate had led them. His real complaint, however, was that the Signoria was letting the man insult and threaten the present occupant of the Holy See, 'unworthy though he may be'. As the days went by, Becchi reported further attacks on Fra' Girolamo, how Cardinal Carafa was urging the union of the San Marco congregation with the new Tuscan–Lombard congregation.

Girolamo remained defiant. 'Don't I have any fear?' he asked himself in the pulpit, answering, 'No, I don't, since they want to excommunicate me because I'm not doing evil. Bring this wretched excommunication to me, carry it high on a lance-head, and open the gates to let it in,' he told his hearers in the Duomo. 'I'm going to answer it and if I don't amaze you, then afterwards you can say just what you like. I shall make the faces all around you blench so much that they will look like a pale sea, and I'll send forth a cry to make the whole world shudder with terror.'[5]

Meanwhile, Piero was planning his new coup. He had wasted vast sums on whoring and gambling, but managed to borrow enough from the Pope and the Venetians to hire 1,300 mercenaries. Despite a secret warning from Bernardo del Nero that he had no chance of success, he and his troops arrived outside Florence on 28 May, at the Porta San Gattolino. However, the city had been alerted by a peasant and was ready for him, with cannon mounted on the walls – del Nero ostentatiously helping to organise its defence. 'Go and tell the Signoria that Piero de' Medici will ride up to the gates and then ride off again,' insisted Fra' Girolamo when informed. In the event, Piero waited outside the walls all day, jeered at by the citizens, but dared not mount an assault, hoping that his supporters inside might open the gate. Humiliated, he gave up at 5 p.m., fleeing to Sienese territory.[6]

For some reason a mistaken report reached Rome that Piero had been successful. His brother, Cardinal Giuliano, ordered a lavish firework display to celebrate the family's restoration and then rushed off to tell Pope Alexander the glad tidings. When he learned what had really happened, Alexander angrily commented that it served Piero right, since he did everything badly, while despite having helped to finance the plot the Holy Father insisted he had known nothing about it. Although Piero continued scheming, his failure resulted in the collapse of the *Bigi* for the time being. The *Arrabbiati* now became the main opposition party.

The next Signoria was dominated by the *Arrabbiati*, led by Piero degli Alberto, the new *Gonfaloniere*. They were in secret contact

Ludovico Sforza, Duke of Milan ('Il Moro'), shown here with his wife Beatrice, daughter of Ercole d'Este, Duke of Ferrara, was another of Savonarola's enemies. From their empty tomb by Andrea Solari. (*Certosa di Pavia*)

A flattering likeness of the gnome-like Charles VIII – said by those who saw him to look 'more a monster than a man' – whose invasion of Italy was prophesied by Savonarola. Polychrome bust of *c.* 1495. (*Museo Nazionale del Bargello*)

The Burgundian statesman Philippe de Commines (1445–1511), who had met Edward IV and Richard III. He took part in the French invasion of Italy, fighting at Fornovo, and in his memoirs describes his conversations with Savonarola. (*Musée d'Arras*)

Botticelli, a follower of Savonarola who went on painting nudes despite his conversion. Self-portrait from his *Adoration of the Magi*. (*Galleria degli Uffizi, Florence*)

Girolamo Benivieni, who wrote the hymns for the Burning of the Vanities. From a cast of his death mask by Bastiniani, 1863. (*Musée du Louvre, Paris*)

Supplizio del Savonarola – Girolamo's execution in the Piazza della Signoria on 23 May 1498, when he and his two companions were hanged in chains and burned. By Francesco Rosselli. (*Museo di San Marco, Florence*)

Savonarolean art: *Magdalen at the Foot of the Cross*, by Botticelli, in which the Magdalen is also repentant Florence, *c.* 1500. (*Fogg Art Museum, Harvard*)

Opposite: Savonarolean art: *Mystic Nativity*, by Botticelli, painted in 1501 during 'the second woe of the Apocalypse' according to the inscription. (*National Gallery, London*)

Nineteenth-century statue of Savonarola outside the Castello Estense, Florence – the plinth is inscribed 'Scourge of vice and tyrants in corrupt and servile times.' (*Assessorato al Turismo di Ferrara*)

with both the Pope and Il Moro, who promised to help them overthrow the Frate. The first step was to stop his sermons, but they had to find adequate grounds.

The night before he was to preach at the Duomo on 4 May, Ascension Day, Doffo Spini and a band of *Compagnacci* smeared the pulpit with excrement, draped it in a rotting donkey skin and lined with upward pointing nails the railing on which he banged his fist – although they abandoned a scheme to blow him up in the pulpit with gunpowder bought from a firework-maker. By the time he arrived at noon with his bodyguard the mess had been cleaned off. However, the Duomo's congregation included sneering rows of scented, foppishly dressed *Compagnacci*. Undeterred, Fra' Girolamo launched into a vigorous sermon. Halfway through, he began to attack his enemies in the congregation. 'Lord, don't be angry with them, forgive them, convert them, for they know not what they do,' he cried. 'Wicked men, you want to fight the Frate and by doing so you're making war on the Lord, while I am not fighting you out of hatred but from love of God. You say I cause strife, but the Lord Christ Himself came on earth to bring strife among men.'[7]

Suddenly there was a deafening crash – the main doors of the cathedral had been broken down. The *Compagnacci* began to howl and scream, banging benches. Terrified, the congregation tried to run out, jamming the doorways, and panicking still further when *Piagnoni* armed with swords and halberds rushed in to protect the Frate. After trying in vain to make himself heard, he was escorted back to San Marco. No one was punished by the Signoria for organising the riot.[8]

It was the first time anybody had showed disrespect. A spell had been broken. Although the uproar in the Duomo was not Savonarola's fault, the *Arrabbiati* tried, unsuccessfully, to use it as a pretext for expelling him from the city. But it gave the Signoria the chance they had been waiting for. Next day, it banned all orders of friars from preaching in Florence without its express permission, besides removing the stools, benches and stands from the Duomo. 'This was done from a grudge they had against the poor Frate,' explains Landucci. He also says that the Signoria's members 'gave themselves over to gambling and indulged in every sort of vice, opening the Frascato, taverns, etc.'[9] (The Frascato was the city's biggest house of ill-fame, a combined brothel and casino.)

By now Florence was pestilence-ridden. 'At this time many people died of fever in the city and at the hospitals, the fever making them rave and lose consciousness,[10] and when that happened they died in two or three days,' noted Landucci on 18 May. 'It was said that during these last days of the waning moon there were 120 cases at the hospitals,' he recorded on 1 June, and, ominously, 'It was also said that there was a touch of plague at the hospital.'[11]

The new administration brought back horse-races. 'The palio of Santo Barnaba was run, which had not happened for years because of the Prophet's predictions,' wrote Landucci on 11 June. 'This [fresh] Signoria decided to let it be run, and no longer paid any attention to what the Frate said, declaring: "We're going to cheer the people up a little – do all of us have to become friars?" Yet still they deprive us of the word of God.'[12]

Since March Becchi had been warning the Ten of excommunication, and that even Fra' Girolamo's former patron, Cardinal Carafa, was making threats. Alexander had postponed his thunderbolt, waiting for Piero's coup to bring down the Frate. He may also have hoped that the riot in the Duomo would do it – forewarned by Fra' Mariano da Genazzano, eager for revenge on that 'instrument of the Devil and perdition of the Florentine people'.

Girolamo attempted to deflect the Pope by sending him a conciliatory letter on 22 May. 'Why is my Lord angered with his servant?' he begins rhetorically. He complains that Alexander has never listened to him while believing the slanders against him. He says that Fra' Mariano once attacked the Pope from the pulpit yet is now accusing him of the same crime, although he himself has never attacked anyone – let alone the Vicar of Christ. He declares that he willingly submits to the Church's authority and cannot possibly be accused of preaching unorthodox doctrine, as will be proved by his book, the *Triumphis Crucis*, soon to be published. 'But if all human aid should fail me,' he ends, 'then I shall put all my trust in God and make plain to the world the wickedness of those who may one day be forced to repent of what they are doing.'[13]

According to Alessandro Bracci in Rome, the Pope was mollified by the Frate's letter, ready to take it at face value and accept his submission. However, on 13 May he had already sent a brief ordering the Frate's excommunication:

We hear from many persons worthy of belief that a certain Fra' Girolamo Savonarola, at present said to be the superior of San Marco in Florence, has been spreading pernicious doctrines, to the great scandal and sorrow of simple souls. We have ordered him to stop preaching and to come and ask our pardon for his errors, but he has refused, making excuses which we accepted out of mistaken kindness.[14]

The Pope also complains of his refusal to merge San Marco with the Tuscan–Roman Congregation:

We now command you, on every feast day and in the presence of the people, to declare the said Fra' Girolamo excommunicated. . . . Under pain of the same penalty, all people are forbidden to help him, speak to him or approve of anything he does or says, since he is an excommunicated person who is suspected of heresy.

Becchi blamed Savonarola's enemies, explaining to the Ten in a letter of 19 May that although Alexander had been angered by the Frate and wanted to punish him, he would never have used his most potent weapon unless encouraged by others. 'I can inform your lordships that the Very Reverend Monsignor of Naples [Carafa] is the real author, together with various other Cardinals.'[15] The envoy was almost certainly correct. Now that the threat from King Charles was over, Savonarola had ceased to be a danger to Alexander and was just a minor nuisance. Only later did the Pope grow enraged. At this stage, he simply wanted him to make the Florentines abandon their alliance with France and join the League. In contrast, 'great prelates' such as Carafa had let themselves be infuriated by Girolamo's diatribes.

The Ten answered Becchi by return of post, saying they were most indignant at the news, insisting somewhat speciously that the Frate had never blamed or chided any single individual by name in his sermons but had merely been attacking vice, and that their city owed a very great debt to him for reforming its way of life.

The excommunication was formally proclaimed in Florence on 18 June 1497, in the city's five major churches. Amid tapers and torches, an old enemy of Girolamo, Fra' Leonardo, pronounced the papal instruction at the Augustinian priory of Santo Spirito – once the home of Fra' Mariano da Genazzano – surrounded by the community, who rang hand-bells throughout the reading to emphasise its solemnity. The city was in an uproar, *Arrabbiati* and *Compagnacci* rejoicing, while the Frate was denounced in a flood of obscene ballads and pamphlets. When the friars of San Marco sang their office, crowds gathered outside to yell insults. Florence's sober aspect vanished overnight, prostitutes returning to the streets.

Yet the document merely described him as 'suspected of heresy'. He had never been formally charged, let alone tried and found guilty. There was also a case, if a dangerous one, for arguing that an excommunication by an illegally elected pope was invalid.

For a time matters were interrupted by news of the murder of Alexander's eldest son Juan Borgia, Duke of Gandia, whose body had been found in the Tiber on 15 June with nine stab wounds. The murderer was never discovered, but the suspects included his brother Cesare. The Holy Father was so distressed that for days he refused to eat or drink. He became a changed man, planning to reform the Church and appointing a short-lived commission of cardinals to identify the problems. Letters of sympathy poured into Rome, among them being one from Fra' Girolamo.[16] However, the Pope soon recovered, abandoning any schemes for reform.

A day after the proclamation of the excommunication, Savonarola had published a letter in reply entitled *Contro la escomunicanze surrettizia* ('Against the Clandestine Excommunication'). Addressed not to Pope Alexander but to 'All faithful Christians and all those beloved of God', this was as much a manifesto as a letter. The author describes himself as:

> The servant of Jesus Christ, sent by Him to the city of Florence to make known the great scourge about to descend upon Italy and especially upon Rome – that scourge which will spread throughout the entire world, in our time and very soon – so that the Elect may be prepared for these terrible afflictions and in consequence escape God's anger. God wants news of our prophecies to be heard all over Christendom.

Moreover, 'God will preserve us from every danger and give us a great victory.'

He explains that his so-called excommunication is based on an unjustified accusation of heresy and a malicious charge of disobedience, and cannot be valid in the eyes of God or man. With reason, he claims that never for one moment has he departed from Catholic orthodoxy in his teaching, and that the Tuscan–Roman congregation – which he refuses to join – has been established solely for the purpose of trapping him. The author reminds his readers that he has always told them he expects nothing but persecution in return for the blessings he is bringing down on Florence:

> Unable to find proper grounds for securing my excommunication, my enemies have given the Pope false reasons, saying that I am spreading harmful doctrines and heresies, although I have only taught what Christ taught. If they accuse me of disobedience, you can rest assured that I have never been disobedient to either the Holy Roman Church or to the Pope . . . you can see the sheer enormity of our foes, who have been shamelessly supplying the Pope with obvious lies.[17]

Shortly after, Girolamo published another, longer letter,[18] printed in Latin, *Contra sententiam excommunicationis*. Aimed at academics, canon lawyers and theologians, it cites precedents for refusing to obey the Pope in certain circumstances, and for ignoring excommunication. Girolamo quotes the famous Jean Gerson, active at the beginning of the century, who had written that the opinion of a single canon lawyer or theologian can provide grounds for disregarding an excommunication. Girolamo also tells his readers that they may be unaware of the advice given by the late Pope Martin V, that the faithful have no obligation to shun the excommunicated, unless given express instructions.

Reading the letter, Alexander can scarcely have been soothed by its reference to Gerson, who had taught that the unity of the Church could only be restored by a general council, not necessarily summoned by a pope, and that a council could depose a pope. Yet Savonarola had convinced himself that he was justified in ignoring what he considered to be an invalid excommunication.

Piagnoni accepted Fra' Girolamo's letter at face value, rejecting the excommunication. Since he no longer preached at the Duomo, they flocked to San Marco to hear him say Mass. The humanists among them went on writing in support. It was now that Giovanni Nesi published his *Oraculum*, praising Savonarola as the Ferrarese

Socrates who has brought back morals. Domenico Benivieni produced a *Dialogo* defending his doctrines, and an *Epistola . . . a un amico responsiva*, refuting 'calumnies against Frate Hieronymo of Ferrara' with the lucidity to be expected from a professor of logic. Before the Frate, Christianity had been moribund – the clergy depraved, God's word denied and neo-paganism rampant. The Church's leaders were so corrupt that he alone showed men how Christianity should be lived. Benivieni rejected any suggestion that prophecy had ended with the birth of Christ, while emphasising that the Frate's golden predictions would come true only if the Florentines persevered with their reform.

Understandably, the *Arrabbiati* greeted the excommunication with joy, telling fellow citizens that an interdict was likely to follow at any moment, with dire consequences for trade, let alone spiritual welfare. It gave force to their demand that the Signoria should banish the Frate before he did any further damage to the city.

At Milan Lodovico Il Moro was delighted, summoning the ambassadors of Florence and Ferrara to his presence. Surrounded by the members of his council, he had the excommunication read out to them, followed by Fra' Girolamo's reply. When the reading was finished, the Duke sneered that he had never heard 'anything so absurd' as the arguments put forward by the Frate. The effect was marred by Fra' Vincenzo Bandelli, an old Dominican friend of Girolamo and a distinguished theologian, who had the temerity to observe that they were very good arguments indeed.

If the Signoria that had presided when the excommunication reached Florence had stayed in power, Savonarola would have been in grave danger, because so many of its members were uncompromising *Arrabbiati*. Instead, led by Domenico Bartoli, the new Signoria elected for July and August were nearly all committed supporters of the Frate, as were most of those of the Signoria during the rest of the year. For the moment he was safe.

On 8 July 1497 the new Signoria wrote to Pope Alexander:

We consider this Frate to be a good and pious man, with a thorough understanding of the Christian religion. . . . He has spent years working for our people's good, and no fault has ever been found with his way of life or his doctrine. But, because virtue is open to envy, there are many among our people who turn the name of honesty upside down and think they become great men by attacking good ones. So we fervently beg your Holiness, in your fatherly and saintly charity, to use your own judgement in this affair and take away the weight of your ban not merely from Fra' Girolamo Savonarola but also from anyone else who may have incurred it. Your Holiness could do no greater kindness to the [Florentine] Republic, especially in this time of pestilence. . . .[19]

On the day the Signoria wrote this letter, the friars of San Marco sent another letter to His Holiness in defence of their prior: 'We number 259, most of us natives of Florence, and we all know him well' they told the pontiff.[20] 'As men of some education and experience, obviously we would not defend and support in this way someone who is a foreigner by birth unless we felt completely satisfied with his way of life and conduct. But we can see clearly that the hand of God is with him, as has been shown by the sheer extent of his conversions.' Every member of the community signed the letter. Throughout that year, each Signoria in turn sent letters to Rome in defence of Savonarola, asking the Pope to withdraw his excommunication. They also lobbied the six cardinals to whom Alexander had entrusted the case, in particular Oliviero Carafa.

During July and August Fra' Girolamo was distracted by a serious outbreak of 'plague', similar to the Black Death of the previous century. (The Black Death was not bubonic plague caught from rat fleas as used to be thought, but a viral, haemorrhagic fever passed directly from one person to another, which resembled today's ebola fever.) Everyone who could afford it left the city. On 24 July Girolamo, writing to his brother the doctor to tell him their brother Fra' Maurelio was away from Florence, gave an assessment of the situation that shows he had not forgotten his medical training:

More people are dying from high, plague-like fevers than true plague, on some days fifty, sixty or seventy, and occasionally as many as one hundred, so they say. I don't know if it's true or not. But things aren't getting any better and you see nothing in Florence save crosses and corpses. We are very well, thank God. I haven't left the priory, but I've sent away over seventy of our friars. I'm not worried about myself since I trust in God's protecting grace, and I'm staying here to comfort those struck down.[21]

Yet there had already been several deaths at San Marco.

The Frate sent Alberto Savonarola another letter on 14 August in which he says he had sent the younger friars away. The citizens were supplying the priory with food and giving up their *palazzi* so that the brethren could use them as hospitals. 'All of us are cheerful, leading a holy life.' He comments, 'It is wonderful to see the happiness of those who are called away, believing in life as well as death. Friars and lay people, men and women, die praising the Lord with their last breath.'[22] Mercifully, the epidemic died down before the end of the month. During the same letter the Frate referred to the excommunication. 'Rome may be against me, but she is against Christ rather than me and is fighting God. Who can resist Him and hope for peace? Don't be in any doubt – God's going to win.'

In the meantime, at some point in July Fra' Girolamo heard from a sympathiser at Ferrara (possibly Fra' Tommaso, the Duke's Dominican confessor) that Ercole d'Este was wavering. He at once wrote to Ercole, on 1 August, telling him not to lose heart. 'The Jews did not believe the Prophets, because they thought that what they predicted took too long to happen, so that in the end they deceived themselves time and again until finally the Romans destroyed them. . . . Read Holy Scripture, or have it read to you, especially such Prophets as Jeremiah and Ezekiel, and you will find that almost everything is the same as today.' He also advised him to reform his court.[23]

The Duke replied a week later, thanking the Frate for his 'sweet letter'.[24] He admits that he is worried that the French King has not done what was predicted. Would Fra' Girolamo please let him know what Charles is going to do, 'because we have such respect for you that we will believe everything you predict as certain to happen and, if you want, we will ensure that what you write will remain unknown to anyone else'.[25] Girolamo hoped for a helpful vision and pored over the Bible for some time, but without much enlightenment since he did not answer Ercole until 29 August. His letter boiled down to little more than saying they must trust in God.

TWENTY-TWO

A Plot

A Roman prelate – *Petrus Aurea . . . commentaria*, 1507

Do justice, therefore, magnificent Signori.
Savonarola, *Prediche sopra Ezechiele*

In December 1497 the Duke of Ferrara opened negotiations with Milan for admission to the Holy League. Privately, however, he remained devoted to 'Our Fra' Hieronymo', who reacted to his defection with considerable subtlety. On 19 November Manfredi reported how Savonarola was defusing Florentine anger at the loss of their last remaining ally[1] in Italy, and how he had suggested that it would be prudent for the Duke to keep on good terms with the King of France, who might yet return.

The *Piagnoni* stayed in control of the Signoria, but while the plague was still raging they had used their power in a brutally inept way that did them lasting damage. 'A priest officiating in Santa Maria Maggiore was arrested by the Eight and confessed to having secretly declared that Fra' Girolamo and Fra' Domenico and all the Frati at San Marco were sodomites, on account of a grudge he had against them,' Landucci noted on 23 July.[2] 'This morning he was sent by the Eight to proclaim the friars' good name; from a pulpit erected on the steps of Santa Maria del Fiore . . . and in the presence of all the people said he had told lies, and publicly confessed his error. Nevertheless, the Eight sent him to the Stinche [prison] where he was confined in a cage.'

It was not a slanderous priest being put in a cage that did the damage, but mishandling a graver business. During the summer a certain Lamberto dell' Antella, had been caught with a letter which showed that until recently he had been a trusted follower of Piero, and had ridden with him in May. However, after the coup's failure Piero had unjustly accused dell' Antella of treachery, imprisoning both him and his brother at Siena, even asking the Sienese to put the pair in a dungeon known as the Carnaio (Charnel House), from which inmates usually came out dead. Only bribery had enabled the brothers to escape with their lives. But Lamberto was a man who knew a very great deal about Florence's former tyrant and his plans. Although aware that he had reason to hate Piero de' Medici and was ready to confess everything, the Eight had him racked four times, just to make sure he would tell the truth. During a lengthy 'questioning'[3] he screamed out some names that were carefully noted down. After the racking was over, the Eight offered Lamberto a full pardon in return for any further information he might have kept back.

He told them that Piero was going to pieces in Rome. Rising late, he dined at his San Severino relations' palace, renowned for its cuisine, gorging himself for hours and then spent the rest of the day in the arms of a whore. The night was passed drinking and gambling until dawn. Any money went on dice, so that he was hopelessly in debt while he quarrelled with everybody, including his brother the cardinal, ill treating his followers and even killing them. He had drawn up a long list of families he would exterminate when he returned to Florence – he thought of nothing but revenge.

In addition, Lamberto dell' Antella revealed Piero's latest scheme. He was plotting another coup, planning to break into Florence on the night of 15 August. As the city was in chaos after the plague, and as many rich citizens had left their *palazzi* to take refuge in country villas, he hoped to win over the mob with handouts of food and money, and by letting them sack the empty *palazzi*, and during the uproar he would install himself in the Palazzo della Signoria.

But the list Lamberto gave of Piero's leading supporters in Florence was, in modern terms, political dynamite. All received a polite summons from the Signoria. The wilier fled at once, but some obeyed and were arrested. Five were charged with treason, then tried for their lives by the Eight, who were assisted by twelve specially appointed citizens. Each rich and high born, the five accused included two gifted young men, Lorenzo Tornabuoni and Gianozzo Pucci, whose wife was a devout *Piagnona*; a prominent merchant, Giovanni Cambi; the head of a distinguished family, Niccolò Ridolfi; and the 75-year-old Bernardo del Nero.

Four were found guilty of involvement in Piero's plot in May, while, if Bernardo del Nero had tried to discourage it, he was condemned for not revealing it to the authorities – this was thought especially deplorable since at the time he had been *Gonfaloniere*. Their case was not improved by a plea for mercy from Il Moro, who was politely told to stop meddling. But the Eight were reluctant to execute them, while four members of the Signoria were openly anxious to spare their lives.

A Pratica of nearly 200 citizens met on 17 August, and again four days later, to discuss their punishment, sitting from morning till midnight. Although it favoured the death penalty, their friends in the Signoria almost managed to save them. However, the implacable Francesco Valori, the 'Florentine Cato', shouted they must die. Even then the noisy debate continued until Valori jumped up from his seat and forced a vote on the Signoria, bellowing, 'Justice must be done or there will be a revolt!' After cowing the Signoria into voting for the death of 'these would-be destroyers of our country', he led the condemned men through the torchlit darkness, barefoot and manacled, into the courtyard of the Bargello, the chief criminal magistrate's palace, which he had had surrounded by 300 troops. Here he saw to their beheading by the public executioner.[4] All died with dignity.

An unrepentant death. From *Predica dell'arte del ben morire*, Florence, 1496

Fra' Girolamo stayed away from the trial, letting the law take its course, apart from asking for mercy for Lorenzo Tornabuoni. He did so with a noticeable lack of enthusiasm, after the youth's family pleaded with him, and refused to intercede for any of the others. He sent Giovambattista Ridolfi, a fervent *Piagnone*, a coldly pious letter of sympathy about his brother. 'Perhaps God has ordained such a penance [as beheading] for his salvation,' he wrote grimly. 'Suffering can save those who might otherwise be damned by prosperity.'[5]

Duke Ercole had realised the danger of too much harshness, ordering Manfredi to try to persuade the Signoria to spare the lives of the accused, but his instructions arrived too late. Far from being irritated, as they were by Il Moro's attempts to interfere, the Signoria was flattered by Ercole's interest. When they asked Manfredi how Ferrara reacted to news of the executions, he replied smoothly that the Duke had complete confidence in the way Florentines conducted their affairs.

The execution of such respected figures was politically inept, arousing revulsion and pity. 'All Florence was sorry for them,' Landucci tells us.[6] 'It seemed too cruel for such men as they were.' Valori, the *Piagnoni*'s leader, earned himself undying hatred while Savonarola's indifference provided his enemies with further ammunition. But, as has been seen, by now the Frate had abandoned the clemency that had proved so successful during Piero's overthrow in 1494. Admittedly, in Villari's words, 'he commanded neither the will nor the power to influence a sentence handed out in the heat and fury of a whirlwind debate'.[7] Yet he must share at least some of the blame. And if the executions deprived the Medicean *Bigi* of leaders, they helped to strengthen the *Arrabbiati*, who were joined by the surviving *Bigi*. Opposition to Fra' Girolamo grew more bitter than ever.

In the short term the affair seemed to do him little harm. According to the *Arrabbiato* chronicler Parenti, Valori's role made him the leading man in the city, while the next three Signorie – those for the following six months – were dominated by *Piagnoni*. Early in September the Milanese spy Paolo Sommenzi reported to his master Il Moro that 'the Frate's party has the government in its hands, without any opposition'.[8] They hoped to persuade the Pope to withdraw his excommunication, telling Bracci at Rome to 'knock at every door and shout out loud, make every effort possible, never relax or stop trying until you have got what we want'. They also lobbied Cardinal Carafa, who advised them to persuade Fra' Girolamo to write a submissive letter to Alexander. He did so on 13 October, his letter being presumably delivered by Bracci.

I am more distressed at having your Holiness's favour withdrawn from me than by any other misfortune and fly eagerly to your feet, begging you to hear my cry at last and no longer let me be torn from your bosom. To whom else can I go as one of his flock except to the shepherd whose voice I love to hear, whose blessing I implore? . . .

I would go at once to cast myself at your feet if only I could be safe on the journey from my enemies' malice and plots. As soon as I can do so without danger I shall set out [for Rome] at once and I wish with all my heart that I could do it now in order to prove myself innocent of these calumnies once and for all. Meanwhile, I most humbly submit in every way to your authority, as I always have done, and if from want of judgement or unintentionally I have been at fault in anything, then I humbly ask forgiveness.[9]

Unsurprisingly, what Ridolfi calls 'this virile act of submission' received no acknowledgement. Savonarola was still refusing to go to Rome, still declining to make Florence abandon her alliance with France and join the League.

Yet even now there was a chance of reconciliation. Cardinal Carafa was owed a large sum of money by a Florentine whose property had been confiscated after dell' Antella's revelations. It appears that the Signoria offered to pay Carafa the money if he secured the 'absolution' and that despite his former hostility he tried to do so. The Pseudo-Burlamacchi says that Cardinal Piccolomini[10] also offered to secure it, for 5,000 *scudi*. We know that Girolamo was optimistic about the outcome. 'He hopes that his business with the Pope will soon be settled,' Manfredi reported on 19 November. 'If so, it will earn him great admiration, especially because he has not given in to the Pope's demands.'[11] Negotiations dragged on into 1498. On 9 January the Signoria told Bonsi at Rome to use every effort to secure the Frate's absolution, and bring pressure to bear on the Cardinal of Naples – Carafa. On 5 February Bonsi reported that he had enlisted the help of the Bishop of Perugia, who would do his best with the Pope.

But on 8 February Bonsi reported that during an audience with Alexander when he tried to speak of Fra' Girolamo His Holiness had interrupted, saying that first he wanted to know precisely what the Signoria meant to do for him if he recovered Pisa for them. With regard to Savonarola, the Pope said that his was a peculiarly grave case because he had insulted the honour of the Holy See, adding that many cardinals thought he had behaved disgracefully over the excommunication. Bonsi replied lamely that the Frate possessed many virtues and had done many good works.[12]

TWENTY-THREE

The Wrath of Pharaoh

Defending Savonarola – *Tractato di maestro Domenico Benievieni*, 1496

'Come, let us wisely oppress them', said Pharaoh of the Israelites.

Savonarola, *Prediche sopra Esodo*

After the excummunication, Savonarola stopped giving sermons for some months. Guicciardini, who saw deeper than most people, believed that had he kept quiet for a little longer he would have obtained absolution – he also thought that when the Pope finally took action against him it was because of lobbying by the friar's enemies than any reason of his own.[1] Ridolfi stresses that as late as November 1497 Manfredi reported a conversation in which

Fra' Girolamo hoped that 'an accommodation will soon be reached with the Pope since matters look promising and His Holiness is inclining towards one'.[2] The Signoria's attitude in January and early February 1498 shows they were still optimistic.

During his absence from the pulpit Fra' Girolamo wrote one of his most important books, *Triumphis Crucis*, an investigation of the Christian faith. Like Aquinas, he starts from an almost agnostic position – 'we are not going to rely on any authority, rejecting what anyone says, however clever, and we will rely solely on natural reason'. At the same time, however, he admits that some truths, such as the Trinity, are beyond reason. He stresses that in every religion there is outer and inner worship, the inner – expressed by a better life – being superior. Nothing is more valuable than a real Christian's inward peace, which enables martyrs to face death without flinching. The book's imagery is typical of the fifteenth century. A mystic chariot drawn by apostles and prophets travels triumphantly through the world, bearing Christ the Conqueror crowned with

An astrologer and a theologian agreeing – but Savonarola considered astrology 'utter foolishness'. From Petrus de Aliaco, *Concordia astronomie*, Augsburg, 1490

thorns and shining with celestial light, smashing down every obstacle in his way.

The *Trattato contra gli astrologi*, written a little later, was aimed at his old foes the stargazers. Designed to show that their 'science' was utter foolishness, it is subtitled 'in corroboration of the refutation of astrology by the Serene Count Giovanni Pico de la Mirandola'. The book made him more enemies than friends, among the many people who conducted their daily lives according to astrological prediction. Early in 1498, responding to a request from the Signoria, Savonarola produced the *Trattato circa il regimento e governo della città di Firenze*, a resumé of what he had said about government in his sermons. He stresses that a republic is best suited to 'the mutable, restless and ambitious temperament of Florentines', dwells on the miseries of life under a despot and recommends a Grand Council as a safeguard against both anarchy and tyranny.

But by the end of 1497 Girolamo's patience was wearing thin. The Pope had not lifted his excommunication. The Frate suddenly emerged from seclusion on Christmas Day, celebrating the three Masses, giving communion to the congregation at San Marco and walking in procession in the Piazza outside. At Epiphany (6 January 1498), 'The Signoria of Florence went to the offering [of gifts] at San Marco and kissed Fra' Girolamo's hand at the altar, to the great surprise of thoughtful men, not only his adversaries but also among his friends,' records Landucci. 'At this time the cold was very severe and the Arno froze.'[3] On 1 February Manfredi reported to Ferrara that the Frate had told him he would preach during Lent, 'when he had received the sign from those who could command him'. Asked if he meant Alexander or the Signoria, he replied that he meant neither: the Pope was still leading an evil life and had no intention of granting his absolution. He was 'awaiting a command from one far greater than the Pope'. Manfredi comments, 'We shall have to wait and see how it all turns out, how the affair ends, since at least we shall know whether Fra' Girolamo's inspiration is divine or merely human.'[4]

Ignoring the cold, Fra' Girolamo's supporters, both boys and adults, had replaced the stands in the Duomo and were begging him to give a sermon. 'Father, when are you going to preach again?' they asked. 'We're dying of hunger for lack of it!'[5] His mind seems to have been made up by a letter to the Signoria from Bonsi at Rome, to the effect that Alexander would not give him absolution until Florence joined the League, but that after that 'he will be well pleasing to you in any way you want'.[6] In response, Girolamo defiantly promised his followers that he would deliver a sermon at the Duomo on Septuagesima Sunday, 11 February. The canons at the Duomo sent their vicar to inform the Signoria that people were banned from attending any sermon by Savonarola, but the Signoria made the vicar resign, replacing him by a *Piagnone*. 'Many people went there and it was much talked of because of his excommunication, and many did not go for fear of being excommunicated,' writes Landucci.[7] 'I was one of those who did not go.'

When the Frate climbed into the pulpit, the congregation sang the *Te Deum*. As expected, he dwelt at length on his quarrel with Rome. 'Tell me this, what was the object of those who used lying to get me excommunicated?' he asked. It was to go back to their vices. 'No sooner was the excommunication announced than they reverted to drunkenness, loose-living and every sort of crime, while the godly way of life was abandoned. . . . Oh Lord, if I try to be absolved from such an excommunication, then may I be sent to hell.' He implied that the Duke of Gandia's murder – 'Someone at Rome has lost a son' – was God's judgement on the Pope, and also that the plotter Bernardo del Nero was suffering eternal damnation.[8]

On 15 February he gave a sermon at San Marco for priests and friars, 'and told them of their failings, according to what was reported to me by one of them', says Landucci:

'The tonsure is the badge of all iniquity,' cried Fra' Girolamo. 'It starts in Rome where the clergy mock Christ and the saints, where they are worse than Turks or Moors. Not only do they refuse to do penance for the Lord's sake, but they even sell the sacraments. Today there is a sale in benefices, which are sold to the highest bidder. Do you really think Jesus Christ will let this continue? . . .

'You've been to Rome and you know the life the priests lead there. Tell me, do you think of them as pillars of the Church or as great noblemen? They have courtiers and lackeys, horses and dogs, don't they? Aren't their mansions crammed with tapestry and silk, with scent and servants? Does it really seem to you that this is the Church of God? Their arrogance fills the whole world, matched by their insatiable greed. They will do anything for gold and ring their bells purely from avarice, when they ask for food, for fuel, for money. They go to Vespers and the Hours in choir as money can be got at these services, but not to Matins where coins don't change hands. They sell benefices, they sell the sacraments, they sell weddings, they sell everything. And yet they're frightened of excommunication!'[9]

The Frate preached twice more before Lent began. On 18 February he told the Duomo, 'You must be crazy to say a Pope can't make a mistake when so many Popes have made mistakes. . . . How many decrees have been issued by one Pope and revoked by the next, how many opinions held by some pontiffs have been denied by others?' He then examined Alexander's briefs in detail, pointing out mistakes and contradictions. 'Why are they so angry with me at Rome? Do you think it's because of religion? Certainly not! They are trying to overthrow our government, they are trying to tyrannize us, they don't care if godly living goes down with it, the godly living inspired by our teaching which will die with it. He who is against our teaching is against Gospel charity and is the real heretic.'[10]

In his sermon on Quinquagesima Sunday he declared, 'This excommunication is the foe of godly living and must come from the Devil. . . . If every unjust sentence had to be regarded as valid, then an evil Pope would be allowed to destroy the Church while we tamely submitted.' Two days later, on 27 February 1498 the second burning of the vanities took place in Piazza della Signoria. Before it began, Fra' Girolamo said Mass at San Marco, giving communion to several thousand men and women. After he had blessed the crowd from a makeshift wooden pulpit outside, shaking with emotion he prayed, 'Lord, if my words are insincere, if my words have not been truly inspired by you, then may you strike me dead at this very moment.'[11] According to Landucci, this time some of the crowd were openly hostile: 'the lukewarm laughed and mocked, saying, "He's excommunicated and gives Communion to others!" And it certainly seemed a great mistake to me, although I had faith in him.'[12]

The bonfire resembled that of the previous year although the Pseudo-Burlamacchi tells us the vanities were more valuable. The summit was capped with effigies of Lucifer and the Seven Deadly Sins.[13] A *Te Deum* was sung by the crowd, then the bonfire was lit, burning to the ground amid loud cheers. After it was over, the crowd marched to the Piazza San Marco where a great crucifix had been erected. Here everybody linked hands with the friars and danced round the crucifix, singing hymns. Yet many of those collecting the vanities had been stoned or beaten with cudgels – some had had their white cloaks torn off and the red crosses wrenched out of their hands.

'His [resumption of] preaching caused bitter disagreement,' says Guicciardini, describing the effect of these latest sermons:

> His opponents, whose influence among the common people was growing stronger by the day, were horrified at his disobedience and rebuked him, since his rashness might alienate the Pope, at a time when negotiations about the recovery of Pisa were being discussed by the pontiff and his various allies, and when it was vital to do everything possible to ensure papal support.
>
> On the other hand, his followers defended him, arguing that spiritual matters should take no account of any fears about the consequences in this world, and that such fears should certainly not be made an excuse for Popes to start interfering in the affairs of the [Florentine] Republic.[14]

This is a fair enough assessment, but Guicciardini omits to explain why Fra' Girolamo resumed preaching. It was because he had finally realised that Alexander would in no circumstances lift the excommunication unless Florence joined the League. Girolamo dared not let her do this since it meant ending the French alliance. He was not prepared to surrender his belief that King Charles would come again. Early in February Gianfrancesco Pico had unwisely published an *Apologia* in Florence, dedicated to Duke Ercole, which insisted that Savonarola's excommunication was invalid. It was seized on by the *Arrabbiati*, who sent it to the Pope. The dedication embarrassed Ercole while the book infuriated Alexander.

When Messrs Bonsi and Bracci attended the Pope's audience on 25 February, two days before the carnival, he called them over in his usual bluff way. After telling the ambassadors of the fatherly affection he felt for Florence and how hard he had been trying to recover Pisa for the republic, his tone changed abruptly. Quoting at length from the Frate's sermon on Septuagesima Sunday (11 February) he complained of the Signoria having so little respect for him as to let Savonarola preach in such a way. 'No Turk or Infidel would tolerate this sort of behaviour,' Alexander informed the unfortunate envoys.

'He ordered me to tell you he is sending a special message to warn you that he will place the entire city under interdict unless effective measures are taken immediately to stop the sermons,' Bonsi reported dolefully to the Signoria. 'He spoke of Fra' Girolamo with great indignation and used very harsh words indeed, repeating that if he did not stop before Lent, the interdict would most certainly be imposed.' He had said so in front of the cardinal of Perugia and other prelates, which showed he had no intention of changing his mind, added Bonsi. When he and Bracci had tried to reply, they were always cut short by the Pope or by some cardinal.

Alexander had then ordered that some comic songs about him, sent from Florence, should be read out to them. 'Am I to be the butt of ballad-mongers?' he demanded. When the horrified envoys protested that if anyone said the Frate was responsible, it was a lie, the Holy Father reverted to the need for an interdict and the unpleasant message he was sending to the Signoria. In the same despatch, Bonsi writes:

No one in Rome will believe what you say about the other-worldly nature of Fra' Girolamo's work. . . . It is no use trying to obtain support from anybody here, especially from those who know what he has been saying about the Pope. And all too many people are ready to throw oil on the flames.[15]

Bonsi would have been even more dejected had he known of a sermon that Savonarola would give on Ash Wednesday:

Oh Rome, Rome! You're going to suffer so much, you'll be sorry you ever fought us. You call yourselves blessed while we are the excommunicated although you fight as the damned do, like infidels. Rome should realize that the friar in Florence and his followers want to fight you evil men in the same way we would fight the Turks, that we want to die and suffer martyrdom. Yes, I really want to be martyred by you. Oh Lord, grant me this grace! You think you can frighten me, Rome, but I don't know the meaning of fear.

This would be a battle between soldiers of Christ and soldiers of Satan, added the Frate. 'If you want to fight me, then you'll fight as a pagan,' he told an unnamed enemy, who was clearly Pope Alexander, 'because here we live in a Christian fashion, while your way of life is contrary to Christ.'

In the same Ash Wednesday sermon he included a story about the saintly Jacopone da Todi who, when invited to preach before 'that wicked Pope', Boniface VIII, had told him, 'I'm amazed, yes, I'm altogether amazed, that the earth doesn't open and swallow you up. God be with you!', and then walked off without another word. It was obvious that the Frate meant his hearers to identify the present pontiff with Boniface.[16]

The message from Alexander to the Signoria, with which he had threatened Bonsi, arrived from Rome next day. It was a papal brief dated 26 February. Having long known of 'the grave and pernicious errors of that son of iniquity, Fra' Hieronymo Savonarola of Ferrara' and having excommunicated him, the Pope had learned that the man was now claiming he had not been excommunicated and was hurling infamous abuse against the Catholic religion and the authority of the Holy See. Even so, a large number of Florentines were attending his sermons with the permission of the Signoria 'from whom better things might have been expected'. The Pope ordered the Signoria to send him immediately to Rome, where, if he repented, he would be kindly treated. Or, at the very least, he should be confined in a safe place 'as a rotten member' and forbidden to see anybody.[17] Another brief (which has not survived) was addressed to the canons of the Duomo, probably ordering them to keep the Frate out of the cathedral.

Preaching on the same day, when Savonarola reached the end of his sermon he commented robustly:

Briefs have come from Rome, haven't they? People are saying they call me *'filius perditionis'*, a 'son of perdition'. Well, you can write back like this. 'The man you call a son of perdition doesn't keep boys or concubines for his pleasure, but spends all his time preaching the Christian religion. . . . He's trying to glorify the Church of Christ while you're trying to ruin it.'[18]

However, his position in Florence had suddenly become much weaker. 'Yesterday the new Signoria took office and six of them are hostile to the Frate,' the spy Sommenzi reported to Milan on 2 March.[19] This was a very serious development since the new *Gonfaloniere*, Piero Popoleschi, was one of the most bitter of the *Arrabbiati*, a man who genuinely loathed the Frate. Only three members belonged to the *Piagnoni*. For months every Signoria had been dominated by Fra' Girolamo's supporters, but all he could do now was to hope that more favourable members would be elected in May.

Sommenzi also says that a large Pratica, summoned to discuss how to answer the Pope's brief, has advised the Signoria to tell Alexander he would never have written in such a way had he been aware of the reformation due to Fra' Girolamo's preaching. They should also inform the Pope that they could not take any action against the Frate unless some really serious scandal occurred, and ask His Holiness to hold them excused. Nor must they forget to say that it was a straightforward calumny to allege that Girolamo was preaching false doctrine.

Despite the new Signoria's hostility, Savonarola still had many influential friends in the city. Each of the Ten in charge of foreign policy, including relations with Rome, was a supporter, while most well-informed Florentines were aware that, regardless of Girolamo, the Pope wanted their republic to fall. They also suspected that he hoped to transform Florence into a principality for his son Cesare.

On 3 March the Signoria sent Alexander a formal reply to his brief, based on the Pratica's recommendations. First, they explained that, abashed at being called 'a son of iniquity', Savonarola would no longer give sermons but had withdrawn inside his priory. The letter continued:

> For eight years he has preached in our midst, foretelling what will happen in the future and working a great moral reformation, as a result of which he has incurred the emnity of many perverse persons, who never cease from making countless false accusations against him. . . . We very much regret that we cannot comply with your Holiness's request.

For the moment, the Signoria could not act against the Frate without running the risk of provoking 'popular disturbances'.[20]

There was a Machiavellian twist to the Signoria's letter. Six of the nine who sent it were openly opposed to Savonarola and everything he stood for. They had no wish to praise him, let alone defend him, but they hoped to goad Alexander into taking drastic action. Sommenzi reports that the letter was designed to infuriate the pontiff and make him issue an interdict, so that it would be easier for them to act against the Frate.

But Fra' Girolamo was doing their work for them. On the same day he himself wrote to the Pope. He had in no way deserved His Holiness's last opposition to all he had tried to do at Florence, he complained. The Pope should have helped him:

Yet you always listened to my calumniators and detractors, and in doing so deprived me of the help that it was not only your duty as a Christian to give but your obligation because of your office. Instead, you opened the door to the wolves and gave them every possible help and opportunity to hinder Christ's work. But God, who uses the earth's weak and humble creatures to thwart the powerful, hears the prayers of his poor children. He is prepared to show that he does now that we are suffering so much evil at your hands, ready to prove it against you and all his other enemies, with natural and with supernatural signs. . . . So, Holy Father, worry about your own salvation.[21]

No one could forgive a letter so full of contempt. Guicciardini says 'the controversy raged for many days, the Pope becoming very angry'.[22] From now on Alexander would do everything he could to destroy him.

Already irritated by Florentine claims to be the new Jerusalem and the comparison of Rome to Babylon, Romans began to see the Frate's defiance of their ruler as an insult. Florentines were beaten up in the streets while a man broke into Bonsi's house and tried to kill him. On Ash Wednesday Mariano da Genazzano, now Master General of the Augustinian friars, gave a sermon at his priory. The church was packed, the congregation including bishops and even cardinals. Everyone knew that he was going to launch a savage attack on his old enemy.

Once again, Fra' Mariano lost his temper in the pulpit. 'The preaching of the friar from Ferrara comes from the Devil,' he shouted:

He has the audacity to say that the Pope is unworthy of his office, a broken reed. Here is a creature who is a filthy Jew, an obscenity, a thief who steals money and hoards treasure. . . . And yet Pope Alexander has pissed less than this man has had medals coined in his honour. . . . You wicked villain, you know perfectly well when you see all those visions of yours – it's after you've swallowed a whole vat of that strong Trebbiano wine. . . .

Oh Pope! Oh you Cardinals! How can you tolerate this monster, this serpent? Can the Church's authority really have sunk so low that a drunkard of this sort is able to trample her beneath his feet? You people don't even know what he's plotting. He's going to say things that will blot out the sun! . . .[23]

To demonstrate his contempt, Fra' Mariano made some sort of pornographic gesture (of a sort that fifteenth-century Italians called 'figs in your face'), but only succeeded in shocking his audience.[24] 'This shows what envy can do!' wrote Landucci when reports of the sermon reached Florence.[25] The Frate reacted in his own way, prophesying the imminent death of the Augustinian – who died before the year was over.

A more effective attack was launched by Giovanni Caroli, in a pamphlet that contained a blistering criticism of Fra' Girolamo's audacity in questioning the excommunication. No human being had the right to question the Vicar of Christ's judgement, he argued. In doing so, Girolamo and his *Piagnoni* were openly demolishing the Church – which, claimed Caroli, was something they had always planned to do in any case, since they possessed a barely disguised agenda and were plotting to build a completely new Church. What they wanted was not renewal but revolution.[26]

A smear campaign had been set in motion. Monsignor Burchard records in his *Diarium* that since the age of twenty the Frate had committed 'many sins of the flesh' he never confessed, deliberately celebrating Mass without consecrating the Host. Burchard also has a story of Savonarola putting poison in a lamprey and then telling his friars he saw a vision of enemies trying to murder him, after which he fed the fish to a goat brought into the refectory – whereupon the goat dropped down dead, much to the brethren's edification. (Interestingly, Cinozzi quotes the Frate as saying that Il Moro had tried to poison him three times, on the last occasion with a poisoned lamprey.[27])

On 7 March Bonsi and Bracci had to endure another very unpleasant audience. The Signoria's letter of four days before was read out to them, after which Alexander said he was astounded to receive such a reply and that it was 'a wicked letter'. Savonarola's sermons were in print, he continued. He had seen passages where the Frate laughed off the excommunication, declaring he would sooner go down to hell than seek absolution, and had described the pontiff as 'a broken reed' and reproaching him with the death of his own son. There was no guarantee the man would stay inside San Marco and that he would be justified in placing Florence under an interdict, although prepared to give the city one last chance. When the envoys tried to defend Girolamo, the Pope said he was not concerned with his doctrine, but only with his disobedience and contempt for the Holy See.

Monsignor Stefano Taverna, Bishop of Parma and Il Moro's ambassador to Rome, had been standing at Alexander's side throughout the audience. Afterwards, appearing to shake with fright at the recollection, he told the two Florentines that when they had left the Pope's presence His Holiness had burst into a truly terrifying fit of rage. Yet he assured them that even now, if they could stop the Frate preaching for a time and make him beg for absolution, Alexander would let him preach at some later date. The wily bishop was no less of a liar than his master in Milan.

'You must appreciate that the entire papal court is hostile to us,' writes an increasingly panic-stricken Bonsi, 'while Parma tells me that Piero de' Medici and the Venetian ambassador are both doing their best to make matters worse.'

'The Pope is certain the Signoria's letter was dictated by Fra' Girolamo', had been the Bishop of Parma's final, Parthian shot. 'He says the style is just like his' (perhaps this was a reference to the Frate's recent communication of the same date). 'Naturally we said we could not believe this was true,' replied poor Bonsi, although he sounds as if he was not entirely sure about it. He ends his despatch by lamenting, 'We are falling deeper and deeper into disgrace.'[28]

While these discussions were taking place, the Frate was continuing his Lenten sermons at San Marco, his texts from the Book of Exodus. Since the priory church was too small to hold the crowds who came to hear him, men were admitted on six days of the week, women on Saturdays. In the seventh sermon he gave Pope

Alexander and his minions the roles of Pharaoh and the Egyptians, giving the roles of Moses and the Israelites to himself and the Florentines:

> Now, just as in those times, the wicked think they are wise and call the city, chosen by God to receive his special graces, 'foolish Florence or the Frate's Florence'. . . . The great rulers of our day make preachers fail in their job of ensuring that Christ is born again in men's souls and, if they refuse, oppress them with excommunication and persecution.[29]

In the eighth sermon he recalled how Pharaoh enslaved the Israelites, making them do servile work:

> If you want to do the servile work of seeking worldly things, Rome won't stop you. Rome will let you heap up plenty of riches worth no more than mud or clay, but she will prevent you from collecting the tools of grace – symbolised by the straw – that you need if you're going to build a true temple of the spirit.

'God says, "I will deliver you from this slavery of wicked priests and prelates",' he declared in his sixteenth sermon. 'Never doubt for a moment that God will raise his mighty arm against Rome and that his awesome judgements will deliver you. One day, all those priests who strut about so proudly shall hide their tonsures in shame. For the scourge will surely come.'[30]

'God has sent his preachers into the vineyard, but nowadays how many people are trying to kill them?' he asked in his twentieth sermon. 'They want to drive the truth away, and I warn you that it's not just the Frate they're trying to drive way but Christ himself, believe me. Mark my words well, Rome, the kingdom shall be taken from you. For soon Christ is going to take the Church out of your hands and entrust it to proper shepherds, who will turn it to good account. *Videbis cito* – soon you will see all this happen.'[31]

Although fully aware of the need to avoid giving the Signoria a chance to attack him, throughout these sermons he had remained as uncompromising as ever, making the same prophecies. Florence was the chosen city, the Turks would be converted and the scourge was certainly coming to Italy – above all, to Rome.

Yet the last sermons of Savonarola were far from being monopolised by prophecies or his confrontation with the Pope. 'The mind of
man is like a bird seeking where to build her nest,' he told a
congregation of women in the penultimate sermon. 'She roams
through the world, trying to find rest in philosophy, in literature, in
science, in anything you like, but only in God can she find true
repose.' He prayed,

> Have compassion on your poor little flock, whom here you see so
> deeply afflicted and persecuted, for you are their shepherd and
> surely you wish them well, Oh Lord? If I'm no longer of any use
> in this world, then take my life. If you find I'm an obstacle, take
> my life and kill me. Yet what have my poor sheep done? They
> have not done any evil. It is I who am the sinner.[32]

Perhaps this prayer reveals a rare moment of doubt, when Fra'
Girolamo feared that his prophetic vision might have deceived him –
that the scourge might not come to Italy and cleanse Rome after all,
and that, instead, he had brought disaster on his followers. But the
mood of weakness, if it really was one, soon passed. The Frate
regained complete confidence in his vision of the future. Yes, the
scourge was coming, and coming very soon. He was ready for what
might well be his final battle with Pope Alexander.

TWENTY-FOUR

The Dialogue

Savonarola and the Devil in disguise – *Compendium Revelationum*, 1496

Despise not prophesying . . .
St Paul's Second Epistle to the Thessalonians, 5: 20

At some time between January and March 1498 Savonarola published *De veritate prophetica dyalogus* (usually known as the *Dyalogus*), written during his period of silence after his excommunication in the previous June. It was an attempt to explain why he felt so confident about his ability to see into the future. He also wanted to provide theological justification for a gift that in his view could benefit all Christendom.

Studying Thomas Aquinas in his youth had given him a strange enthusiasm for everything the Father had written on the way in which angels operate and on the nature of the Prophets' visions; he had pored long and hard over minute, hair-splitting distinctions drawn by the Angelic Doctor, while at the same time studying the Old Testament and the Apocalypse in such depth that he was familiar with every dream of the Prophets and Patriarchs. . . . Even as a child he had been accustomed to seeing spectres; now they intensified, haunting him even in public by day, and becoming almost threatening at night. When he found that these ghostly visions grew more frequent in reading the Bible and the Fathers of the Church, in deep prayer and lengthy vigils, he began to believe that they were sent from Heaven, mental pictures brought to him by angels, just like the visions of the prophets as they were described by St Thomas. From then on, he let no dream or fantasy pass without searching for a parallel in the Bible and applying the criteria that had been laid down by the Angelic Doctor.[1]

Highly coloured though it may be, this passage from Pasquale Villari's life of Savonarola cannot be bettered. It is almost certainly an accurate reconstruction of how the Frate spent his nights in those three tiny rooms at San Marco. Some of the visions came to him when he was sleeping, others when he was awake.

Villari is wrong, however, in attributing the way in which Girolamo interpreted the dreams to St Thomas, who implies that foreknowledge cannot be depended on and that great caution is needed in using it. The *Summa Theologica* contains five densely argued chapters on the subject. 'Light from prophecy extends also to the directing of human acts,' Aquinas tells us. 'In this sense prophecy is needed for the ruling of a people' – an observation no doubt noted by the Frate. St Thomas also says, 'The gift of prophecy is granted to a man for the utility of others and the enlightenment of his own mind.' He tells us that 'some people when asleep naturally foresee events', that 'Foreknowledge of the future which comes in dreams is either from a revelation of spiritual beings or from a bodily cause.'[2]

Yet Aquinas warns of the unreliability of foreknowledge. 'It seems that what is prophetically known or announced can be false. Thus prophecy can be subject to error.'[3] Still more disturbing, he says, 'we must conclude that some prophecy comes from demons'. At best, insists Thomas, 'Prophecy is a transient gleam, not a steady light.'[4]

Villari is correct in emphasising that Savonarola's main instrument of prophecy was the Scriptures. It was a common belief in fifteenth-century Europe that the Bible was full of secret messages which might change the world. The Frate shared this belief, and his interpretation of his own visions were based on what he considered Biblical precedents. As Ridolfi comments, the people and the words of the Old Testament that filled his mind suddenly sprang to life, making him clairvoyant and giving him glimpses into the future – although often he was puzzled by what he saw there.

Presumably, he read any contemporary writings that might elucidate the interpretation, such as Jean Gerson's *De Revelationibus* or the interminable works of Denis the Carthusian.[5] Yet Gerson advised that no vision should be accepted as genuine until after the visionary's death, and although Denis claimed to have seen demons and ghosts by the hundred he did not explain how or why. No doubt Marsilio Ficino and his Platonist friends were all firm believers in visions of the real, other world, but, tainted by neo-paganism and astrology, their views could not be taken too seriously. Nothing so far written on the subject appears to have been of much use to Girolamo.

Although the Church's official view was that prophecy possessed far less importance than it had in the Old Testament, Fra' Girolamo believed it still had a vital role. In one of his sermons on Ezekiel, delivered in 1497, he had insisted that 'natural light is not enough'. There was 'a need for the supernatural light' that only prophecy could supply. Now he claimed that it guided the Christian community, preparing it for the future so that eventually it might achieve the fullness of God.

He was not alone in his belief. The recent schism in the Church, with one Pope at Rome and another at Avignon, had deeply disturbed Catholicism. One consequence was a revival of prophecy by such figures as Queen Brigit of Sweden and Joan of Arc, among the best-known Dominican prophets being Catherine of Siena and Vincent Ferrer. In the 1490s Florence was full of less impressive examples. They included women such as the half-insane Camilla Bartolini Rucellai, who predicted that Giovanni Pico would become a Dominican 'at the time of the lilies' – accurately enough, if one identifies 'lilies' with the French invasion. The men tended to be even crazier, dishevelled madmen who howled at street corners that soon the thoroughfares would run red with blood.

Fanatics like this made Girolamo seem comparatively restrained. Quite apart from his prophecies and preaching, as head of one of the most respected religious houses in the city, a community that was attracting an increasingly high calibre of recruits, he had earned a name for sanctity and a brilliant mind, while his friends included the best intellects of the day. All these factors helped to inspire confidence in him.

As has been seen, not only had predicting the French invasion won him an impressive reputation, but it convinced him beyond doubt that he could see into the future. It was widely known how he had already foretold the deaths of Lorenzo, Pope Innocent and King Ferrante, and that they duly died. If sceptics suggested he had heard of the invasion talk in Paris or quibbled it had taken longer than expected for Ferrante to die although an old man, the Frate's holiness argued in his favour.

Under increasing pressure from critics, he decided to give his revelations a theological basis. Divided into nine books but only sixty pages long, the *Dyalogus* is a treatise in elegant, humanist Latin, which shows an extraordinary knowledge of the Bible. Its underlying theme is the reinterpretation of St Thomas's concept of man sharing in the divine light, as man sharing in the light of prophecy.

The structure consists of a dialogue in a lonely place with seven fantastically named interrogators, Urias, Rechma, Iechimham, Eliphaz, Thoralmed, Abbacuc and Saphtham, each representing a particular gift of the Holy Spirit, with whom he discusses the problems of prophecy in depth. The frontispiece to the first edition shows them seated round the hooded Frate in his black mantle under a tree in a garden, with a dove hovering overhead, while Florence with its Duomo can be seen in the background.

Fra' Girolamo allows the seven to raise objections which he then demolishes, just as he had done with those of the Tempter in the *Compendium*. When they suggest that he has been pretending to be a prophet in order to make people believe more strongly in religion, his outraged answer is that lying to the people in Christ's name would be turning the Lord Himself into a liar. Accused of playing the part of a prophet from diabolical pride under a cloak of false

Savonarola's dialogue with Urias, Rechma, Iechimham, Eliphaz, Thoralmed, Abbacuc
and Saphtham. From *De veritate prophetica dyalogus*, Florence, 1498

humility, even of being possessed by a demon, he calmly replies, 'Man does not acquire any merit in God's eyes from revelation, so what grounds could I possibly have for pride?'

When one of Girolamo's interrogators, Eliphaz, puts it to him that he may have been deceiving himself, if with the best intentions, he retorts:

> No, impossible. I know that my purpose is always a pure one. I worship the Lord in all sincerity, and I do my best to follow in his footsteps. I spend my nights in prayer and vigils, while I sacrifice my peace of mind and waste my health and strength with the object of helping my neighbour. No, it is impossible God would deceive me. This light [seen in his visions] is truth itself, the light that comes to the aid of my intelligence and fills me with charity.

Eliphaz then reminds him that many men have been deceived by visions of whose truth they convinced themselves. The Frate's reply to this is that if only such men had been purer of heart and taken proper care in interpreting what they saw, they would never have been deceived. While assuring Eliphaz that he himself has set sail 'on this extremely dangerous sea' with the utmost reluctance and after preparing himself by long prayer, he insists that his judgement is incapable of letting him down.

'But why are you so sure your revelations are true?' the seven ask Fra' Girolamo. In response he refers them to such precedents as the gifts of prophecy in both the Old and the New Testament and the 'angelology' of Thomas Aquinas, which accepts the existence of angels who function as divine messengers, as, for example, the angel in the Annunciation to the Virgin Mary, and he backs up these precedents with a wealth of quotations from the Bible and the *Summa*. He also quotes Gianfrancesco Pico della Mirandola, adding that he took after his late uncle, who had 'towered over all the cleverest, most learned and most distinguished men of our age just as the cypress tree does over rose bushes'. He insists that prophecy can be neither proved nor disproved by reason, but only by the divine light, which is infused by God.

He cites the best-known fruits of his own prophetic gift, the growth of San Marco and Florence's renewal. Many have entered the priory, highly educated men, to accept a ruler stricter than any other – a fair number have joined since his excommunication. Something similar has happened to the Florentines. No one can say that prophecy is bad if it achieves results like these. Perhaps there are people who oppose him, but even if they seem good these are the lukewarm and they resemble the Pharisees.

The world may well be approaching the Last Times and antichrist could appear at any moment. Whatever happens, it is plain that the corruption of Christianity has made it necessary for God to intervene. There is wickedness everywhere. Christ, 'if he came to Rome in its present worldly state', would be put to death in the way the Jews had killed him and 'you would not find one but a thousand crosses'. Just as the decadence of Israel's faith helped to prepare the way for belief in Christ, so the evil state of the Church is preparing men for renewal. In the end, the seven agree that Girolamo has proved the truth of his visions beyond any possible doubt.

Yet he had not fully admitted his gifts until 1496. In the *Prediche sopra Amos e Zaccaria* of March that year, he had denied he was a prophet. 'I am neither a prophet nor the son of a prophet,' he declared, adding that he was able to see into the future simply by the light of Christian charity and Christian learning. But in an *Epistola a uno amico* (the friend in question being Domenico Benivieni) printed two months later, he stated unequivocally, 'It is your sins, Italy's sins, that make me a prophet and ought to make prophets of you yourselves.'

An uncanny number of his prophecies came true, not just the invasion of Italy and the death of the three Italian rulers but the death of the dauphin. If Charles VIII was not to lead another French invasion, his successor would. Girolamo also prophesied with a fair degree of accuracy the sack of Rome and Florence in the next century and certain other events. The best example is the way he died, which he foretold from the start of his career as a popular preacher – most notably in 1491 during a sermon on the Psalms.

Yet even in his own day people rejected the *Dyalogus*, which soon found its way on to the list of books Catholics were forbidden to read. There is no doubt that he had visions, however. The most plausible explanation is (as Villari suggests) that the tendency to 'see things' which he displayed as a child was exacerbated by fasting and lack of sleep.[6] In his *Compendium Revelationum* he mentions an occasion when a voice spoke to him as he prayed 'sleepless until daylight' and 'weary from long wakefulness'. We also know that asceticism weakened him to such an extent that after delivering a sermon he sometimes had to spend days in bed.

Neither in the *Dyalogus* or the *Compendium* does he mention a friar at San Marco, Silvestro Maruffi, who suffered from mental disorders and hallucinations that were caused by an inability to sleep. He told Fra' Girolamo that they must be afflicted by the same malady and that he was less prone to see apparitions after being bled by the doctor. However, Girolamo decided that Fra' Silvestro's visions were genuine, although he only mentioned them when they tallied with his own.

For most people the real mystery is how could an intelligent man deceive himself in such a way. Nevertheless, Joseph Schnitzer, one of Fra' Girolamo's finest biographers, was convinced that he had possessed the power of prophecy, insisting that anybody who fails to accept this cannot understand him.[7] Roberto Ridolfi, who spent years studying the Frate, also believed that he had been 'a great prophet'.[8]

As Aquinas warned, clairvoyance is unreliable, a view with which Girolamo secretly agreed. At the end of the *Dyalogus* he reveals a fear that his powers may one day abandon him. '*Vos denique, sacratissimi dona, numquam patrocinio me verbo destituite,*' he implores. 'Oh you, most holy gifts, never end by depriving me of your protection.'[9]

TWENTY-FIVE

'This little worm'

A friar preaching – German, sixteenth century

. . . the insults of this little worm . . .
Pope Alexander VI, *Numquam putavimus*

The Holy Father now decided to eliminate the Frate. His methods have best been defined by the historian Jacopo Nardi who, although writing years later, had been in Florence at the time as a very young man. Nardi is always remarkable for objectivity, and the great eighteenth-century historian Muratori accepted his assessment of Savonarola's career without qualification:

The Pope, who wanted a different government in our country from the government of the day, finally threatened the city with interdicts, using condemnation and censure to make it look as if the city was rebelling against the Holy Church and the Holy See; while at the same time promising the Signoria, publicly in letters and secretly in messages, to do all that he possibly could as a good friend to help the city, if the said Fra' Girolamo were delivered into His Holiness's hands.[1]

We do not know the names of Alexander's spies, the men who delivered the messages, or how they operated, but they were certainly in Florence, working tirelessly. And, like Il Moro's sinister Sommenzi, they too were in contact with the *Arrabbiati*, striving to bring down the Frate.

On 9 March 1498 the Pope prepared a further brief for the Signoria, *Numquam putavimus*, which Ridolfi calls 'a terrible brief'.[2] From the tone of barely controlled fury there is reason to think that Alexander dictated it himself. Only by quoting it in full can one convey its ferocity:

We would never have thought it possible your impertinence could reach such a point that you would dare to argue with us about the business of Fra' Girolamo Savonarola almost as if it were some personal quarrel and completely ignore your duty of rendering to Caesar that which is Caesar's and to God that which is God's. It is time we put an end to all these letters and briefs which are multiplying *ad infinitum*.

Please understand, once and for all, that this Fra' Girolamo has been definitively excommunicated by us, not because of any slanders or promptings by other persons, but because he has disobeyed our command to join the Tuscan–Roman Congregation, and because of the open contempt he has shown for our decree of excommunication by continuing to preach as if he were some angel sent by the Lord. We are not condemning him for his good works and their effect on your city. On the contrary, we applaud him for them, but we want him to come and beg our pardon for his wilful pride, after which we might be prepared to forgive him, if he has abased himself before us.

Not only have you encouraged this friar in his disobedience, but by preventing anyone else from preaching you have set him up as your own oracle of Apollo. We shall never cease in our efforts until full satisfaction has been given to the honour and dignity of the Holy See for the insults of this little worm whom you harbour.

You should take better care of your own affairs, because not until you are properly obedient will we deign to listen to all the various requests you are currently making to us about the (political) interests of your republic. In any case, we insist you answer us by actions, not by letters. We are determined not to tolerate your disobedience any longer but have every intention of placing your entire city under an interdict and keeping it in force for as long as you go on patronizing and protecting this monstrous idol of yours.[3]

What makes it so likely that Alexander dictated this thunderbolt himself – and that we are hearing the Holy Father's own voice – is the angry sarcasm, with such touches as the Latin word *vermiculo* (little worm). Suspicion becomes certainty on learning that *Nunquam putavimus* was never sent. A consummate diplomat, he realised on reflection that if he upset the Florentines too much he would never destroy the Frate.

On 10 March Cardinal Ascanio Sforza wrote to his brother Il Moro at Milan that he must already have heard of His Holiness's violent indignation about the sermons and outrageous behaviour of Fra' Hieronymo at Florence. It had been hard for Sforza to restrain the Pope's fury and stop him sending the original brief intended for the Florentines. Such evil-natured letters had arrived from Savonarola that Alexander had been beside himself with rage and the Bishop of Parma had had the utmost difficulty in calming him down. Ascanio adds that he has now managed to convince the Pope it would be wiser to send a gentler brief which would have a better chance of putting an end to the 'wickedness' of Fra' Hieronymo.

Expectantibus nobis, also dated 9 March, is harsh enough but designed to argue rather than browbeat the Florentines into cooperation. Repeating that, while of course, he respects the Frate's teaching and upright life, Alexander says it is impossible to put up any further with his insolence. The new brief states:

He has not merely refused to submit to excommunication but declared it invalid, and has had the audacity to challenge God to send him to hell if he asks to be absolved from it. We are no longer prepared to tolerate him or waste more time on correspondence. You will make sure that he ceases to preach and then hand him over to us or, at the very least, keep him imprisoned until he is ready to come to us and abase himself at our feet to beg for absolution. We would be graciously prepared to grant this after receiving his submission so that, after being absolved, he could go on preaching the word of God.[4]

Villari comments that, had Fra' Girolamo gone to Rome, 'he would at once have been seized and strangled in the Castle of St Angelo'.[5]

The Pope ends by saying that he has every intention of placing Florence under an interdict, or of 'doing something even worse' (which he does not name), should the Signoria refuse to do what he requests – although it is hard to see what could be worse in the papal armoury than an interdict.[6]

Understandably alarmed by *Expectantibus nobis*, the Signoria summoned a large Pratica for 14 March to debate what should be done. Twenty-five citizens from each *quartiere* of the city attended, as well as all the principal officials. The minutes have survived and give a fascinating insight into the minds of well-to-do Florentines. Giovanni Canacci reminded the assembly that their republic was 'the weakest of the five powers of Italy', and that an interdict would ruin their trade everywhere. In his opinion, the Frate should be handed over to the Pope. 'Remember,' he added, 'how Troy was burned and destroyed because of refusing to surrender Helen of Troy.'[7]

Paolantonio Soderini disagreed. The whole affair was political, got up by enemies to cause discord among Florentines. Pope Alexander must be told firmly that they would never join the League, while 'Fra' Girolamo ought to be cherished like a rare and precious jewel since all Italy has not his equal'. Lorenzo Lanzi, an official at the Monte di Pietà, thought the Frate's sermons had saved the republic, reminding the assembly that it owed the Grand Council to him. 'We should rinse our mouths out before speaking of Fra' Girolamo instead of proposing to give him up. Where would we be without his help? Why are you so frightened of an interdict? Let it come, as others did in the past.'

Subtly hostile, Guidantonio Vespucci, a wily patrician lawyer, saw the problem from a different perspective. Asking Alexander to help the republic recover Pisa while opposing his wishes would be self-defeating. 'Whether Fra' Girolamo is right or wrong, you will get nothing out of the Pope without giving him what he wants,' he argued smoothly. 'And if he does declare an interdict, then your entire commerce is going to be wrecked.' If the Frate submitted, it might be possible to appease Alexander, but whatever happened, it would be wisest to obey His Holiness.

Antonio Malegonelle said that all this trouble had been stirred up by enemies of the republic, who had turned Alexander against 'Hieronymo'. Either he was a fraud or a good and holy man, in which case he should certainly not be banned from preaching – to forbid him would bring down a curse. Enea della Stufa agreed. The Frate's teaching was divinely inspired and the attack on him the work of malevolent 'potentates' – the city would be in an uproar if they obeyed the Pope, who would be sure to demand further concessions. Giovanni Cambi thought so too, saying that Fra' Girolamo was probably sent by God and they would be punished for persecuting him, while even if Alexander might make promises about Pisa, it was not in his power to fulfil them.

However, Giuliano Gondi wanted the Signoria to obey the brief. 'This man preaches there is no Pope,' he claimed. 'He will bring into being a sect of fraticelli of a sort we've seen here before, a heretical sect.' An interdict would be a disaster. 'Messer Enea [della Stufa] would talk in a different way if he had anything to lose. I myself have wine all over Italy and if such a sentence were to be imposed I should go bankrupt.'

In contrast, Francesco Valori, for once persuasive rather than bullying, insisted that forbidding the citizens of a free city to attend San Marco would be intolerable. 'The priory is more of a school of virtue than it has been at any time these last fifty years, and I advise you to show the Frate more honour and respect than you have shown anyone for two centuries,' declared the *Piagnone* leader. 'Instead of meddling with his preaching, we ought to give him better opportunities for spreading the word of God. These Briefs did not originate from the Pope, but were slyly extracted from him by our enemies, who are doing their best to destroy us.'[8]

Valori was supported by Antonio Canigiani, afraid of neither interdicts nor excommuncations because he knew 'certain Florentines were at the bottom of them all'. 'The Old and the New Testaments are surely enough to prove that Fra' Girolamo is a true prophet,' said this fervent *Piagnone*, adding that whether the excommunication was valid or not, the city's liberties must not be surrendered to a pope.

On the other hand, Giacomo Pandolfini agreed entirely with what Guidantonio Vespucci had argued, pleading that the brief should be obeyed in regard to the Frate's preaching, which should be banned. However, he said nothing about handing him over to Alexander. This seems to have been the majority view, but the Pratica broke up without taking a decision.

Meanwhile, Savonarola's sermons at San Marco were showing a certain desperation. On 7 March he claimed that the first brief could not have been written by the Pope as it was so 'ill-conceived'. A week later, referring to *Expectantibus nobis* while the Pratica was sitting, he said of Alexander, 'He is not to be called Pope and not to be obeyed when he issues commands against the will of God.'[9]

During these weeks a dissatisfied young bureaucrat called Niccolò Machiavelli, an *Arrabbiato* excluded from the Grand Council because of his inadequate background, saw Fra' Girolamo as a ruthless fraud. After attending two sermons at San Marco, he reported in a letter of 9 March how the Frate had acted the part of Moses,[10] shouting from the pulpit, 'Oh Egyptian, I want to give you a thrust with my sword', adding that he would like to give him an even greater blow – the Egyptian being presumably the Pope. He also quoted him as saying, 'Don't you realise what it means to cry "Interdict! Interdict! Interdict!"? It means "Tyrant! Tyrant! Tyrant!"' Machiavelli thought that Girolamo was implying that, should Alexander put Florence under the ban, a tyrant must take over – his henchman Francesco Valori.

He was wrong. Fra' Girolamo was warning the Florentines of the far from unlikely possibility of a Medicean restoration. Since Piero de' Medici was completely discredited, the *Bigi* had found a new leader in his cousin, Lorenzo de Pierfrancesco de' Medici, who had secured the backing of Lodovico Il Moro after marrying his niece. Girolamo is known to have been nervous about Lorenzo for some time and, to a certain degree he was a prophet in this, too, since eventually the Medici, if not Lorenzo himself, would return to Florence in triumph.

Another Pratica met on 17 March.[11] It consisted of only nineteen citizens but, as each was rich and influential, it was able to describe itself with a certain exaggeration as the 'heart of the city'. Its conclusions were that the Frate must be made to stop preaching immediately, but that the Pope's other demands were an insult to the honour of the republic. The Signoria followed its advice, sending word to San Marco.

In his last sermon, on 18 March, Fra' Girolamo told his followers, who still packed the priory church:

> The message of the Lord has long been a consuming fire in my bones and in my heart, and I could never control it but was always forced to speak out, because I felt almost as if I were burning, as if set alight by the Lord's spirit. Yet sometimes after coming down from the pulpit, I would say to myself, 'I shall never talk like this again.' . . . So I must let the Lord's will be done, for the more we suffer on earth, the greater will be our crown of glory in heaven.

At the end of the sermon he finally explained what had happened: 'Yesterday, at the third hour after sunset a message came from our rulers to say that, after much deliberation, they had decided they would like me to stop preaching.' He had promised to give them their answer today. Yes, he announced, the Lord would let him stop. But there was something else he must announce:

> Bad news is coming to Florence, of a misfortune that will overwhelm her. You may be afraid of an interdict decreed by the Pope, but the Lord is about to lay one upon you, of a sort that is going to take away the lives and all the riches of the wicked.
>
> We obtain through prayer what we cannot obtain through sermons, and we fervently encourage all good men to do this. Oh Lord, I beseech you to have mercy on the good and delay your promises no longer.[12]

A Council of the Church?

Savonarola writes a letter – *Prediche sopra Ezechiel*, 1517

Now I hereby testify, in verbo domini, *that this Alexander is no Pope, nor can he be considered one.*

Savonarola, *Lettere ai Principi*

Just over a year before these events, on 7 January 1497, in response to a request from Charles VIII, the lawyers of the Sorbonne had given their opinion that a King of France possessed the right to summon a council of the Church, convincing Charles that he could depose the Pope. The Dominican network would have informed Fra' Girolamo, well aware that the King was his only hope. No help would come from any of the cardinals.

Girolamo must also have known that Charles was again thinking of recrossing the Alps. 'He always set his heart on returning to Italy, readily admitting he had made some very serious mistakes and listing them, but he thought that next time, when he was able to go back and regain what he had lost, he would be much more careful,' says Philippe de Commines.[1] He adds that Charles had 'turned his thoughts towards living according to God's commandments and ensuring that there was justice in the Church'. As a start, the King had been trying to make the French clergy lead more upright lives. It looked, to those closest to him, as if he wanted to initiate a full-scale reform of the entire Church and not just in France – as further justification for his next expedition to Italy. But it was also clear that he might take a long time to make up his mind.

Unlike King Charles, Savonarola could not afford the luxury of waiting, as may be seen from Bonsi's despatch to the Ten from Rome on 18 March. Alarmed, the envoy reports that the Pope has spoken to more than a few cardinals of his extreme indignation at the shocking abuse hurled by Fra' Girolamo at both him and the entire papal court, and is no less angry with Florence for allowing it to happen. His Holiness's advisers have now told him that a ban on preaching is not enough. He must insist on the Frate being sent to Rome without further delay. Besides laying Florence under interdict, he should arrest every Florentine in Rome, impounding their goods, and if the Frate has still not been handed over by a certain date, then he should imprison the more important in Castel Sant' Angelo and confiscate their property.

The Pope agrees with all this, continues Bonsi, adding that Alexander is so furious that he is ready to inflict as much harm as he possibly can on the republic. Bonsi begs the Ten to act quickly, 'for the love of God'. They must understand that by himself he can do nothing to save the situation.[2]

On 19 March a group of Florentine merchants at Rome sent an urgent letter to the Signoria, confirming Bonsi's report. They are in grave danger because of the favour shown by the Signoria to the 'venerable Fra' Hieronimo' – Florence will not just be humiliated but seriously damaged if they have to suffer as a consequence. Will the Signoria please take action to rescue them? Like Bonsi, they imply that it has to be action against the Frate.[3]

External observers suspected that his days were numbered. On 26 March Duke Ercole wrote to the Pope, fulsomely disassociating himself from Gianfrancesco Pico's embarrassing *Apologia*, and saying that never for a moment had he doubted the excommunication's validity. The Duke assured His Holiness that, 'as God is my witness', he had never even discussed the subject with Pico, whose dedication implying this was either a lie or a literary fiction. He insisted that he himself invariably spoke of the Pope 'with the utmost honour'.[4]

On 27 March Sommenzi reported to Il Moro that the outlook was very promising indeed. The Frate's supporters had failed in an attempt to set members of the Signoria against each other, while more magistrates hostile to him had been elected. If only the Holy Father keeps up the pressure, 'the Frateschi will soon be cowed by our friends and unable to go on intriguing with the French'.[5] The alliance with France was, of course, the fundamental reason for Il Moro's paranoiac hatred of Savonarola.

Fra' Girolamo was not yet beaten, even now. But shrewd politician that he was, he saw his growing peril, recognising that the odds against him worsened every day, fully aware that more and more of the *Grandi*, the bankers and merchants, were beginning to agree with those who regarded him as bad for business. He ordered three friars from San Marco to preach against the excommunication at churches all over Florence. Some, especially Domenico da Pescia, whom Sommenzi calls 'impertinent and loutish', used fiercer language than their prior.[6] Sommenzi adds that an eloquent Franciscan friar, Fra' Francesco, was disputing their claims. 'There was just as much disagreement among priests as laity,' comments Guicciardini, 'and members of other religious orders never stopped delivering fervent sermons against him.'[7]

Although Girolamo had stopped preaching, it was clear that the Pope's wishes were still being flouted. On 28 March the Bishop of Parma wrote to Il Moro that everybody in Rome was saying that the Frate must be dealt with. Some of the Florentine colony had been promising His Holiness the Signoria would do just as he wanted, while the Roman clergy were hoping he would send a prelate to Florence to arrest the man and send him to Rome.[8] But so far the Pope had not reached a decision. Two days later, Bonsi heard that 'His Holiness has decided to put an end to all this.'

In the meantime, the Milanese envoy at Bologna, Francesco Tranchedino, had reported to Il Moro on 20 March that the *Frateschi* (the *Piagnoni*) were in contact with France, offering big sums of money if the King would come to their rescue. Tranchedino also claimed that agents in Florence had informed him that revolution was in the air as people realised the French had left them in the lurch while conditions in the city were deteriorating 'as a result of the Frate's hypocrisy and vanity' – but this was standard *Arrabbiati* abuse.[9]

Savonarola's reaction to the growing crisis was an appeal to the rulers of Christendom. In a circular letter addressed to the Holy Roman Emperor and the Kings of France, Spain, England and Hungary, he did not mince his words:

> The moment of vengeance has come and the Lord commands me to reveal new secrets, making clear to the world the danger that threatens the Barque of Peter because of your neglect. The Church is full of abominations, from the crown of her head to the soles of her feet, yet not only do you fail to apply any sort of cure but you even pay homage to the source of the evils that pollute her. In consequence, the Lord is deeply angered and for a long time has left the Church without a shepherd. . . .[10]

> Now I hereby testify, *in verbo Domini*, that this Alexander is no Pope, nor can he be considered one because – leaving aside the mortal sin of simony by which he bought the Papal Chair and sells the Church's benefices to the highest bidder every day, and ignoring his other all too obvious vices – I declare that he is not a Christian and does not believe in the existence of God, which goes beyond the bounds of infidelity. . . .

He begged the rulers to summon a council of the Church, as was their right. It must meet as soon as possible, 'in some free and suitable place' – God was sure to send signs and portents to encourage them. He added a few lines to each copy of his letter, addressed to the recipient. He reminded Maximilian that nothing was more fitting for a Holy Roman Emperor than to come to the rescue of the Church when she was in danger. And he told Charles VIII:

> You cannot have forgotten all the many opportunities of doing good the Lord has given you, and should you fail to join this holy enterprise you will be punished more severely than the others. You who bear the title of Most Christian King, whom the Lord has chosen and armed with his vengeance, will you allow the ruin of the Church? Can you ignore the many grave dangers that surround her?

As for Ferdinand of Spain: 'What good can come of your victories over the infidels?' he asked, referring to the recent conquest of Granada. 'You have raised a building that is hollow, for inside the foundations of the Church are collapsing and the whole edifice is falling into ruin.'[11] Copies of the letters to the Kings of England and Hungary have not survived, but presumably they contained similar messages.

Savonarola chose five reliable supporters to deliver the letters. Each would send a preliminary letter, of which he supplied a draft, to influential contacts whom he had identified at the main courts. These would be asked to give the main letter to the ruler in question, together with a copy of a letter he had written to Alexander. 'I employed Giovanni Cambi to contact the Emperor,' he afterwards explained.[12]

> Domenico Mazzinghi would write in his own name to Giovacchino Guasconi a letter that was to be shown to the King of France. [Mazzinghi was a former *Gonfaloniere* while Guasconi was Florence's ambassador to Charles.] Simone del Nero was to write to his brother Niccolò to approach the King of Spain. The business of the English letter was handled by Francesco del Pugliese, who had an English friend in Florence whom he could persuade to write. As for the letter destined for the King of Hungary, I sent copies to Madonna la Minuta at Ferrara and a friend of mine there. The drafts of all these letters I had sent to the various people mentioned by Fra' Niccolòda Milano.[13]

Domenico Mazzinghi despatched two copies – to make certain that at least one arrrived – to Guasconi in France. Later, he described how he had become involved:

> Towards the end of last March Fra' Girolamo asked me to come and see him, saying 'I want you to do something for me. I know you're full of zeal wherever God's work is concerned, and I would like you to write a letter to Giovacchino [Guasconi] of which I shall supply a draft, and to accompany it with a letter I have written to the Pope.'

Fra' Niccolò had given Mazzinghi the draft, which he had rewritten as a letter from himself. 'Besides what was in the draft, I added, on my own account, that on the day of the Carnival more than 3,000 had confessed and communicated while the rest were abandoning themselves to dissipation.'[14]

Mazzinghi also sent a letter of his own[15] to Guasconi that has survived and which gives a vivid insight into how a fervent *Piagnone* regarded the Frate:

> You will have heard of the persecution directed against our father, Fra' Hieronymo da Ferrara, especially at Rome, for having exposed those vices of the clergy that are an abomination before God and the world. The Pope has excommunicated him and threatened our city with an interdict, to stop him preaching. He was persuaded to do it by certain vicious men from the city, but all good people and lovers of truth have a very high opinion of this man. It is wonderful to see what fervour he inspires, in particular by his predictions of the renovation of the Church and the conversion of the heathen, and by the terrible threats he has made concerning the scourges that are about to fall on Italy, and above all on Rome because of her intolerable wickedness. . . .

Guasconi must show the Frate's letters to King Charles, continues Mazzinghi. His Most Christian Majesty is bound to summon a council or God will punish him. It will be a far greater thing for him to have done than conquer infidels, since if the Church's foundations collapsed it would mean the ruin of Christendom. 'May God inspire His Majesty and others who have power, so that they do not let the most precious blood of Christ to be insulted in such a way for, speaking truthfully, it is managed more disgracefully by these wicked priests and prelates than it would be by Jews or Moors. . . .'

Another messenger has left an account, Simone del Nero:

> On 24 March Giovanni Spina came to my house, saying that Fra' Girolamo wanted to talk to me. I went to San Marco at once where I found Fra' Girolamo in the infirmary with the ambassador of Ferrara. Leaving the ambassador, he said to me, 'You know how I've been preaching the renovation of the Church and the conversion of the infidels – it's God's will that the work should succeed. So I want you to write a letter to your brother Niccolò, your agent in Spain, of which I shall give you a draft . . . and also to send him a copy of a letter to the Pope.

Simone told Spina that there was no point in sending the letters. 'Niccolò won't be there as I gave him permission to leave some months ago. In any case he has written to me saying that the kings [of Spain and Portugal] are busy with their African expedition.'[16]

But Fra' Girolamo insisted, and in the end Simone promised to write to his brother. In his letter he praised the Frate no less fervently than had Mazzinghi.

Everything went wrong. It is likely the *Arrabbiati* and the *Tiepidi* heard rumours of what was going on and alerted the Pope who realised this was the meaning of Savonarola's words, 'Someday, I shall turn the key' – the key being the Key of Peter. Then the courier carrying Mazzinghi's correspondence was robbed by a band of Milanese bandits, who sold it to Il Moro. The Duke forwarded the letters to his brother in Rome, who passed them on to His Holiness. Nor did any of the other letters reach their destinations.

Yet if Fra' Girolamo's appeal had reached Charles VIII and the King had marched on Rome, Christianity might have had a very different future.

TWENTY-SEVEN

The Ordeal by Fire

A Franciscan friar – *Speculum fratrum minorum*, 1524

To appeal to heaven for a miracle by a rash acceptance of a challenge, which is a mere snare prepared for me by ignoble foes, would be a tempting of God, and the appeal would not be responded to.

George Eliot, *Romola*

After reading the letters found on Mazzinghi's courier, Pope Alexander was keener than ever to crush the 'little worm'. Yet despite the ban on his preaching, ever more savage attacks by *Arrabbiati* and *Compagnacci* and the election of a hostile Signoria (the new *Gonfaloniere*, Piero Popoleschi, openly wanted to get rid of him as soon as possible), Savonarola still had plenty of support in Florence. For all the pontiff's threats, an interdict was a weapon of last resort whose use might seriously damage Roman commerce. However, events were to play into Alexander's hands.

By now other religious orders were attacking the Frate, particularly the Franciscans. At their church of Santa Croce, ever since the beginning of Lent Fra' Francesco di Puglia had been calling him a heretic, a schismatic and a false prophet. Then, during a sermon on 25 March, Francesco was so carried away by his own eloquence that he challenged Girolamo to prove by an ordeal by fire that he was not a fraud. A precedent was enshrined in Florentine history. In 1068 one of the city's great saints, Giovanni Gualberto, abbot of Vallombrosa, had told one of his brethren to walk through a fire in the presence of the citizens in order to prove the unworthiness of a new bishop of Florence. The monk had been unhurt by the flames.

The challenge was at once accepted by Domenico da Pescia, the most fervent of the three Dominicans who were preaching in Girolamo's place. In 1497, when Domenico and the Franciscan were giving sermons at Prato, Francesco had suggested a similar duel, but had been called away before it could go any further, so Domenico's acceptance is to some extent understandable. It was not clear, however, whether Fra' Francesco was challenging Savonarola in person or merely anyone who agreed with him.

At first Fra' Girolamo did not take the idea seriously and in any case he regarded the Franciscan as a nonentity. He said afterwards that he had disapproved of Fra' Domenico's acceptance. But, without consulting him, two days later Domenico published *Conclusiones*, a defence of his prior, in which he repeated his readiness to undergo the ordeal, 'hoping by the power of God, our Saviour, and for his glory, to prove the truth for the good of souls and emerge from it safe and sound'.[1]

Horrified at his challenge being taken seriously, Fra' Francesco backed down. 'His quarrel was only with Savonarola,' he insisted. 'Yet while of course expecting to be consumed [by the flames], he was prepared to enter the fire with him to bring about the destruction of a man who was spreading scandal and false doctrine.'[2] But he declined to have any dealings with Domenico. This should have ended the matter.

According to the Pseudo-Burlamacchi it was the *Compagnacci* who refused to let the matter drop, after a discussion at one of their banquets, which took place on the evening of the publication of Fra' Domenico's *Conclusiones*. 'If Savonarola goes into the fire, he will certainly be burned,' they decided. 'But if he doesn't, he is bound to lose all credibility with his followers – and then we'll have a good chance of causing a riot and capturing him during the uproar.'[3] They not only persuaded Fra' Francesco to persevere with his challenge – Doffo Spini promised him they would see he never entered the flames – but involved the Signoria.

The Frate's enemies in the Signoria leapt at the chance to discredit him. Next day, the contents of Domenico's *Conclusiones* were recorded by the official notary – the need to reform the Church, her inevitable scourging and reform, the scourging and rebirth of Florence, the fulfilling of these things in a short time and the invalidity of Fra' Girolamo's excommunication. They were then signed by their author who later signed a commitment to enter the fire or undergo any other sort of ordeal.

The unhappy Fra' Francesco signed a declaration stating that while ready to go through the flames with Savonarola he was not concerned with Domenico and could find another Franciscan who would enter the fire. He only signed after much prevarication and considerable pressure, adding that he did so 'at the desire and request of the Magnificent Signoria'.[4] To confuse matters, another friar from San Marco, Mariano Ughi, stated that if need be he was ready to take Domenico's place.

On the following day Fra' Francesco returned to declare, somewhat surprisingly, that he was 'conscious of his inferiority to Fra' Girolamo in scholarship and virtue'. He then produced another Franciscan, the obviously terrified Fra' Giuliano Rondinelli, who declared before the Signoria that he would enter the flames although certain he was going to be burned alive – he would do so 'for the salvation of his soul'.[5]

On 30 March the inevitable Pratica met at the Palazzo della Signoria. Predictably, Domenico Mazzinghi had no reservations, telling the assembly that the ordeal must take place, 'because such a miracle will surely redound to the glory of God and the peace of the city'. Piero Guicciardini, the historian's father and another *Piagnone*, was another in favour of the ordeal. Although an old enemy of the

Frate, Giovanni Canacci was one of the few who showed humanity. 'I honestly believe that if our ancestors who founded this city had foreseen that a question of this sort would be discussed here, and that we were going to become a laughing stock and disgrace to the entire world, they would have refused to have anything to do with us,' he protested sorrowfully. 'I implore your Excellencies to save these people from such wretchedness at any cost, whether from fire, air or water.'

'Why not let them try a method that doesn't risk lives?' suggested Antonio Strozzi. 'Perhaps they might take an oath to cross the Arno without getting wet.' 'If people think the ordeal might bring back harmony to the city, then they should not only go through fire, but into the water, up into the air or down into the earth', was the view of Girolamo Rucellai. 'Our first concern is our city, not these friars.'[6]

It appears that most members of the Pratica privately agreed with Filippo Giugni when he said that the wisest course of action would be to hand the Frate over to the Pope without further delay. Rich men, they were alarmed by the prospect of an interdict – they had too much to lose. The tide was turning against Fra' Girolamo.

In accord with the general opinion among the Pratica that there was no point in stopping the ordeal,[7] the Signoria decreed that it should take place on 6 April, no doubt with secret satisfaction. The superior of the contender who perished in the flames (meaning Fra' Girolamo or Fra' Francesco) would be banished from Florence. If both contenders died, then the Frate was to be deemed the loser and sentenced to perpetual banishment.

Bonsi reported that Rome seemed displeased by the news. In submitting the excommunication to divine judgement, the ordeal was questioning the sentence. His Holiness had informed the envoy that it was 'wholly to be condemned'.[8] Yet after the ordeal he wrote to thank Fra' Franceso and he may have foreseen that it would discredit the Frate. Some writers even suggest that he encouraged the Franciscans. On the other hand, the Pseudo-Burlamacchi claims that the Signoria wrote to ask for Alexander's approval, but 'the Pope feared he might lose his tiara if the trial succeeded,[9] which is why he refused permission'. In fact, the Signoria never asked him. Given Savonarola's alarming reputation, it is not inconceivable that Alexander was afraid the Frate might be justified by the ordeal.

Meanwhile, at San Marco Silvestro Maruffi had a vision in which he was told by the guardian angels of both Fra' Girolamo and Fra' Domenico that Domenico would go through the fire without being touched by the flames, while on 2 April two of the friars, Malatesta Sacramoro and Roberto Salviati, called at the Palazzo della Signoria to register their readiness to enter the fire. Next day all the brethren, together with a large number of *Piagnone* laymen, wrote a letter[10] to the Holy Father in which they too declared their readiness.

Frustrated by being unable to preach, the Frate published a *Riposta* explaining his own attitude towards the ordeal:

The work I am busy with is too important for me to bother about joining in such wretched quarrels. If the enemies who insult us and then make all sorts of excuses, would promise publicly to use this to obtain a verdict on our cause and on the reform of the Church, I wouldn't hesitate for a moment to enter the fire and feel certain of going through it unharmed. But if they want to use it to prove the excommunication valid, then they might do better to answer my arguments. Or do they hope to use the fire as a means of disputing my prophecies? I am not trying to bully or beg anyone into believing them against his will. All I ask is that everybody should live a Christian life, and for that the fire of charity and the miracle of faith are needed – nothing else helps.

The enemies who started this business say they are certain to die, admitting they are their own murderers. In contrast, we've been forced into it, compelled to accept because the honour of God and religion is at stake. Those who know themselves to be genuinely inspired by the Lord are bound to come out of the flames unhurt, if the experiment ever takes place, which is far from certain.

As for me, I keep myself for a greater cause, for which I am always ready to lay down my life. The time is coming when the Lord may favour us with supernatural signs and portents, but it will not be at man's command or pleasure. In any case, they should be satisfied that by sending some of our brethren we shall be no less exposed to the anger of the multitude if the Lord decides not to let them go through the fire unhurt.[11]

That last sentence, 'no less exposed to the anger of the multitude if the Lord decides not to let them go through the fire unhurt', is

scarcely confident. Yet despite his misgivings, the *Piagnoni*'s behaviour at the services in San Marco was full of frenzied optimism.
Thousands – not just friars, but secular priests, nuns, laymen,
women and children – could be heard shouting, 'I will go into the
fire for your glory, Lord!'

During the days immediately before the ordeal no one was
admitted into the priory, where the community was engaged in a
continuous prayer of intercession. On 5 April the ordeal was
postponed for a day. On 6 April the Signoria issued a new decree,
announcing, 'Should Fra' Domenico be consumed [by the flames]
Fra' Girolamo is to leave Florence within three hours.'

A huge stage of brick and rubble, covered with earth, had been
built in the Piazza della Signoria, 7 feet tall, 90 long and 16 wide. It
was heaped with two banks of wood soaked in oil, pitch and resin,
divided by a path about 5 feet broad. Starting from opposite ends at
the same moment, the contenders would walk down this path
through a blazing pyre.[12] Florence was looking forward to the best
free entertainment for a very long time. Even the burning of some
unlucky sodomite could not compete with such a spectacle.

When the day came, Saturday 7 April, Fra' Girolamo said Mass at
San Marco. His brief sermon beforehand hints at secret misgivings:

> I can't promise you that the trial will take place, because it doesn't
> depend on us, but I can tell you that, if it does, we shall certainly
> win the victory. . . . Oh Lord, we don't need miracles to believe
> what is true, but we've been forced into this ordeal, made to
> accept it in order to save our self-respect. We are certain that the
> Evil One will be unable to turn this business into blasphemy or
> denial of your will, so we are marching out to do battle for you.
> Surely, our opponents must worship another God, since their
> ways are so different from our ways? Oh Lord, your people here
> only want to serve you.[13]

Summoned by the Signoria's mace-bearers, the contingent from
San Marco marched to the Piazza two by two, led by a cross-bearer.
First came a serene Fra' Domenico in a crimson cope with a crucifix
in his hand, and after him Fra' Girolamo, carrying a silver
monstrance which contained the Host; he was flanked by Fra'
Malatesta Sacramoro and Fra' Francesco Salviati. After them came

two hundred friars who were followed by *Piagnoni* of all ages, each holding a little red cross in one hand and a lighted taper in the other. They were chanting a psalm: 'Let God arise, let his enemies be scattered: let them also that hate him flee before him. As smoke is driven away, so drive them away: as wax melteth, so let the wicked perish at the presence of God.'

The Piazza was a sea of people when the Dominicans reached it, every roof-top packed with spectators. A thousand men-at-arms kept order, including several hundred *Compagnacci* in full armour under Doffo Spini.[14] The Franciscans from Santa Croce had arrived half an hour before, not in procession but in small groups, and showing a distinct lack of commitment.

It became clear at once that the Franciscans were less than enthusiastic. First they objected to Fra' Domenico's crimson cope on the grounds that it might be enchanted with a spell to protect him from the flames. After he removed it, they objected to his habit for the same reason, so, stripping to the skin, he changed it for that of another friar. Then they complained that he was surrounded by Dominicans, so he agreed to wait among the Franciscans.

Fra' Francesco di Puglia and his understudy Fra' Giuliano Rondinelli were late, however. When they arrived, they asked for another meeting with the Signoria. Their brethren outside now complained that Fra' Domenico's crucifix was bewitched, but when he offered to replace it by the Host they protested that this would endanger the Body of God. Fra' Francesco and Fra' Giuliano showed no sign of emerging from the Palazzo della Signoria.

By now the atmosphere in the Piazza had become unbearably tense. The delay went on, yet nobody explained why. Despite their confidence, the Dominicans waited with growing anxiety while the dense crowd, many of whom had been there since dawn, became restive. A riot broke out in one corner, quelled by men-at-arms. Unexpectedly, a savage storm blew up. Thunder and lightning, hail and heavy rain drenched everybody, soaking the pyre. But the crowd and the friars still waited for the ordeal.

Finally, when evening came and darkness had begun to fall, a spokesman emerged from the Signoria to announce that the ordeal would not take place after all. People began to shout that the Frate had made fools of them. Whipped up by the *Arrabbiati*, the mob in the Piazza errupted. Girolamo and his Dominicans got back to San

Marco with the greatest difficulty, only the swords and halberds of some friendly men-of-arms enabling them to find a way through the enraged crowd.

It was more than the end of Savonarola's Florence: it was the end of Savonarola.

TWENTY-EIGHT

The Siege of San Marco

A Renaissance grotesque – Florentine, sixteenth century

Fra' Girolamo Savonarola . . . ruined with his new order of things immediately the multitude believed in him no longer, and he had no means of keeping steadfast those who believed, or of making the unbelievers believe.

Machiavelli, *Il Principe*

Both the Dominicans and the Franciscans sang a *Te Deum* when they returned to their friaries. Yet there was little to be thankful for at San Marco, apart from the fact that nobody had been hurt. The crowd's behaviour showed the Dominicans they were in imminent danger. In the past there had been several attempts on Fra' Girolamo's life, but it was the first time the friars had been attacked as a body. Luca Landucci, a supporter, if admittedly lukewarm, noted ruefully that the fiasco of the ordeal had deeply upset the people, 'who almost lost faith in the prophet'. He adds that it was being discussed throughout the city, 'especially by those against the Frate, who were much encouraged'.[1]

It was obvious that the *Arrabbiati* were going to attack the priory. Some *Piagnone* leaders proposed that they should arm themselves, but Francesco Valori, always a man of rigid principle, disagreed – they must not start the bloodshed. The wiser among them decided to leave the city at once, saying that if they were not allowed to fight it would be better to run.

Trouble broke out on the following evening, that of Palm Sunday, with a riot at the Duomo. Armed *Compagnacci* prevented the Dominican preacher from delivering his sermon at Vespers, banging the benches with their swords and howling abuse, shouting, 'Get out, you damned *Piagnoni*!' until the congregation broke into a panic-stricken stampede for the doors. Anyone who tried to remonstrate was knocked down. Cheered on by the *Compagnacci*, boys stoned the *Piagnoni* as they fled from the cathedral, using the lethal skill banned by the Frate. Outside, anyone who looked like a *Piagnone* was attacked, several people being wounded and one or two killed. A young man was chased and run through with a spear, merely for singing a psalm as he walked along the street, while an unfortunate spectacle-maker, who had nothing to do with the *Piagnoni* but had come out of his shop to protest at the noise, was cut down with a sword.

The uproar grew. Within a very short time several hundred armed men had joined the boys and the *Compagnacci*, and a mob was raging through the streets. They stoned the house of Andrea Camboni, a leading *Piagnone*, but were driven back by a hail of missiles from inside. Rallying, they stormed Camboni's house, burning it to the ground.

Meanwhile, to yells of 'Get the friars! Burn San Marco!' a band of youths led by *Compagnacci* rushed into the Piazza outside the priory as Vespers was ending. They hurled stones through the church door but, still being comparatively few, were not bold enough to enter the building. Inside, there was panic, women screaming. 'I chanced to be there,' records Luca. 'And if I hadn't managed to get out through the cloister, I might have been killed.'[2] A wax-chandler named Paolo said afterwards that he too had fled from the stones. 'I didn't see where or from whom the violence was coming, but I could hear the shouts about wanting to kill everyone who was in San Marco.'[3] The friars evacuated the church, barring the doors into the priory. The noise outside became deafening since the mob, which was growing bigger all the time, howled threats, threw missiles and hammered on the doors. However, the priory's strong walls and narrow windows made it an excellent fortress.

Preparations for defence had been made, without Fra' Girolamo's knowledge. Aware that a crisis was imminent, helped by several of the friars some *Piagnoni* had turned a disused cell in the cloister into a small arsenal that contained eighteen halberds and six crossbows with bolts, besides a dozen helmets and breast-plates and a few bucklers. There were also firearms, a keg of gunpowder and a box of bullets. The firearms consisted of two *bombardelle* or small cannon (which in the event were never used) and eight arquebuses – crude matchlocks but deadly at short range.[4]

Thirty laymen remained inside San Marco, including Valori, ready to defend the priory with their lives, as were some of the friars. The defence was led by Francesco Davanzatti, who, aided by Baldo Inghirami, had provided the arms. But instead of merely guarding the entrances and waiting for the authorities to arrive, they made the mistake of attacking the mob. An armed group of sixteen friars and four laymen went out into the Piazza and tried to drive away the crowd, firing and even fighting hand to hand, the friars making a bizarre spectacle with breast-plates and helmets on top of their white robes. Among them was Fra' Luca della Robbia, son of the artist Andrea. Above the din the Piagnona (San Marco's great bell) pealed incessantly, ringing desperately for help.

However, their enemies were increasing all the time and after an hour they were forced to retreat inside, hurling tiles from the roof on to the besiegers. Infuriated, the crowd piled bales of flaming straw against the doors. The only action taken by the Signoria was to send mace-bearers with the message that the defenders must lay down their arms and Savonarola must leave Florentine territory within twelve hours.

Donning his chasuble and stole, taking a cross in his hand, Fra' Girolamo announced that he was going out into the Piazza to surrender. 'Let me go,' he begged. 'The storm has blown up solely because of me.'[5] His brethren forcibly held him back. Seeing that he could not leave, he led them into the church, insisting that prayer was the only weapon for a priest and rebuking those who had taken up arms: 'They must not stain their hands with blood, they must obey the precepts of the Gospel, the commands of their superior.' Not every friar was ready to listen.

As soon as it grew dark, Francesco Valori escaped over a garden wall, hoping to rally the *Piagnoni* and bring help. However, things looked so hopeless that for a time he hid in an attic. When he finally reached his house he found it besieged by another mob, and was just in time to see his wife shot dead by a crossbow bolt in the head as she looked out from a window. Recognised and seized, he was being taken to the Signoria, who had promised to spare his life, when he was seen by some kinsmen of the Mediceans he had executed in August. They struck him from behind with a halberd, another *Arrabbiato* knifing the Florentine Cato as he lay dying on the ground.

By this time the besiegers at San Marco had dragged up three mangonels which fired large rocks against the priory doors, as well as through the windows and over the walls. Eventually, at about 2 a.m.,[6] weakened by the flaming straw, the doors gave way under the fusillade of rocks and repeated blows by makeshift battering-rams, whereupon the enraged rabble poured in. But, still hoping that Valori would return with reinforcements, the defenders put up a surprisingly stubborn resistance. Fra' Enrico, a young German, proved to be a remarkably good shot with an arquebus, using the pulpit as a sniper's nest as the church filled with smoke and flames, shouting at each discharge, '*Salvum fac populum tuum, Domine!*' ('Save thy people, oh Lord!').[7] He was not the only friar who turned out to be a marksman. Others hurled tiles or stones, or hit their enemies in the face with heavy crucifixes. The Frate did his best to restrain them, telling the miniaturist Fra' Benedetto to lay down his halberd, but he could not be everywhere. More than a few went on fighting until the very end.

Together with the bulk of the community, Fra' Girolamo withdrew to the Greek library, where, despite the hellish noise outside and likelihood of the mob breaking in, they chanted their office as if in choir. At the last moment, despite being badly wounded and covered in blood, a small Florentine tradesman, Girolamo Cini, who had long wished to join the Dominicans and had stayed on after Vespers to defend the priory, begged for admission. He was immediately clothed with the habit.

Then Girolamo addressed the friars his farewell:

> All I have said came to me from God, and He is my witness in heaven that I am not lying. I hadn't foreseen that the city would turn against me so soon, but may the Lord's will be done. My final command to you is this – let faith, prayer and patience be your weapons. I am leaving you with grief and anguish, to surrender myself into the hands of my enemies. I don't know if they will kill me, but you can be certain that once I'm dead I shall be able to help you better in heaven than I have been on earth. Take comfort, embrace the cross and through it you'll find salvation.[8]

The besiegers, who by now had guns and crossbows, had been reinforced by a detachment of men-at-arms from the Signoria whose commander, Gioacchino della Vecchia, announced that he was ready to bring up cannon if the friars did not surrender.

For a moment Fra' Girolamo thought of fleeing through the garden as Valori had done. He was dissuaded by Fra' Malatesta Sacramoro, who had secretly gone over to the enemy – the only traitor in the community. 'Shouldn't the shepherd be ready to risk his life for his flock,' Malatesta reminded him slyly. Yet had he tried to escape he would certainly have been caught and lynched – the uproar had spread all over Florence, every citizen arming himself, and few *Piagnoni* would have dared to shelter him.

At about 3.00 a.m. two friars went into the cloister and asked to speak with the men-at-arms. 'We agree to hand over the Frate if you promise to take him safely to the Palagio [Palazzo della Signoria],' they said. The men-at-arms promised. Accompanied by Fra' Domenico, Savonarola came out of the library and surrendered to the Signoria's mace-bearers, who manacled their hands.[9]

They were dragged through the cloisters and out of the smoking ruins of the priory into the sea of hostile faces in the Piazza San Marco, to be pushed through the jeering mob along the street towards the Palazzo. Blows and spittle rained on them all the way, while in the darkness besiegers waved lanterns or thrust torches into Girolamo's face, yelling, 'Behold the true light!' Just before he reached the Palazzo, beaten and bruised, a man kicked his backside, screaming, 'That's the seat of his prophecies!'[10]

At the Palazzo della Signoria, the triumphant *Gonfaloniere* Piero Popoleschi asked with heavy sarcasm if the two friars still believed they were divinely inspired.[11] Both men answered that they did, most certainly. Then they were confined for the night in separate prisons, Fra' Girolamo in the Alberghettina – 'little inn' – which was a small cell carved into the massive wall of one of the upper storeys of the Palazzo's bell-tower, with a tiny window looking over the city to the wooded hills far away. Like Joan of Arc's voices, in the end Girolamo Savonarola's visions had failed him.

TWENTY-NINE

The Rack

The Florentine lily – Florentine, sixteenth century

Take me down, and I will write you the story of my whole life.
Savonarola, according to Landucci, *Diario fiorentine*

On the day after, Monday in Easter Week, Florence was still in tumult, even if the rioters had laid down their arms. According to Luca Landucci, 'hell seemed open', while citizens never tired of cursing Savonarola as *'ladro e traditore'* ('thief and traitor'). 'No one dared to say a word in the Frate's defence,' adds Luca, 'or they would have been killed.'[1] For the moment the *Piagnoni* had been reduced to a hunted remnant. A score were arrested – not only two or three more Dominicans and wealthy figures such as Andrea Camboni or Domenico Mazzinghi, but men like 'Niccolò the shoemaker' and 'Paolo the wax-chandler'. The political leaders of the *Piagnoni* were dead, in prison or in hiding.

A Pratica was summoned immediately, and was dominated by *Arrabbiati* and *Compagnacci*. Anybody who sympathised with the *Piagnoni* or felt pity for them, if any were present, remained silent. Since nearly all members of the Ten and the Eight, were *Piagnoni*, and since this was a political revolution, the Pratica insisted they must be replaced at once, before the expiry of their legal term of office. The most outrageous election was that of Doffo Spini, leader of the *Compagnacci*, who now became one of the Eight – and one of the Frate's judges.

The Pratica told the Signoria what it wanted done with Savonarola. The three friars were to be examined in secret – the Frate himself, Fra' Domenico and Fra' Silvestro Maruffi (who had been arrested after emerging from a hiding place, betrayed by Malatesta Sacramoro). Only suitable extracts from the reports of their interrogation should be made available to the public, and because of fears that he might reveal political secrets, Savonarola must not be sent to Rome, although the Pope should be informed that he was being held in a secure prison. Seventeen commissioners were to be appointed to question him. The commissioners, chosen on 11 April, consisted of his worst enemies, among them being Doffo Spini. Another was the chronicler Pietro Parenti, who had always disliked the Frate.

That the Signoria were taking no chances was evident from the man they put in charge of the interrogation, Francesco di Ser Barone, known as 'Ser Ceccone'.[2] A former Medicean involved in one of Piero's plots, Ceccone had been saved by the friars at San Marco where he had taken refuge. Despite being hired by Doffo Spini to record the conversation at the *Compagnacci*'s dinners – and spying for Il Moro to whom he sent reports in cypher – until now Ceccone had pretended to be a *Piagnone*, attending the sermons at the Duomo. Although as a notary instead of a magistrate he was not legally qualified to report on interrogations, he could be relied on to twist the evidence and ensure a verdict of guilty.[3]

At 5 p.m. on 10 April Landucci watched Fra' Girolamo being carried by two men from the Palazzo della Signoria to the Bargello prison next door – carried because his legs were in irons.[4] He had already been questioned and racked, but so far they had not managed to break him.

From a legal standpoint the Signoria had no right to torture a cleric unless they obtained permission from the Pope, but they assumed that the Holy Father would have no objection. They had guessed rightly. A brief arrived from Rome, dated 12 April. 'It gave us the utmost pleasure to learn from your ambassador of the well-timed efficacy of the steps you have taken to crush the mad fury of that son of iniquity, Fra' Hieronymo Savonarola, who has not only deluded the people with vain and empty promises, but has resisted both your commands and ours by force of arms', purred the gratified pontiff. 'At last, however, he is confined, for which we give thanks to our loving Saviour, who, because He is the light that enlightens the world, would not suffer your truly religious city to remain sunk in darkness.'[5] As well as sending congratulations, His Holiness graciously gave permission to use torture when examining the friars. In addition, he absolved anybody who might have broken some ecclesiastical law by attacking a religious house or by attending the sermons of an excommunicate. Only later did he make it clear that he wanted Savonarola sent to Rome: Ridolfi comments, 'the Signoria's stubborn resistance to his request cast a shadow over the Borgia's joy'.[6]

The method the Signoria employed for questioning was the *strappado*, the Italian rack. This was a rope attached to a pulley on the ceiling. (If rumour be true, it was occasionally used by the Italian army during the Second World War.) Stripped and bound, his hands tied behind him, the suspect was hoisted up to the ceiling to hang by his wrists and then suddenly dropped so as to dislocate his arms, after which he was generally left hanging for the time it took to say the Creed. A surgeon was present to reset the arms in their sockets. Although the injuries seldom proved fatal, the pain was excruciating, made worse by a *tratto* or tug on the rope. Someone as frail as Fra' Girolamo, weakened by fasting and chronic ill health, suffered horribly.

Interrogations never began with torture, as there were three formal preliminary stages. The accused was asked to confess. Then, if he did not make a satisfactory confession, he was threatened with being tortured. Finally, if the accused's statements were still thought to be unsatisfactory, the order was given for torture.

As has been said, the Frate's interrogation began on 9 April, using the pretext that he was a cleric to deprive him of counsel for his defence, on the grounds that ecclesiastics were never provided with defence counsels. The logic is hard to grasp since, according to canon law, as laymen the Signoria had no right to try a churchman.

Landucci was told he had been hoisted three times and Fra' Domenico four. 'Right-minded men who had faith in him wept on hearing how he had been tortured,' he observes.[7] Three hoists was an underestimate. Filipepi claims that on one day alone during the week that followed the Frate was hoisted and dropped fourteen times, after being lifted up to the ceiling, but between four and six seems more likely – fourteen would have killed him. In addition, red-hot coals were applied to the soles of his feet while he was dangling from the rope.

No doubt Fra' Girolamo's interrogators gave him news from France that reached Florence on 13 April. Charles VIII had died at Amboise on the day of the ordeal by fire. The 'New Cyrus' had struck his head against a latrine doorway, and would never again cross the Alps.

'Take me down, and I will write you the story of my whole life,' Girolamo is said by Landucci to have told his interrogators.[8] But that was not what they wanted. Their object was to extract admissions that could be distorted into treason and provide grounds for the death penalty. A scheme to summon a council of the Church could scarcely be twisted into a plot to betray Florence. When examining him, Ser Ceccone hammered away at the fiction that he had deliberately tried to deceive the Florentines with his visions, but while he managed to extract plenty of interesting information none of it could be described as incriminating.

He went on to politics. The Frate admitted that he would have liked to see Valori become *Gonfaloniere* for life, like a Venetian Doge but with more power – although there had been no talk of a coup. He had never been directly involved in domestic politics, leaving them to laymen like Valori, even if he had made his wishes known to him through Andrea Camboni. Yes, he had had other allies among the Frateschi, people such as Girolamo Benivieni, Piero Cinozzi and Francesco Davanzatti, but he had never tried to arrange for supporters to be elected to the Signoria or to the Grand Council. Nor had he ever contemplated an alliance with Piero: 'I strongly opposed him.'

As for external politics, yes, he had tried to persuade the King of France to return, sending him letters, but it would have benefited

Florence since he had asked Charles to restore her lost lands. His Bible readings, not his visions, had convinced him that the 'barbarians' would come to Italy to renew the Church and that the Turks would be converted. He described his attempt to summon a council of the Church, and how afterwards he would have persuaded the princes to conquer the infidels. No, he had not wanted to be Pope – although if elected he would not have refused the office.

He had never asked his friars to tell him what they heard in confession. Nor had he wanted the ordeal by fire, which put him in 'great difficulty and danger', only agreeing to it for the sake of his reputation. In any case, he had suspected that ultimately the Franciscans would be too frightened of the flames.

Throughout, Fra' Girolamo resisted in his own subtle way. After all, Aquinas says there is no obligation to tell the whole truth to unjust judges.[9] He denied having been a prophet, just as Christ had done, while, talking as much as possible, he obscured his answers with a flood of verbiage. During a later interrogation a papal expert at such examinations observed how he would pretend to answer a question, first by telling some of the truth and then obscuring it, but always without lying.

He then signed a 'deposition' drawn up by Ser Ceccone, who inserted compromising additions. Certain recurring phrases are obvious interpolations by the notary, such as 'this was my hypocrisy', 'this was my pride' or 'I did it for the sake of worldly glory'. On 19 April the deposition was publicly read out in the Sala Grande of the Grand Council, as was customary, in the absence of the accused.[10]

'He whom we had held to be a prophet, confessed that he was no prophet, and had not received from God the things which he preached; and he confessed that many things which had occurred during the course of his preaching were contrary to what he had given us to understand,' recalls Landucci, continuing:

I was present when this protocol was read, and I marvelled, feeling utterly dumbfounded with surprise. My heart was grieved to see such an edifice fall to the ground on account of having been founded on a lie. Florence had been expecting a new Jerusalem, from which would issue just laws and splendour and an example of righteous life, and to see the renovation of the Church, the conversion of unbelievers, and the consolation of the righteous; and I felt that everything was exactly contrary.[11]

Yet the deposition made Savonarola look so guiltless that the Signoria tried to stop it circulating. Sending an extract to Pope Alexander, in a covering letter they claimed he had not confessed because his body was unusually tolerant of pain – although we know from Ceccone's reports that the reverse was true. Sommenzi reported despondently to Milan that what had been read out was of no importance, that 'neither by the application of the cord or by any other sort of torture have his examiners been able to discover any crime in him . . . had they uncovered anything useful, they would not have let an hour go by without announcing it'.[12]

The Ferrarese chronicler Bernardino Zambotti informs us that Duke Ercole wrote to the Signoria interceding for the Frate, but that his letter was ignored by 'those very cruel Florentines'. Girolamo had to suffer further interrogation and torture, from 21 to 22 April, after which Ceccone polished up one or two new answers he had given and these, too, were read out in the Sala Grande. But, once again, the Signoria realised that they were inadequate.

They were also disconcerted by the behaviour of Fra' Domenico, who proved so stubborn that his interrogators used the ghastly *stranghetta* (iron boot) on him besides the *strappado*. 'I may easily die if you torture me more, because I am so shattered that my arms are useless, especially the left one which . . . is dislocated for a second time,' declared Domenico. But they tortured him again, and again. He still refused to say what they wanted if this meant lying. 'I have always thought him an altogether upright and extraordinary man', was his final deposition.[13]

Fra' Silvestro Maruffi was not so brave, as was perhaps to be expected from an insomniac valetudinarian, his overriding objects being to save his life and escape any more torture. Obediently, he denounced Girolamo and gave lists of everyone who had visited San Marco. Yet none of the information he provided was sufficient for a capital charge against the Frate.

Silvestro was not alone among the friars at San Marco in deserting his prior. On 21 April most of them signed a letter to the Pope that makes painful reading. 'Not only ourselves but men of much greater gifts were deceived by Fra' Girolamo's cunning,' they pleaded:

The impressive quality of his teaching, his upright life, the holiness of his behaviour, what seemed to be his devotion, and the excellent results he achieved in cleansing the city from immorality, usury and every kind of vice, and the events which appeared to confirm his prophecies in a way beyond human power or imagination, and were so frequent and of such a sort that, had he not retracted and admitted what he said was not inspired by God, we would never have been able to renounce our belief in him. For our faith in him was so strong that all of us were ready to go through the fire in support of his doctrine.[14]

They begged the pontiff to absolve them from the excommunication they had incurred by supporting the Frate and the guilt of taking up arms to defend San Marco. They ended their letter by saying, 'May your Holiness be satisfied with the arrest of Fra' Girolamo Savonarola, the source of all the trouble. Let him suffer fitting punishment if there is any sufficient for wickedness such as his, and may we sheep who have strayed return to the one true shepherd.' Yet they said nothing about any crime against Florence.

The *Arrabbiati* became desperate at failing to find evidence that would destroy Fra' Girolamo once and for all and, with him, the *Piagnoni*. There was a fresh wave of arrests and interrogations, of both friars and laymen. On 27 April Landucci noted, 'All the citizens arrested for this cause were scourged [i.e. tortured], so that from 15 in the morning [11 a.m.] till evening there was ceaseless screaming at the Bargello.'[15] These interrogations, too, produced nothing of value.

On 5 May a Pratica composed entirely of *Arrabbiati* debated whether or not to send the friars to Rome. The majority view, however, was that they should be put to death in Florence – 'the execution can take place here so much more quietly' being Giovanni Canacci's view.[16] The minutes of the debate reveal beyond doubt that ever since the fall of San Marco the Signoria had been planning a judicial murder.

Accordingly, the Signoria instructed Bonsi – who was still ambassador to Rome, having deserted the Frate – to implore the Pope's help. In an explanatory letter to His Holiness, they pointed out that if the friars went to the scaffold in Florence, it would deter their followers and help to put an end to the *Piagnone* movement. But the Holy Father was welcome to send his own officials to examine Fra' Girolamo.

THIRTY

A Papal Commission

Prelates arriving at a city – Livy, *Les décades*, 1487

I don't know who you are, and I don't want to. You may be He Himself or just his likeness, but tomorrow I shall find you guilty of being a heretic and have you burned at the stake. People who've been kissing your feet today will pile faggots on the flames.

Dostoyevsky, *The Brothers Karamazov*

In a brief of 12 May Alexander waived his demand for Savonarola to be brought to Rome. In the same brief he granted a request from the Signoria that normally he would have considered outrageous, giving them permission to tax ecclesiastical property for the next three years. Clearly, he was pleased with the Florentines.

His Holiness sent two 'Apostolic Commissioners' to Florence, to 'investigate the crimes and iniquities of these three children of perdition', and to arrange for the friars' condemnation and degradation from their orders so they could be handed over to the secular authorities for execution. The commissioners were also to see if more convincing grounds for condemnation could be extracted. They must make sure that nobody at Rome was implicated in Savonarola's appeal to the European sovereigns – the Pope had not forgotten how many cardinals had been in favour of deposing him in 1495.

One of these commissioners was the Master General of the Dominicans, Fra' Giovacchino Torriani, until recently Savonarola's friend and patron. Chosen purely for the sake of appearances, he would play a muted part in the proceedings. The other commissioner was a Catalan canon lawyer who had made a formidable reputation for himself as a magistrate at Rome, Francisco Remolins, Bishop of Lerida. Known in Italy as 'Romolino', he was a favourite of the Pope and, as a careerist with his eye fixed firmly on a red hat, he could be counted on to see that matters ended in the way Alexander wanted. When the pair rode into Florence the mob yelled, 'Are they going to die?' The Bishop shouted back, 'Yes, they're going to die all right!' The *Arrabbiati* had sent a beautiful whore to his lodgings, disguised as a page. (Afterwards, he took her home to Rome, still dressed as a boy.) 'We shall have a good bonfire,' he told his hosts. 'I've brought the verdict.'[1]

Knowing the Holy Father's interest in the case, Romolino wasted no time, summoning the torturers on the morning after his arrival. This was for a third examination of Fra' Girolamo, which was to be attended by an unusually large group of senior Florentine officials. Aware that Ser Ceccone had done a bad job, the Signoria hoped that an experienced canon lawyer from Rome would be able to extract a more satisfactory confession.[2]

Romolino concentrated on Savonarola's scheme for a council. 'Did you have any dealings with princes?' he asked. 'Which of them did you trust, and why?'[3]

'I had no dealings with the Italian princes, because I considered all of them to be my enemies,' Girolamo told him. Instead, he had placed his hopes in the late King of France 'because I had spoken with him', in the Emperor Maximilian 'because I heard he was easy to win over', in the King of Spain 'because I heard he was hostile to the Curia', and in King Henry VII of England 'because I heard he was a good man'. But 'I knew nothing about the King of Hungary'.

'Which cardinals were your friends, and what contact did you have with them?' was the next question. 'I used to regard the Cardinal of Naples [Oliviero Carafa] as my friend, but didn't have much confidence in him. Although he was responsible for our securing the separation from Lombardy, this was really due to Piero de' Medici's intervention. After Piero's departure [from Florence], I learned that he and his brother the Cardinal had turned [Carafa] against me. Lately, I have had no contact with him at all, or with any other Cardinal.'

After further questions, Romolino ordered that Girolamo should be stripped for the rope. He threw himself on his knees, pointing to his left arm which dangled uselessly from earlier rackings. 'Hear me, God!' he cried. 'You've caught me – I confess that I've denied Christ, that I've told lies. Signori of Florence, bear witness that I denied Him from fear of torture. If I have to suffer, then I will suffer for the truth, which is that which I said came from God. Oh God, grant me repentance for denying you because of my fear of torture.' Hoisted up, he screamed, 'Don't tear me!' and, 'Jesus, help me! This time you've caught me!' Hanging from the rope, he was asked why he said this. 'To seem like a good man,' he answered and, when the question was repeated, 'Because I'm mad.' Throughout, he begged, 'Don't torture me, I'll tell the truth – Yes! Yes! Yes!'[4]

The most likely explanation for his behaviour is that he was admitting he had made false confessions while being racked, in the hope it might persuade his interrogators to stop torturing him; but that, since the ruse had failed, he was now trying to make the new interrogators realise he had been genuinely inspired by God, so that they would have mercy on him. On the other hand, it is also possible that his words have been twisted by the interrogators.

'Why did you deny just now what you had confessed?' was Romolino's next question, while he was still hanging on the rope. 'Because I'm a fool', was the reply. After being let down, he said, 'When I'm confronted with torture, I lose all my self-control, but when I'm in a room with a few men who deal gently with me, then I'm able to express myself better.'

He appeared to be so confused that Romolino then put some seemingly ridiculous but loaded questions to him, presumably with

Papal propaganda – the Frate inspired by demons. From G.F. Poggio Bracciolini, *Contra Fratrem Hieronymum Savonarolam processus*, Nuremburg, *c.* 1498

the intention of eliciting compromising replies from a man who was in such a muddled state of mind. 'Did you ever argue that Jesus Christ was just a man?' he enquired. 'Only a fool could think that,' answered Girolamo. 'Do you believe in magic charms?' was another question of this sort. 'I've always laughed at them.'

Romolino resumed a more fruitful approach: 'Did you write contemptuous letters about the Pope?' he asked. 'I did not actually write such letters myself, but I persuaded others to write them,' answered Fra' Girolamo. 'It was only recently that I thought of doing so. Others did not incite me to do this – it was I who instigated them.'

'What good did you think you were going to do? Didn't you realize what a scandal you would cause?' The broken man replied, 'It was all because of my pride and folly.'

In a tactful gesture towards his hosts, Romolino then switched to Florentine affairs. 'Did you cause dissension in the city through your preaching and did you show partiality for your own party?' 'Certainly I favoured my own party, but I never encouraged murder', was Girolamo's response. 'What about those five citizens who were put to death last August?' 'I was content with their being punished with death or exile, but I never meddled in the business – except for interceding with Valori, if not very enthusiastically, on behalf of Lorenzo Tornabuoni.'[5]

The report of a reply next day is so satisfactory for Romolino that one suspects it has been rewritten:

> Monsignor, what I said yesterday as a denial [of my previous admissions] was said by a man who was overwrought, because I wanted to deliver myself from such great trouble, since this bodily suffering is so much that even the sight of it frightens me far more than actual torture by rope frightens most men. Everything I wrote down and signed during my first and second examinations was true, and I ought to thank my fellow citizens for handling me so gently. If I didn't tell the truth to begin with, it was from pride. Yet, since they handled me so gently, I decided to tell the truth.

If we can believe the report, he added: 'I have been a wicked man, and now I want to clear my conscience and am going to confess everything in as much detail as I can.'[6]

'What dealings have you had with women about their supposed visions?' asked Romolino. 'At the start, I used to talk to women and pick up things from them, which I then used as visions of my own,' answered Savonarola. 'Recently, however, I have avoided all speech with them. The ones from whom I learned things were Madonna Vaggia Bisdomini, Madonna Camilla Rucellai, Madonna Gianfigliazi, but I didn't pay much attention to the last of these as she seemed crazy.'[7] (Girolamo had told Ceccone that Camilla sent him a message saying she had a vision that Bernardo del Nero should be killed by being thrown from a window of the Palazzo della Signoria.)

Threatening to use the rope again, Romolino returned to the council, clearly the most important feature of the case from Rome's point of view. 'Oh brother, what a mess you're in,' Fra' Girolamo is supposed to have muttered. Then he began to weep, saying, 'When I think that I ever managed to set such a business in motion, I can only regret it. I don't know how I came to start on it – it all seems like a dream.'[8] He had begun his scheme for a council less than three months ago, he explained. Nothing was to be hoped from the Italian states – he had no influential contacts in Venice, the King of Naples was too weak to do anything and the Florentines were split. He could not trust the cardinals, who would report him to the Pope. So he had decided that his only hope lay in the European sovereigns.

All this was already known to Romolino. However, the Bishop succeeded in extracting further details about Girolamo's efforts to find support among the cardinals. He had tried but failed to contact the cardinals of San Piero in Vincoli and St Malo – Della Rovere and Briçonnet. The former had once sent him a message saying that 'a group of cardinals bent on holding a council' would come to Florence, while the latter had spoken to him about the Church's reform. He had been more hopeful about the 'Cardinal of Naples' – Carafa – and had written to him, but only to revive their friendship in preparation and without mentioning a council. However, he had spoken to a certain Michelangelo de Orvieto, one of Carafa's men, about the possibility of a council. In addition, he had received an anonymous letter of carefully phrased encouragement from the city of Naples, telling him to 'light the fire'. Romolino leapt on the word 'Napoli', hoping to involve Cardinal Carafa. 'Naples! Naples!' cried Girolamo, apparently after being hoisted again. 'I sought his advice and that of others too.' But he refused to compromise his old patron unjustly and on the following day, while confirming everything else he had said, insisted that Carafa had not been involved, despite being threatened with further torture. 'I never said one word about the council to the Cardinal of Naples, or to any of the others.' He had only mentioned Carafa 'out of fear'. Nothing more could be got out of him on the subject.

Before the commissioners had finished, a Pratica met to discuss the sentence.[9] A lawyer, Agnolo Niccolini, said it would be a crime to kill Fra' Girolamo:

> This man would not only succeed in restoring faith to the world, should it ever die out, but he would spread all the learning with which he is so richly gifted. I advise keeping him in prison, if you must, but spare his life and give him writing materials, and he will produce wonderful works to the glory of God.

But the Pratica was dominated by *Arrabbiati*, fearful that a *Piagnone* Signoria might return to set him free and punish them. 'Let's blame all the city's evils on the Frate and get rid of the lot together,' suggested Bernardo Rucellai. The chronicler Piero Parenti, now a member of the Eight, writes no less bluntly, 'We were determined that he wouldn't come out of it alive.'[10]

Simone Filipepi relates how, eighteen months after these events, Doffo Spini called at Sandro Botticelli's studio one night, at about 3 a.m. When he was sitting by the fire Botticelli asked him about Fra' Girolamo. 'Sandro, do you want to know the truth?' he answered. 'We found no sin in him, mortal or venial.' 'Then why put him to such a filthy death?' enquired Botticelli. Spini explained that if they hadn't condemned Girolamo and his friends to die, letting them go home to San Marco, 'the mob would have put us all in a sack, torn to pieces. The business stirred up too much hatred – we condemned them to save our own skins.'[11]

Even so, when the Apostolic Commissioners had a final meeting with Florentine officials on 22 May before completing their report, Romolino suggested sparing Fra' Domenico's life, to give a graceful impression of clemency. 'All Savonarola's doctrines might be kept alive by that particular friar,' objected a Florentine. 'Losing one little friar doesn't matter much,' agreed the Bishop. 'He can die too.'[12]

Because Fra' Girolamo had planned to depose Pope Alexander through a council of the Church summoned by temporal rulers, he was guilty of contravening the Bull *Execrabilis* of Pius II of 1459, which specifically condemned an appeal from a pope to a council. But the Bishop was not content with this. A letter to the Holy Father of 23 May, signed by both Romolino and Torriani, but almost certainly written entirely by the former, contains a farrago of lies.

First, Fra' Hieronymo admits that for fourteen years he never confessed his sins properly yet went on saying Mass. Further, he declares that he arranged for Fra' Silvestro and many other friars to hear confessions and report to him what they found out, and that afterwards, publicly in the pulpit and privately in conversation, he denounced the sins made known to him in this way, pretending that he knew of them by divine revelation. In addition, he has committed such grave and detestable crimes that for the moment it would be wrong to mention them. He confesses to spreading sedition among the citizens, to causing food shortages which have resulted in the death of the poor, and to murdering many people of rank. . . .

Romolino reserved his highest indignation for the attempt to summon a council:

> He also confesses that, through letters and messages, he tried to urge Christian princes into schism against your Holiness. To such depths of wickedness did this most evil and many-sided monster sink that his entire appearance of goodness was merely pretended, a disguise for his ambition and thirst to gain glory in this world. He has been accustomed to turning to the crucifix and saying to our Lord, 'If I lie, then you lie.' So enormous are his crimes that the hand shrinks from writing them down, the mind from contemplating them.

The Bishop had some words about Fra' Domenico, that uncooperative witness. 'He has often dared to say in the pulpit that the angels would sooner fall from heaven than that anything predicted by Fra' Hieronymo should not come to pass.' As for the abortive ordeal, 'We shall not mention the errors of which this friar might have been guilty when he wanted to enter the fire carrying the Body of Christ.'[13]

During these weeks of torture Girolamo wrote two meditations, on the Psalms *Miserere mei Deus* and *In te Domine, speravi* – dictating them, since his arm was broken. The first echoes his sermons: 'Look at your Church and see how it contains more infidels than Christians, each one making a God of his belly . . . Hell is full.' The second describes despair and hope battling for his heart. 'Despair lays siege to me . . . my friends fight under his banner as enemies. Everything I see and hear is shaped by despair . . . but if I turn to Heaven, hope shall come to my rescue.' They were swiftly printed, in secret.

He cured his gaoler's syphilis so effectively that the man thought it was a miracle and begged him to write a rule of life for ordinary people. The result was his *Regola del ben vivere cristiano, composta mentre era in carcere* ('A Rule for a Christian Life, written while in prison') in which he stresses the need of good works and contempt for this world. The *Regola* was smuggled out, to be printed secretly at Florence before the end of the year.

On 22 May the Apostolic Commissioners condemned the three friars as 'heretics and schismatics, and for preaching novelties', charges which had nothing to do with anything they had admitted during their interrogation. They were to be degraded from their priesthood then handed over to the secular authorities for punishment.[14]

George Eliot imagines Girolamo's state of mind:

He endured a double agony: not only the reviling, and the torture, and the death-throe, but the agony of sinking from the vision of glorious achievement into that deep shadow where he could only say, 'I count as nothing: darkness encompasses me: yet the light I saw was the true light.'[15]

THIRTY-ONE

The Final Burning

The *Battuti* – Florentine, fifteenth century

They will take the just men and burn them in the midst of the city, and what the fire does not consume and the wind does not carry away, they will throw into the water.

Savonarola, *Prediche sopra i Salmi*

Alexander VI could easily have saved the lives of Girolamo and his friends, since they had been found guilty of offences against the Church,[1] not against the Florentine republic. But, as Girolamo Benivieni heard in April from banker friends at Rome, the Pope had been determined that Savonarola should die. Admittedly there is no other evidence of His Holiness's intentions, although the eighteenth-century historian Giovanni Domenico Mansi says, without giving any source, that the Pope wanted 'the extreme penalty'.[2] However, judging from the behaviour of Bishop Romolino, whose courtier's ear was carefully attuned to papal wishes, the only possible conclusion is that the Holy Father was more than ready to condone the friars' judicial murder.

On the afternoon of 22 May Romolino sent formal messages to Savonarola and his two brethren, summoning them to appear before him on the following day when he would pronounce sentence. 'I am in prison, but if able I will come,' he told the messengers sardonically. Late on the night of the same day a group of senior Florentine officials, accompanied by two notaries – one was Ser Ceccone – entered Girolamo's cell and curtly informed him that he was to die next morning. The Frate was at prayer and did not even bother to ask in what way he was to be executed, immediately resuming his devotions. Fra' Domenico, however, did enquire, and, on being told they would be hanged and then burned, at once begged to be burned alive in honour of Christ's sufferings on the Cross. But poor Fra' Silvestro broke down at the prospect.

After eating a hearty supper, Fra' Domenico wrote a letter to the friars of his order at Fiesole, where he had been prior. Having affectionately said goodbye, he asked for their prayers and, somewhat optimistically in view of the circumstances, gave instructions for his burial – 'in some obscure corner, not inside the church'. He also left a last request. 'Collect all the pamphlets of Fra' Girolamo that are in my cell, have them bound, and put a copy in our library. Keep another copy for reading [aloud, during meals] placed on the second table in the refectory, fastened to it by a chain, so that the lay brothers may have an opportunity to read it sometimes.'[3] Then he lay down and fell into a deep sleep, as if unaware that anything of importance was to happen next day. In contrast, Fra' Silvestro Maruffi cried desperately that he wanted to throw himself on the Florentines' mercy – surely they would spare his life?

Luca Landucci says that preparations for the friars' execution started even before they were told they were going to die:

In the evening a scaffold was put up, covering the whole *ringhiera*, the marble terrace of the Palazzo della Signoria, and then a scaffolding which began at the *ringhiera* next to the 'lion' and reached into the middle of the Piazza, towards the *Tetto de' Pisani*; and a block of wood many *braccia* high was set up here, and around it a large round platform. On top of this piece of wood they placed another horizontal piece in the shape of a cross, but people noticing it, said, 'They've decided to crucify him'; and after hearing their remarks orders were given to saw off part of the wood, so that it should not look like a cross.[4]

A man robed and hooded in black entered Savonarola's cell. This was a member of the fraternity called the *Compagnia de' Neri*, or sometimes the *Battuto* (from scourging themselves in atonement for their sins), whose calling was to console those going to the scaffold. The man, Jacopo Niccolini,[5] had been selected by the Signoria because he did not belong to the *Piagnoni*, but now that he met the Frate, he was at once converted. No less obviously, Girolamo took an immediate liking to Jacopo. Declining the offer of supper, he asked for a confessor. A Benedictine monk came and gave him absolution.

Meanwhile, Jacopo Niccolini had been to the Signoria and obtained leave for the three friars to meet in the Sala Grande of the Gran Consiglio. 'I hear you've asked to be thrown into the fire alive,' Girolamo told Fra' Domenico. 'That is wrong, because it's not for us to choose what sort of death we die – we have to accept willingly whatever end has been destined for us by God.' He spoke to Fra' Silvestro more sternly. 'As for you, I know you want to tell the crowd you're innocent. But I order you to do no such thing and instead to follow the example of Jesus Christ, who refused to proclaim His innocence even when on the cross – we must do the same since everything He did is something we should copy.'[6] Then he gave the pair his blessing.

Fra' Girolamo was taken back to prison where, crippled by torture, he knelt on the floor next to Niccolini and then fell asleep with his head on Jacopo's lap. It was a tranquil sleep, since he had a smile on his face. When he awoke, he prophesied that disaster would befall Florence. 'Remember carefully,' he is said to have told Niccolini, 'that it will all happen when there is a Pope called Clement.'[7]

Early next morning the Frate was allowed to say Mass in the chapel at the Palazzo della Signoria, giving communion to the two others. He prayed 'To thou my lord, to thou my saviour, to thou my comforter', for forgiveness for any harm that he might unknowingly have brought on the city of Florence and its people. He ended by begging God 'to give me strength during my last moments and not to let the Enemy have any power over me'.[8]

Then the gaolers came for them. They had already removed the manacles from round their wrists, but not the leg-irons on their ankles, so that the friars could only hobble. Stumbling down the stairs, they were seized by Dominicans from Santa Maria Novella, who on the Master General's instructions made them take off their white habits and black mantles, to demonstrate their formal expulsion from the Order. Girolamo showed some emotion when he surrendered his habit, like a degraded army officer forced to strip himself of his uniform. In their white undershirts, they shuffled out into the Piazza, which was as densely crowded as on the day of the ordeal by fire. Three tribunals stood on the *ringhiera*. One was led by Bishop Pagagnotti, a Dominican and former friar of San Marco, who was armed with a brief from Pope Alexander giving him the power 'to degrade the three friars about to die' – it had been issued before Romolino left Rome. Another consisted of the Apostolic Commissioners who would pronounce them heretics, while a third included the *Gonfaloniere* and the Eight of Justice.

Then, 'The sacrifice of the three Frati was made,' says Landucci, a sorrowing spectator. 'They were robed in all their vestments, which were taken off one by one, with the appropriate words for the degradation, it being lastly affirmed that Fra' Girolamo was a heretic and schismatic, and on this account condemned to be burnt; then their faces and heads were shaved, as is customary in this ceremony.'[9]

Avoiding Savonarola's eye, Monsignor Pagagnotti mumbled the words of the degradation. When he said, 'I expel you from the Church militant and the Church triumphant', the Frate interrupted. 'From the Church militant, yes, but you cannot speak for the Church triumphant.' (He meant the Church in heaven.) Solemly, Romolino absolved the three, bestowing a plenary indulgence sent by His Holiness. The Eight condemned them to be hanged and burned 'for their atrocious crimes'. Then, escorted by black-hooded *Battuti*, they were led along a long wooden walkway over the heads of the mob, many of whom were jeering, to the gibbet. Despite shortening the cross-bar, it still looked like a cross.

As the friars went along the walkway, stumbling because of their leg-irons, a priest in the crowd asked Fra' Girolamo what was his state of mind towards God, to which he answered, 'The Lord suffered so much for me.' Meanwhile, Fra' Domenico was singing the *Te Deum* in a low voice. When he ended, he told the *Battuti*, 'Remember, all Fra' Girolamo's prophecies will come true, and we die innocent.' Having reached the gibbet, in turn, each was pushed up a ladder, to have a noose fastened around his neck and an iron chain around his waist. One after another, the hangman threw the friars off the ladders. Silvestro went first, crying, 'Into your hands, Oh Lord, I commend my spirit!' His rope was too short and the drop insufficiently violent, so that he took some time to die and repeated the word 'Jesu' many times.

Domenico, still smiling serenely, was turned off next, likewise saying, 'Jesu, Jesu', although he died fairly quickly.

Finally, it was the turn of Girolamo, and a voice cried out from the by now silent crowd, 'Oh prophet, now is the time for you to work one of your miracles!' Before he climbed the ladder, he had recited the Creed, his last audible words. He showed no emotion and, although apparently praying, said nothing that could be heard as he fell, to hang between his two brethren – the hangman jerking the rope to make him dance.

Bundles of faggots had been heaped beneath the gibbet, to be lit before they died so that the flames would engulf them while they were conscious. An eyewitness, the 22-year-old historian Jacopo Nardi, tells us that before the hangman could get down the ladder to light the pyre, someone who had been waiting since dawn rushed forward from the mob with a torch, shouting, 'Now I can burn the man who wanted to burn me!' (Presumably he was a sodomite.) To hasten the blaze, others began hurling small bags of gunpowder on to it, and these exploded with a noise like fireworks.[10]

A breeze suddenly blew up while the three were writhing and kicking, to blow aside for a moment the leaping flames. 'A miracle! A miracle!' cried spectators.[11] But the wind died down and they were set on fire, although dead by this time. Then, for a few long seconds it seemed as if Fra' Girolamo was blessing the crowd, after the rope tying his hands burned away – his right arm rose up and the hand opened, displaying two fingers and the thumb. Women in the throng sobbed hysterically at the spectacle while some people fell on their knees and many others fled panic-stricken from the Piazza.

Held in place by chains, the bodies 'black as rats' went on burning for several hours, arms, legs and organs falling into the fire below, the torsos left hanging on the chains being pelted with showers of stones thrown by boys paid by the hangman's men. The friars' friend, the former miniaturist Benedetto Bettuccio, who was watching from the Piazza, tells us that 'it rained blood and entrails'. When nothing seemed to be left, the hangman and his crew pulled down the gibbet, and bringing more firewood, stoked up the flames to make absolutely sure that it and everything else had been consumed. Finally, they shovelled up the ashes and took them in carts to the Ponte Vecchio, to be tipped into the Arno. This was done to frustrate relic hunters.

According to Luca Landucci, who had been there in the Piazza with the crowd, 'good and thoughtful people', by whom he means other *Piagnoni*, were deeply disappointed that the friars had not been saved by a miracle. 'Many, in fact, fell away from their faith.'[12] Even so, at dawn three days later, several women were found kneeling in the Piazza on the spot where they had been burned, doing so 'out of veneration'.

By dying in silence, without saying anything on the scaffold to indicate his guilt or his innocence, the Frate baffled the Florentines. Many continued to think he had been a fraud, while just as many others believed that his confession had either been forged or extracted by torture. He left a divided city.

THIRTY-TWO

Savonarola's Legacy

The Frate preaches – *Compendio di rivelazioni*

*No longer is there anyone like Fra' Girolamo, so gifted with so
much learning, so much wisdom, so much saintliness.*
Donato Gianotti, *Della Reppublica fiorentina*

Everything Savonarola had stood for seemed to have perished.
'Now we can practise sodomy!'[1] gloated a member of the Ten.
Both the *Piagnone* Luca Landucci and the *Arrabbiato* Piero Parenti
record the excesses in Florence after his death. 'Everyone was
indulging in a vicious life, and at night-time one saw halberds or
naked swords all over the city, and men gambling by candlelight in
the Mercato Vecchio [until just before dawn], and everywhere
without shame,' notes Luca, only a month later. 'Hell seemed open,

and woe to him who should try to reprove vice.'² The *Compagnacci* let goats loose in churches, placed foul smelling asafoetida in censers, ink in holy-water stoups and tore a diadem off a statue of the Madonna at San Marco to crown a prostitute. On Christmas Eve a donkey was led into the Duomo with a truncheon rammed up his fundament, slashed with swords and beaten with clubs as he fled, braying round the cathedral, and then left dying on the steps throughout Christmas Day. Nobody dared to remove him.

Prominent *Piagnoni* citizens were fined ruinously, *Piagnoni* officials lost their jobs. Someone who profited was the young Machiavelli, promoted by the Signoria. (In his letter of 9 March he had referred to the Frate as 'an opportunist and a very inventive fraud', although later he would comment, 'Of a man as Savonarola we can only speak with reverence.'³) San Marco's great bronze bell and the Medici library were confiscated, while many of the friars were banished from Florentine territory. The bell was ceremoniously whipped through the streets.

A large number of *Piagnoni* fled from the city, men such as Botticelli's brother Simone and the artist Baccio de Montelupo. 'Many good men were forced to flee from Florence, finding shelter at some villa in the countryside or at Bologna or Siena or elsewhere, so as not to be persecuted by those who held power and who were nearly all enemies of the said father [Girolamo]', the former tells us. 'I myself, Simone di Mariano de' Filipepi, went to Bologna, where I found many of our party. Among those who stayed behind, some were arrested and tortured every day, declared incapable of holding public office.'⁴

When the Master General of the Dominicans, Giovacchino Torriani – one of the papal commissioners who had condemned Fra' Girolamo – visited Ferrara, people in the streets had to be forcibly restrained from stoning him. The Ferraresi had observed events at Florence with mounting horror.⁵ Shortly after the execution, Savonarola's meditations on the Psalms were published at Ferrara, possibly with Duke Ercole's encouragement, while the diarist Bernardino Zambotti, who gives a summary in his diary of what had been happening to 'our Ferrarese citizen', wrote that all the Frate had done was to try to make the Pope appear before a council by writing to the rulers of Christendom. The three friars had been 'disgracefully put to death without just cause . . . lamented by all good Christians, and most of all by the Ferraresi and His Excellency our Duke'.

However, in November 1499, despite the measures taken by the *Arrabbiati*, Florence elected a *Piagnone Gonfaloniere*, and the *Piagnoni* party swiftly revived. This was because all Florentines accepted the need for unity on learning that Cesare Borgia was marching towards their city. San Marco regained its privileges while Doffo Spini was accused of sodomy. Even if the *Arrabbiati*'s lawyers managed to save Spini's life, the *Arrabbiati* had lost control of the city.

The year 1499 was also when the French returned to Italy under Louis XII and it began to seem that Savonarola might have been right after all. New editions of his books poured off the presses. A sculptor named Pietro Bernardino dei Fanciulli (from leading processions of children through the city on feast days) tried to assume his mantle, preaching that the Frate's scourge was about to descend. Telling everybody not to go to confession because no good priests remained, he founded a sect known as the *Unti* (the 'Anointed') from his custom of anointing them. Accused of heresy, in 1502 he took refuge at Mirandola with Gianfrancesco Pico, but his host's brother, a *condottiere*, stormed the castle and Bernardino was burned at the stake.[6]

The young friars recruited by Fra' Girolamo had begged for Pope Alexander's forgiveness in 1498, but this had been a panic-stricken reaction to his 'confession'. On realising it was a forgery, they saw him as a martyr. When they grew older and held office in their Order they spread his message, stressing Florence's destiny as an 'elect nation'. Their leader was a friend of Savonarola, Fra' Bartolomeo da Faenza, a highly respected theologian, who was several times elected prior of San Marco. An alliance against the Medici was forged between *Piagnoni* and *Arrabbiati* – the latter now accepting that Fra' Girolamo had been both saint and prophet.

In 1502, as he had advised, a *Gonfaloniere* was appointed for life, Piero Soderini, a skilful politician who worked hard to bridge the gap between *Piagnoni* and *Arrabbiati*. Despite the Frate's executioner being stoned to death in 1503 – his corpse was kicked through the streets before being thrown into the Arno – Soderini consolidated the alliance between the two parties, helped by Florence's recovery of Pisa in 1509. This was the year when the great bell, the Piagnona, was formally restored to San Marco.

Alexander VI grew increasingly corrupted by his ruthless son Cesare Borgia. His Holiness's death in August 1503 was rumoured to have been due to absentmindedness – people said that by mistake he had drunk poisoned wine or eaten poisoned sweets that were intended for a cardinal to whom he had taken a dislike. In reality, he almost certainly died from a fever, probably a local form of malaria, accompanied by cardiac complications. But the summer was unusually hot that year and the rumours of poison seemed to be confirmed by the revolting speed with which Alexander's corpse decomposed, his skin turning black and his swollen tongue hanging out of his mouth. There was some grim gossip about the Vicar of Christ's likely fate in the next world. Francesco Gonzaga, Marquess of Mantua, wrote to his wife a month after Alexander died:

> During his last illness the Pope spoke in such a strange way that people who were unaware of what was in his mind thought that he was rambling, yet he was speaking quite clearly. . . . His words were, 'I'm coming – it's only fair, but wait just a little.' Those who knew his secrets explained that at the conclave after [Pope] Innocent's death he had sold his soul to the Devil in return for the Papacy, their understanding being that he was to keep the See [of Peter] for twelve years. . . . Some even swear that they saw seven demons in the room at the moment when he was drawing his last breath.[7]

However far-fetched, the story tells us what many of Papa Borgia's contemporaries thought of him – Guicciardini's verdict on his career was that he had 'envenomed' the entire universe.

Della Rovere, who became Pope Julius II in the autumn, quickly swept away Cesare Borgia and his 'Duchy of the Romagna', so that all that survived of Alexander's ambitions for his family was a sinister legend. Besides issuing a Bull that invalidated the election of every simoniac pontiff, Julius refused to live in the Borgia apartments at the Vatican, saying they reminded him too much of 'those *marranos* of accursed memory'. The fact that Michelangelo was a *Piagnone* did not deter the Pope from commissioning him to decorate the Sistine Chapel, while on one occasion he told some Dominicans that Fra' Girolamo had been a saint and that he would like to canonise him.

Although Ercole d'Este had let his heir Alfonso marry His Holiness's daughter, Lucrezia, for whom the Duke developed a deep affection, he rejoiced at the news of Pope Alexander's death. As he put it in a letter of 24 August to his ambassador at Milan, he was delighted 'so great a scandal should be taken away from the Church'.[8] But instead of repudiating his daughter-in-law as he was urged to do by the French King – on the grounds that her father's demise deprived her of any political value – Ercole continued to cherish Lucrezia. Until the end he went on feeding and clothing the beggars of his capital, and staging annual miracle plays, besides patronising a nun with the stigmata (the wounds of Christ). Early in 1505, Duke Ercole – 'who, in spite of many unworthy deeds, had truly striven to tread the paths upon which the beacon-light of the martyred Fra' Girolamo had shone', as a nineteenth-century historian puts it – died peacefully at Ferrara.[9]

It looked as if the 'new Cyrus' was King Charles's successor, Louis XII, who claimed not only Naples but Milan, leading army after army into Italy. In 1500 he deposed and imprisoned Lodovico il Moro. ('Tell the Florentines that the Frate had the date right, and was a true prophet where I'm concerned,' the captive duke told some Florentine merchants.) In 1509 Louis very nearly smashed his way into Venice. However, in 1511 the fearsome Julius II revived the Holy League against the French, putting on silver armour and leading the papal troops into battle. Louis retorted by persuading a handful of cardinals to summon a council at Pisa and depose Julius. Using Savonarola's arguments against Borgia, they claimed they had the right to do so because the Pope was 'given to simony and infamous, dissolute behaviour'. They also promised to canonise the Frate. But the council failed and Julius placed France under interdict.

By allowing the council to take place on her territory, Florence enraged Julius. The Holy League's troops occupied the city in 1512 and the Medici returned in triumph, guarded by a thousand men-at-arms – without Piero who had been ignominiously drowned in 1503 when fleeing from a battle. For over a decade Florence was ruled by men appointed by the Medici Popes, Leo X and Clement VII, but there was no overt persecution of the *Piagnoni* who kept a low profile.

A few *Piagnoni* welcomed the news of Martin Luther's rebellion against the papacy in 1517, but most rejected it. Two writers who had been close to the Frate, Pico and Girolamo Benivieni, attacked the new doctrines – Pico accused Luther of wrecking the basis of Christian worship, while Benivieni denounced him for splitting the Church. Ironically, Dr Luther admired Savonarola, for defying the papacy and for his meditations on the Psalms which contain the words, 'Faith is His gift and not to be obtained by our works, lest anyone should take glory to himself.' In 1524 he published an edition of both meditations with a preface claiming that Girolamo had shared his doctrine of salvation by faith alone. Yet *A Rule for Christian Living*, written at the same time as the meditations, stressed the need for good works in a way that would have shocked Luther, who does not seem to have read anything by the Frate other than the meditations. There was little in common between Girolamo and a man who, allegedly, declared:

> Who loves not wine, women and song
> Lives a fool his whole life long.

During the early 1520s Bishop John Fisher (later beheaded by Henry VIII for his loyalty to Rome) denied that Fra' Girolamo had been a Lutheran. He was condemned for defying an excommunication, not for his beliefs, said the Bishop, and had accepted the Pope as head of the Church. 'On the sacraments he speaks for every Catholic. On the priesthood, on the eucharist, on penance, he is in complete agreement with the Fathers.' Rejecting Luther's own private revelation, Fisher wrote that while the Frate had been discredited 'because his prophecies did not come true, although he believed – and he wanted us to believe, too – that they came from God', he should 'be venerated for his words and his life'. He argued that 'if so great a man and such a good Catholic can be deceived, how can we trust in Luther?'[10]

Unlike Luther, Fisher had probably read Girolamo's *Triumphis Crucis*. He may have read the *Compendium Revelationum* or the *Dyalogus*.[11] However dismissive the Bishop may be about prophecies, we know he was interested in them – such as those by the 'Holy Maid of Kent' which so angered King Henry.

The *Piagnoni* came into their own when Emperor Charles V's Lutheran *landsknechts* sacked Rome in 1527 and besieged Pope Clement in the Castel Sant' Angelo. Many Florentines believed that this was the Frate's scourge from over the Alps. 'It is almost impossible to imagine the sheer gladness,' writes the republican historian Benedetto Varchi, who was in the crowd.[12] (Varchi was the friend whom Michelangelo later asked to give his funeral oration.) 'Men and women, young and old, patricians and plebeians, priests and laymen, all broke into wild rejoicing and the conviction swiftly revived, multiplied by a thousandfold, that Fra' Girolamo really had been a saint and a prophet.'

The Medici garrison was evicted, after which the *Piagnoni* installed a genuinely republican government, restoring the office of *Gonfaloniere*, to which they elected Niccolò Capponi. The priory of San Marco again became the city's spiritual centre, Dominican preachers taking over the Duomo as in the Frate's heyday, among the most fervent being Fra' Zaccaria da Lunigiana from San Marco and Fra' Benedetto da Foiano from Santa Maria Novella – whose conventual Dominicans had seen the light and turned *Piagnoni*. The new *Gonfaloniere*, capable and devout, was the son of Piero Capponi of the Bells. If not an openly commited *Piagnone* until now, Niccolò was an old friend of Fra' Bartolomeo da Faenza at San Marco and had long been an admirer of Savonarola.

Himself an eyewitness, Varchi describes how in the Sala Grande of the Gran Consiglio Niccolò Capponi repeated, word for word, 'one of those sermons in which the Frate predicts and promises great evil, then great good, for the city of Florence'.[13] The *Gonfaloniere* knelt down, cried '*Misericordia!*' in a loud voice and demanded that Christ should be proclaimed King of Florence, as Fra' Girolamo had demanded. Welcomed by the entire Grand Council, the demand was subsequently commemorated by an inscription on the parapet of the tower of the Palazzo della Signoria where it may still be read – '*Jesus Christus Rex Gloriae venit in pace . . .*' – a declaration that Christ was their sovereign. (This was the tower that had been Girolamo's prison.)

The *Piagnoni* rebuilt the Frate's New Jerusalem[14] as they had long been planning, certain their time would come again. New laws invoking Holy Scripture were passed. Jewish money-lenders had to leave the city within a year, both sexes were forbidden to wear expensive clothes or visit taverns, gambling was outlawed and prostitutes faced grim penalties, while it became impossible for sodomites or blasphemers to escape the death sentence. Long religious processions marched through the streets daily, and everybody was forced to kneel at the ringing of the Angelus bell.

In 1529 the Signoria proclaimed that 'the present popular government and most holy liberty are extraordinary gifts of His Most Divine Majesty', the Crown of Thorns becoming the city's emblem in token of her Messianic destiny. In 1530 it would unanimously adopt a resolution that 'everything done by Florentines against the Frate had been done against God', expunging the record of his trial. Yet while the *Piagnoni* had no hesitation in believing that the Florentines were an Elect Nation and that Rome would be razed to the ground, there was never any hint of social revolution or redistribution of wealth. They were Catholic fanatics, sectarians perhaps, but not millenarians even if they anticipated a glorious future for their city. Even so, the regime was harsher than Fra' Girolamo's. He had always refused to allow persecution of Mediceans, whether members of the family or supporters, except in cases when they posed an obvious threat, but now there was a witchhunt. Mediceans were imprisoned, banished or fined, several being accused of Lutheranism – one was executed for saying the city had been better governed by the Medici.

However, the sack of Rome in 1527 and Niccolò Capponi's election had been the highwater mark of the *Piagnone* revival. The papacy soon recovered and, as a realist, Capponi realised that Clement would send an army to besiege the city. Unfortunately, Capponi's policy of compromise and negotiation, a policy which Savonarola would certainly have encouraged, proved too subtle for his fellow citizens, especially when he omitted to explain why he had rejected Michelangelo's offer to fortify the hill of San Miniato. The discovery that he was secretly corresponding with Clement was the last straw – even Varchi suspected him of disloyalty.[15] Forced to resign in 1528, Capponi died shortly after, the one man who might have saved the Florentine Republic.

Late in the summer of 1529 an army of papal mercenaries, 40,000 strong and led by the Prince of Orange, camped on the left bank of the Arno opposite Florence, while in December 20,000 imperial troops occupied the right bank. The citizens demolished every building outside the walls, while Michelangelo designed new fortifications. However, apart from methodically bombarding the bastions, the enemy made no attempt to launch an assault and settled down to starve the city into submission.

Venice sent friendly messages to the sister republic, but nothing else. In desperation, the Signoria's envoys approached Henry VIII, Florentine merchants in London lobbying the Earl of Wiltshire – Anne Boleyn's father. In the hope that military intervention might force the Pope to grant him his divorce from Catherine of Aragon, Henry eventually agreed to despatch an expedition, but he was overtaken by events. The citizens had a better chance of help from Francis I, who promised to send troops as soon as his sons returned from captivity in Spain.

Some *Piagnoni* gave themselves over to blind superstition after the situation started to deteriorate, insisting that no enemy could defeat a city of God which was inhabited by an elect nation, so long as its citizens were genuinely pure. Even when men, women and children began dying in large numbers from starvation and it made sense to expel 'useless mouths' if the citizens were not to be forced into surrender by hunger, the most abject beggars were allowed to stay inside the walls, only prostitutes being driven out, since the Signoria thought that this was what the Frate would have done.

They knew now that they could expect no help from Francis I despite his earlier promises, because he had made peace with Emperor Charles V and had agreed to leave Italy alone. One of the friars, Santi Pagnini, wrote frantically to Henry VIII,[16] beseeching him to come to the rescue. However, many of the *Piagnoni* could see no need for allies, believing that the Frate would return at the head of an army of angels, to drive the besiegers away in panic-stricken confusion.

Untrained civilian volunteers commanded by *condottieri*, the Florentines sallied out gallantly if ineffectually every night, trying to harry the besiegers. But on 2 August 1530 their last hope, Francesco Ferrucci, was defeated and hacked to pieces while attempting to relieve the city. Not only was everyone starving but plague had broken out. 'Some attempted to escape, others to hide or to find a refuge in the Palazzo della Signoria or in a church,' writes Varchi. 'Most people saw no hope except to place themselves in God's hand and wait for the end from one hour to the next, anticipating not merely death but death from the most horrible tortures.'[17] Michelangelo hid in the *campanile* of San Niccolò. Mobs marched through the streets, demanding surrender, while the militia deserted, leaving the walls unmanned. Finally the *condottieri* trained cannon on their employers and let in the enemy troops.

Florence capitulated formally on 12 August 1530. Escorted by the troops of their cousin Pope Clement, the Medici family returned in force. Guicciardini records that as soon as the soldiers had left, torture and persecution began – without mentioning that it was he who directed the reprisals. Arrests and beheadings took place every day, the friars being dispersed and in some cases imprisoned for years. Fra' Benedetto da Foiano was thrown into a dungeon of Castle Sant' Angelo and starved to death, the fate that might have been Girolamo's had he accepted Alexander's invitation to Rome.

It was the end of Savonarola's 'godly city'. The Florentine Republic became a duchy and then a grand duchy. Soon, all those who had followed the Frate during the 1490s would be dead. (That most faithful supporter, Gianfrancesco Pico was brutally murdered with his son in 1533, stabbed to death by Gianfrancesco's nephew for the sake of their inheritance as they were praying in a church before the high altar.) Yet Fra' Girolamo's cult survived for a long time. Gathering secretly in small groups, fanatical *Piagnoni* insisted that Florence's apotheosis had not yet come because her citizens had failed to purify themselves. They relied on their own visions and new prophecies of their own, while praying to the Frate.

The new Medici rulers were aware of the *Piagnoni*'s hostility and that Dominicans were involved. In 1545 Cosimo I evicted the San Marco community but Pope Paul III made him reinstall them. When one of Cosimo's would-be assassins, Pandolfo Pucci, was caught in 1560, it was discovered that he regularly read the Frate's books. 'Fra' Girolamo's memory has revived, is spreading widely and has become more flourishing than ever,' Archbishop Alessandro Medici reported to Francesco I in 1583. He complained that friars said an Office for him as if he were a saint, that people treasured his relics as those of a martyr – there were statuettes and portrait medallions of him in bronze or gold, cameos and prints, all inscribed 'martyr' or 'prophet'.[18] In response, not only had the Archbishop forbidden the Frate's likeness to be painted among the Dominican saints at Santa Maria Novella, besides preventing his books from being printed – even to the extent of smashing the presses – but, as he boasted, he had 'put real fear into the friars'. The Grand Duke thanked him warmly.

Yet Savonarola continued to be revered by the Oratorian Philip Neri, who kept a portrait of him wearing a halo in his bedroom, as well as eight books by him in his library. He told his own followers to read the *Triumphis Crucis*. A Florentine born in 1515, St Philip's parents appear to have been *Piagnoni*, or to have sympathised with them, and he had received his early education from the friars of San Marco, besides experiencing the *Piagnoni* regime of 1527–30. He contemplated writing Girolamo's life, and felt sure he was going to be canonised soon – as he almost certainly would have been, but for Medici opposition. So, too, was Philip Neri's contemporary, Caterina Ricci, a Dominican prophetess and saint, who spoke of Fra' Girolamo as that 'victorious martyr, blessed Hieronimo' when she was cured of a bad illness after praying to him.

On the other hand, some very impressive figures detested Savonarola's memory, and not just the Medici. In their eyes his unforgivable sin was that he had tried to depose a pope, however deplorable Alexander VI might have been, and to revive the conciliar movement. Among these latterday *Arrabbiati* was the founder of the Jesuits, Ignatius Loyola, who would not allow any of Girolamo's books in Jesuit libraries. But this was only to be expected from Jesuits, dedicated to defending the papal monarchy.

Even so, in the 1590s it seemed likely Fra' Girolamo would be canonised, during the pontificate of Clement VIII (Aldobrandini). On one occasion, the Pope – whose mother had been a *Piagnona* – said he was prepared to do so as soon as proofs of sanctity were properly presented, but then the cause was blocked by the Medici. None the less, the Dominicans at Florence did not stop praying to 'The martyr Blessed Fra' Girolamo Savonarola' during Masses on his feast day until 1634 when they were specifically forbidden to do so by the Vatican, while on the night of every 23 May until 1703 flowers were laid by unknown hands on the spot where he had been burned. An edition of his works appeared at Lyons in 1633–40 and Pico's life of him at Paris in 1674. However, by the end of the seventeenth century Catholic interest in Savonarola had faded, confined in the eighteenth to a few antiquarians, although the Pseudo-Burlamacchi was published in 1764.

In contrast, Protestant esteem for the Frate never waned. Extracts from his meditations on the Psalms appear in an English Primer of 1534 which was approved by Cranmer. Cyriacus Spangenberg published a short, highly misleading life of him at Wittenberg, in 1556, a work that inspired John Foxe to include him in *The Book of*

Martyrs and claim he had predicted the Reformation. 'This man foreshadowed many things to come, as the destruction of Florence and Rome, and the renewing of the church; which three things have happened in these times within our remembrance.' (The 1570 edition contains a woodcut of his execution.) Lutherans went on regarding him as one of their own until the end of the nineteenth century – a vast monument to Luther erected at Worms in the 1860s shows the Frate standing shoulder to shoulder with Huss and Wycliff.

Victorian England was determined to see Fra' Girolamo as Martin Luther's Italian forerunner, a gallant enemy of 'Popedom', forgetting that the Frate had condemned one particular pope for his morals, unlike Luther who had condemned all popes without exception for their doctrines. In 1856, while freely admitting 'the true Christian grandeur of Fra' Girolamo', Dean Milman of St Paul's argued that his 'monkish reformation . . . could not have satisfied the expanding mind of man'.[19] In 1881 Mrs Oliphant published her *Makers of Florence: Dante, Giotto and Savonarola and their City*, and during the same year the Poet Laureate Alfred Austin was responsible for *Savonarola: a Tragedy*, a play in verse which somehow never reached the stage. Clearly, both Mrs Oliphant and Austin regarded the Frate as a proto-Protestant. George Eliot, on the other hand, had read Villari's recent biography of him and – despite her agnosticism – at moments her novel shows an extraordinary understanding of his personality. Even so, its success owed a lot to the myth of his 'Lutheranism', regardless of its demolition by Villari.

In 1875 John Addington Symonds wrote that Savonarola's 'prophecy, his insight into the coming of a new age for the Church and for Italy, is a main fact in the psychology of the Renaissance'.[20] Symonds was echoing Villari. However, Burckhardt, intent on finding a break between the Renaissance and the Middle Ages, saw him as stuck in the past.

A friar of San Marco, Vincenzo Marchese, had revived Savonarolean studies during the 1840s, but was prevented from publishing a definitive edition of the Frate's writings when the Tuscan authorities decided he was a political liability and sent him into exile. He was the forerunner of a group of brilliant scholars who, on account of their enthusiasm for Girolamo's memory, became known as the 'New *Piagnoni*'. One of these was Pasquale

Villari, whose *La Storia di Girolamo Savonarola e de' suoi tempi* appeared in 1859–61. In Villari's view, Fra' Girolamo had helped to start the Renaissance. 'Columbus discovered the paths of the sea, Savonarola those of the soul,' he claims. The Frate had 'tried to reconcile reason with faith, religion with liberty'.[21] Impressively researched and well written, the book transformed history's view of Savonarola, and – despite demolishing his role as the Italian Luther – an English translation was several times reprinted. George Eliot owed a lot to Villari, for guiding her research and helping her readers to appreciate the background to *Romola*.

Another fine study is Joseph Schnitzer's *Savonarola* (1924). Its author was an unfrocked German priest, a 'modernist' liberal, who had been excommunicated by Rome for his views, his own unhappy experiences being reflected in his book. 'A man dreadfully sinned against in his lifetime and after his death', is his verdict on the Frate. 'He has not yet been beatified or canonised, but his day will come as it did for Joan of Arc.'[22] The Florentine Roberto Ridolfi was an even greater scholar than Schnitzer. His magnificent *Vita di Girolamo Savonarola* (1952) reveals that he, too, was convinced that Fra' Girolamo could see into the future – he criticises Villari for not having believed in his prophetic powers. He wrote of 'a devotion, an admiration, and an interest that have lasted for over four hundred and fifty years and can never be extinguished'.[23]

In recent times Savonarola has attracted the interest of historians in Italy (and in America) who publish many learned articles about him, but for an exclusively academic readership. As a result, he is widely misunderstood, popularly remembered only as a repellent fanatic, a philistine who burned works of art. However, he remains a hero to the Dominicans, who have not given up hope of his canonisation. The radical Catholic thinker Ivan Illich (d. 2002) considered his attitude towards his Church wholly admirable and that 'he knew in an extraordinarily beautiful way how to die'.[24] He fascinates more than a few Florentines, who suspect that he has not been fully understood and that a secret remains to be revealed – an apocalyptic warning about the future of the West.

Every 23 May, early in the morning before tourists emerge, his execution is commemorated by a Mass in the chapel of the Palazzo Vecchio (once Palazzo della Signoria), where he said his final Mass, followed by a procession to the Piazza where flowers are strewn where the scaffold stood. This strewing of flowers was revived in the 1950s by the mayor of Florence, Giorgio La Pira, and on one occasion Ridolfi's account of his last moments was read out. The church of San Marco contains a fine nineteenth-century statue of Savonarola in bronze, before which votive candles are constantly lit. The priory has been meticulously restored, and not just because of its beauty.

If short-lived, his achievements were extraordinary. Realising the Church was heading for disaster and finding himself leader of Florence, he tried to avert it by turning the city into a beacon of renewal through making men and women live as Christians. The constitution which he introduced, however clumsy, was arguably the most representative between antiquity and the American Revolution. Even if clairvoyance failed him at the end, to a large extent most of his predictions came true, especially those about himself.

In the last analysis Girolamo Savonarola had much in common with Francis of Assisi, although no two human beings could have been more different. Like the Poverello, he was simply putting Christianity into practice – but while the Franciscan appealed to the heart the Dominican spoke to the intellect. In many ways he stood for Catholicism at its best, just as the Borgia embodied Catholicism at its worst.

Notes

Preface

1. George Eliot, *Romola*, Oxford, 1994, p. 198.
2. Jacob Burckhardt, *Civilisation of the Renaissance in Italy*, London, 1944, p. 292.
3. Pasquale Villari, *La storia di Girolamo Savonarola e de' suoi tempi*, Florence, 1898 (rev. edn).
4. Eliot, *Romola*, p. 431.

One

1. Villari, *La storia*, vol. 1, p. 14.
2. Torquato Tasso, *Gerusalemme Liberata*, Canto XVII, 477.
3. L.N. Cittadella, *La nobile famiglia di Savonarola in Padova e in Ferrara*, Ferrara, 1867, p. 1.
4. For his career, see A. Segarizzi, *La vita e le opere di Michele Savonarola*, Padua, 1900.
5. A. Sauto, 'La casa dove nacque e abito fra Girolamo Savonarola', in *Studi Savonaroliani, Atti e memorie della Deputazione Provinciale Ferrarese di storia patri*, n.s., vol. 7, 3, Ferrara, 1952–3.
6. Villari, *La storia*, vol. 1, docs, pp. iii, iv.
7. G. Pardi (ed.), *Diario ferrarese dall' anno 1409 sino al 1502, di autori incerti*, in *Rerum Scriptores Italicarum*, vol. 24, vii, I, Bologna, 1928, p. 73. The liveliest account of Duke Borso is still E.G. Gardner, *Dukes and Poets in Ferrara*, London, 1904.
8. Gardner, *Dukes and Poets*, p. 80.
9. P. Burlamacchi, ('Pseudo-Burlamacchi'), *Vita del P.F. Girolamo Savonarola, riveduta poco dopo ed aggiunta dal P.F. Timoteo Botonio*, Lucca, 1764, p. 5.
10. *Ibid.*, p. 4.
11. *Ibid.*
12. R. Ridolfi, *Vita di Girolamo Savonarola*, Rome, 1952, vol. 1, p. 4.
13. G. Savonarola, *De divisione omnium scientiarum*, Bk III.
14. Gaspare da Verona, quoted in C. Fusero, *I Borgia*, Milan, 1966, p. 147.
15. Pardi (ed.), *Diario ferrarese*.

Two

1. Pseudo-Burlamacchi, *Vita*, p. 4.
2. G.K. Chesterton, *St Thomas Aquinas*, London, 1935, p. 217.
3. G. Savonarola, *Prediche sopra l'Esodo*.
4. Fra' Benedetto, *Vulnera diligentis*, in A. Gherardi (ed.), *Nuovi Documenti e Studi intorno a Girolamo Savonarola*, Florence, 1887, pp. 7–8.

5. Pardi (ed.), *Diario ferrarese*, vol. 24, vii, 1, p. 43.
6. Guicciardini, *Storie fiorentine*, ed. C. Panigaglia, Bari, 1931, p. 108.
7. Pseudo-Burlamacchi, *Vita*, p. 5.
8. G. Savonarola, *Poesie*, ed. G. Guasti, Florence, 1862, p. 7.
9. Villari, *La storia*, vol. 1, p. 12.
10. Savonarola, *Poesie*, p. 10.
11. He mentions them in *Predica XIX sopra Aggeo* (19 December 1494).
12. B. Aquarone, *Vita di fra Jeronimo Savonarola*, Alessandria, 1857, p. 25.
13. G. Savonarola, *Le Lettere*, ed. R. Ridolfi, Florence, 1933, p. 1.
14. *Del Dispregio del Mondo*, in Villari, vol. 1, docs, p. viii.
15. Savonarola, *Lettere*, p. 4.

Three

1. Dante, *Paradiso*, Canto XII, 70.
2. *Summa Theologica, Quaestio 188 de differentia religionum.*
3. Chesterton, *Aquinas*, p. 219.
4. Pseudo-Burlamacchi, *Vita*, p. 5.
5. Savonarola, *Lettere*, p. 11.
6. Pseudo-Burlamacchi, *Vita*, p. 13.

Four

1. W.L. Gundersheimer, *Ferrara: the Style of a Renaissance Despotism*, Princeton, 1973, p. 212.
2. Thomas Tuohy, *Herculean Ferrara*, Cambridge, 1996, p. 3.
3. Burckhardt, *Civilisation in Italy*, p. 31.
4. E. Garin, *Giovanni Pico della Mirandola: vita e dottrina*, Florence, 1937.
5. Niccolò Machiavelli, *Le istorie fiorentine*, ed A. Panella, Florence, 1843, p. 398.

Five

1. *Il Convivio*, I, 3.
2. D. Weinstein, *Savonarola and Florence: Prophecy and Patriotism in the Renaissance*, Princeton, 1970, p. 27.
3. Thomas Hobbes, *Leviathan*, 1651, Pt 4, Ch. 47.
4. Morgante Maggiore, XVIII, 115.
5. R.C. Trexler, 'La prostitution florentine au XV siècle: patronages et clientes', in *Annales* 36, 1981, p. 984.
6. *Ibid.*
7. *Ibid.*, p. 989.
8. Villari, *La storia*, vol. 1, p. 47.
9. L. Polizzotto, *The Elect Nation: the Savonarola Movement in Florence 1494–1545*, Oxford, 1994, p. 27.
10. Pseudo-Burlamacchi, *Vita*, p. 18.
11. Michael Levey, *Florence: A Portrait*, London, 1996, p. 4.
12. G. Vasari, *Le vite de' più eccellenti pittori, scultori ed architetti*, Florence, 1881.
13. Ridolfi, *Vita*, vol. 1, p. 22.
14. Machiavelli, *Storie fiorentine*, p. 332.
15. Villari, *La storia*, vol. 1, pp. 109–10.
16. *Ibid.*, p. 80.
17. *Estratto d'una epistola . . . de vita et moribus reverendi patris fratris Hieronimus Savonarola . . .* in P. Villari and E. Cassanova, *Scelta di prediche e scritti de Fr' Girolamo Savonarola*, Florence, 1898, p. 10.
18. In Ridolfi's view he had lectured rather than preached, *Vita*, vol. 1, p. 146.

19. Machiavelli, *Storie fiorentine*, p. 364.
20. Savonarola, *Poesie*, p. 4.

21. Villari, *La storia*, vol. 2, docs, pp. cxlix, cl.

Six

1. Savonarola, *Lettere*, p. 5.
2. R. Ridolfi, *Studi Savonaroliani*, Florence, 1935, p. 45.
3. *Ibid.*, p. 47.
4. Pseudo-Burlamacchi, *Vita*, p. 14.

5. Savonarola, *Lettere*, p. 24.
6. Pseudo-Burlamacchi, *Vita*, p. 15.
7. *Ibid.*
8. *Ibid.*

Seven

1. Guicciardini, *Storie fiorentine*, p. 80.
2. Machiavelli, *Storie fiorentine*, p. 398.
3. *Ibid.*
4. M. Bowra 'Songs of Dance and Carnival', in E.F. Jacob, *Italian Renaissance Studies*, London, 1960, p. 343.
5. Machiavelli, *Storie fiorentine*, p. 398.
6. J. Ross and E. Hutton (eds), *Poesie volgari di Lorenzo de' Medici*, Edinburgh, 1912, vol. 2, p. 35.
7. Pseudo-Burlamacchi, *Vita*, p. 19.
8. Letter of Domenico Beniveni, in B. Varchi, *Storia fiorentina*, Florence, 1858, vol. 3, p. 307.
9. Cinozzi, *Estratto d'una epistola.*
10. F. Myers, 'Savonarola', in H.H. Milman, *Savonarola, Erasmus and Other Essays*, London, 1870, p. 32.
11. G. Savonarola, *Prediche sopra Ezechiele*, cited in Ridolfi, *Vita*, vol. 2, p. 101.
12. G. Savonarola, *Prediche sopra i Salmi*.
13. Ridolfi, *Vita*, vol. 1, p. 57.
14. G. Savonarola, *Compendium Revelationum*, in G. Pico della Mirandola, *Vita R.P. Fr. Hieronymi Savonarolae*, ed. J. Quétif, Paris, 1674, p. 277.

15. G. Savonarola, *Sermones sulla Prima Epistola di San Giovanni*.
16. Guicciardini, *Storie fiorentine*, p. 108.
17. *Ibid.*, p. 108.
18. Savonarola, *Lettere*, p. 15.
19. G. Pico della Mirandola, *Ioannis Pici . . . Vita*, trans. Sir T. More and A.S.G. Edwards, in A.S.G. Edwards, K. Gardiner Rodgers and C.H. Miller, *The Complete Works of St. Thomas More*, Yale, New Haven and London, 1997, p. 331.
20. For Girolamo Benivieni, see A. Pelizzari, *Un asceta del Rinascimento (Della vita e delle opere di Girolamo Benivieni)*, Genoa, 1906.
21. Villari, *La storia*, vol. 1, p. xxxiii.
22. Cinozzi, 'Estratto d'un epistola'.
23. Pseudo-Burlamacchi, *Vita*, p. 25.
24. *Ibid.*, p. 20.
25. *Ibid.*, p. 21.
26. *Ibid.*, p. 23.
27. *Sermone sulla prima Epistola di San Giovanni*, quoted by Villari, *La storia*, vol. 1, p. 146.
28. Ridolfi, *Studi Savonaroliani*, p. 98.
29. Ridolfi, *Vita*, vol. 1, p. 72.

Eight

1. Ridolfi, *Studi Savonaroliani*, p. 100.
2. Savonarola, *Compendium Revelationum*, in Quétif, p. 244.

3. Villari, *La storia*, vol. 1, pp. 158–60.
4. The Latin text of Poliziano's letter is in P. Godman, *From Poliziano to*

Machiavelli: Florentine Humanism in the High Renaissance, Princeton, 1998, p. 15, n. 52.

5. Savonarola, *Compendium Revelationum*, in Quétif, p. 231.
6. Letter of Niccolò Guicciardini, Ridolfi, *Studi Savonaroliani*, p. 100.
7. Machiavelli, *Storie fiorentine*, p. 399.
8. Guicciardini, *Storia d'Italia*, vol. 1, p. 7.
9. J. Burchard, *Diarium sive rerum urbanum comentarii*, ed. L. Thuasne, Paris, 1883–5, vol. 3, p. 167.
10. Niccolò Machiavelli, *Il Principe*, Florence, 1857, p. 52.
11. See C. Shaw, *Julius II, the Warrior Pope*, Oxford, 1988, p. 89.

12. Savonarola, *Compendium Revelationum*, in Quétif, p. 231.
13. Villari, *La storia*, vol. 1, p. 201.
14. Pseudo-Burlamacchi, *Vita*, p. 26.
15. Machiavelli, *Storie fiorentine*, p. 390.
16. Pseudo-Burlamacchi, *Vita*, p. 44.
17. Savonarola, *Predica II sul Salmo Quam Bonus.*
18. Savonarola, *Predica VII sul Salmo Quam Bonus.*
19. Savonarola, *Predica X sul Salmo Quam Bonus.*
20. Savonarola, *Predica XXIII sul Salmo Quam Bonus.*
21. *Ibid.*

Nine

1. Guicciardini, *Storia d'Italia*, vol. 1, p. 21.
2. See H.F. Delaborde, *L'expédition de Charles VIII en Italie*, Paris, 1888.
3. Guicciardini, *Storia d'Italia*, vol. 1, p. 27.
4. Philippe de Commines, *Mémoires*, ed. J. Calmette and G. Durville, Paris, 1924, 1925, vol. 3, p. 34.
5. *Ibid.*, vol. 3, p. 41.
6. *Ibid.*, vol. 3, p. 44.

7. B. Cerretani, *Storie fiorentine*, in J. Schnitzer, *Quellen und Forschungen zur Geschichte Savonarolas*, vol. 3, Munich, 1904, p. 12.
8. Commines, *Mémoires*, vol. 3, p. 53.
9. *Ibid.*
10. G. Savonarola, *Prediche sopra Aggeo e Trattato circa il Reggimento e Governo della città di Firenze*, ed. L. Firpo, Rome, 1965.
11. Villari, *La storia*, vol. 1, p. 86.

Ten

1. Villari, *La storia*, vol. 1, p. 230.
2. Guicciardini, *Storia d'Italia*, vol. 1, p. 68.
3. Delaborde, *L'expédition de Charles VIII en Italie.*
4. Commines, *Mémoires*, vol. 3, p. 258.
5. The text is in the *Compendium Revelationum.*
6. E. Duffy, *Saints and Sinners: A History of the Popes*, London, 1997, p. 177.
7. Ridolfi, *Vita*, vol. 1, p. 147.
8. Pico, *Ioannis Pici*, pp. 333–8.
9. *Ibid.*, p. 333.

10. *Ibid.*, p. 334.
11. Burckhardt, *Civilisation in Italy*, p. 215.
12. Godman, *Poliziano to Machiavelli.*
13. L. Landucci, *Diario fiorentine del 1450 al 1516 continuato da uno anonimo fino al 1542*, ed. I. del Badia, Florence, 1883, p. 80.
14. Cerretani, *Storia fiorentina*, quoted by Villari, *La storia*, vol. 1, p. 246.
15. Pseudo-Burlamacchi, *Vita*, p. 64.
16. Savonarola, *Predica XXVI sopra Rut e Michea* (28 December 1496).

Eleven

1. Savonarola, *Predica XXVI sopra Aggeo* (28 December 1496).
2. Guicciardini, *Storia d'Italia*, vol. 1, p. 122.
3. *Ibid.*, p. 130.
4. Savonarola, *Predica VII sopra i Salmi* (25 January 1495).
5. Quoted by N. Rubinstein, 'Politics and Constitution at the end of the Fifteenth Century', in *Italian Renaissance Studies*, ed. E.F. Jacob, London, 1960, p. 153 (my translation).
6. Savonarola, *Predica XIX sopra Aggeo* (19 December 1494).
7. *Ibid.*
8. *Ibid.*
9. *Ibid.*
10. Landucci, *Diario fiorentine*, p. 91.
11. A. Cappelli (ed.), 'Fra Girolamo Savonarola e notizie intorno il suo tempo', in *Atti e Memorie delle*
R.R. *Deputazioni di Storia Patria per le provincie Modenesi e Parmensi*, 4 (1869), p. 337.
12. Guicciardini, *Storia d'Italia*, vol. 1, p. 131.
13. *Ibid.*
14. Landucci, *Diario fiorentine*, p. 93.
15. *Ibid.*, p. 118.
16. Rubinstein, 'Politics and Constitution', p. 155.
17. Savonarola, *Predica XIII sopra Aggeo* (12 December 1494).
18. *Ibid.*
19. Landucci, *Diario fiorentine*, p. 93.
20. *Ibid.*, p. 94.
21. *Ibid.*, p. 95.
22. *Ibid.*, p. 97.
23. *Ibid.*
24. Guicciardini, *Dialogo del Reggimento di Firenze*, quoted by Villari, *La storia*, vol. 1, p. 321.

Twelve

1. Guicciardini, *Storia d'Italia*, vol. 1, p. 101.
2. *Ibid.*
3. Commines, *Mémoires*, vol. 3, p. 87.
4. *Ibid.*, p. 98.
5. Guicciardini, *Storia d'Italia*, vol. 1, p. 103.
6. Commines, *Mémoires*, vol. 3, p. 91.

Thirteen

1. Commines, *Mémoires*, vol. 3, p. 144.
2. *Ibid.*, pp. 144–6.
3. Sir Francis Bacon (ed. J.R. Lumby), *History of the Reign of King Henry VII*, London, 1888, p. 131.
4. P. Balan, *Storia d'Italia*, Modena, 1895, 1896, vol. 5, p. 414.
5. Cappelli, 'Fra Girolamo', p. 345.
6. *Ibid.*, p. 347.
7. *Ibid.*, p. 351.
8. Zambotti: G. Pardi (ed.), *Diario ferrarese*, vol. 24; vii, 2, p. 279.
9. Pico, *Iohannis Pici*, p. 329.
10. Villari, *La storia*, vol. 1, docs, p. xcvii.
11. Guicciardini, *Storia d'Italia*, p. 155.
12. Villari, *La storia*, vol. 1, p. 381.
13. Landucci, *Diario fiorentine*, p. 107.
14. *Ibid.*, p. 109.
15. Commines, *Mémoires*, vol. 3, p. 309.
16. *Ibid.*, p. 155.
17. Guicciardini, *Storia d'Italia*, vol. 1, p. 204.
18. Commines, *Mémoires*, vol. 3, p. 311.
19. Villari, *La storia*, vol. 1, docs, pp. xxi–xxii and xcvi–ciii.

Fourteen

1. Villari, *La storia*, vol. 1, docs, p. xcix.
2. Rubinstein, 'Politics and Constitution', p. 183.
3. Weinstein, *Savonarola and Florence*, p. 34.
4. Guicciardini, *Storia d'Italia*, p. 153.
5. *Ibid.*, p. 123.
6. Polizzotto, *The Elect Nation*, p. 12.
7. *Ibid.*, p. 13.
8. Villari, *La storia*, vol. 1, p. 309.
9. Polizzotto, *The Elect Nation*, p. 19.
10. Pseudo-Burlamacchi, *Vita*, p. 75.
11. Weinstein, *Savonarola and Florence*, p. 186.
12. See Garin, *L'Umanesimo Italiana*, Bari, 1952, p. 137; Polizzotto, *The Elect Nation*, p. 102; Godman, *Poliziano to Machiavelli*, p. 135.
13. Quoted in Godman, *Poliziano to Machiavelli*, p. 136.
14. Quoted by Polizzotto, *The Elect Nation*, p. 106, n. 16.
15. Landucci, *Diario fiorentine*, p. 103.
16. Pseudo-Burlamacchi, *Vita*, p. 76.
17. *Ibid.*, p. 78.
18. Landucci, *Diario fiorentine*, p. 162. Violi lived to a great age and in 1545, still inspired by the Frate's memory, he composed a vivid account of events in Florence during Savonarola's day, *Le Giornate*.
19. Savonarola, *Predica III sopra i Salmi* (13 January 1495) – '*predica della rinnovazione*'.
20. G. Savonarola (ed. R. Ridolfi), *Predica XIII sopra Giobbe* (March 1495), Rome, 1957.
21. Savonarola, *Predica XVI sopra Giobbe* (March 1495).
22. Polizzotto, *The Elect Nation*, p. 35.
23. Landucci, *Diario fiorentine*, p. 124.
24. Cinozzi, *Estratto d'una epistola*, p. 7.
25. Polizzotto, *The Elect Nation*, p. 31.
26. Savonarola, *Predica XXVI sopra i Salmi* (28 July 1495).
27. Polizzotto, *The Elect Nation*, p. 41.
28. A.F. Verde, 'La Congregazione di San Marco dell' ordine dei frati Predicatori. Il "reale" della predicazione Savonaroliana', in *Memorie Dominicane*, 14, 1983, pp. 151ff.
29. Landucci, *Diario fiorentine*, p. 106.
30. His recently discovered letter-book gives a vivid insight into his life at San Marco. See Verde, 'La Congregazione', p. 34.
31. Ridolfi, *Vita*, vol. 1, p. 192.
32. B. Luschino (ed. V. Marchese), *Cedrus Libani*, in *Archivo Storico Italiano*, vol. 7, Florence, 1849.
33. Villari, *La storia*, vol. 1, p. 317.
34. G. Savonarola, *Prediche sopra Aggeo* and *Prediche sopra Amos e Zaccaria*, quoted by Villari, *La storia*, vol. 1, p. 290; and Polizzotto, *The Elect Nation*, pp. 27, 45.
35. Polizzotto, *The Elect Nation*, p. 36.
36. U. Cassuto, *Gli Ebrei a Firenze nell' età del Rinascimento*, Florence, 1918, p. 76, n. 1.
37. Landucci, *Diario fiorentine*, p. 114.
38. See E. Armstrong, 'English Purchases of Printed Books from the Continent, 1465–1526', *English Historical Review* (1979), pp. 269–90.
39. Pseudo-Burlamacchi, *Vita*, p. 72.
40. Villari, *La storia*, vol. 1, p. 313.
41. *Ibid.*
42. Weinstein, *Savonarola and Florence*, p. 173.
43. Savonarola, *Predica I sopra Amos e Zaccaria* (17 February 1496).
44. Cerretani quoted by Villari in *La storia*, vol. 1, p. 313.
45. Landucci, *Diario fiorentine*, p. 124.

Fifteen

1. L. von Pastor, *The History of the Popes*, trans. F.I. Antrobus, vol. 5, London, 1938–61, p. 203.
2. Burckhardt, *Civisilation in Italy*, p. 295.
3. Landucci, *Diario fiorentine*, p. 106.
4. Pseudo-Burlamacchi, *Vita*, p. 70.
5. Savonarola, *Predica VII sopra i Salmi* (25 January 1495).
6. Landucci, *Diario fiorentine*, p. 99.
7. For Caroli, see Polizzotto, *The Elect Nation*, pp. 59–64.
8. Landucci, *Diario fiorentine*, p. 113.
9. *Ibid.*, p. 122.
10. *Ibid.*, p. 129.

Sixteen

1. Ridolfi, *Vita*, vol. 1, p. 176.
2. Villari, *La storia*, vol. 1, docs, p. civ.
3. Burchard, *Diarium*, vol. 2, p. 411.
4. Savonarola, *Predica XXVI sopra i Salmi* (28 July 1495).
5. *Ibid.*
6. Villari, *La storia*, vol. 1, p. 395.
7. Savonarola, *Predica XXVI sopra i Salmi* (28 July 1495).
8. Villari, *La storia*, vol. 1, docs, pp. xxiv and cv.
9. P. Luotto, *Il Vero Savonarola*, Florence, 1900, p. 606 (the Pope's brief).
10. Savonarola, *Lettere*, p. 61.
11. Villari, *La storia*, vol. 1, p. 404.
12. Savonarola, *Predica XXVIII sopra i Salmi* (11 October 1495).
13. *Ibid.*
14. Gherardi, *Nuovi documenti*, p. 390.

Seventeen

1. Savonarola, *Lettere*, p. 61.
2. I have used Quétif's edition.
3. Villari, *La storia*, vol. 1, p. 339.
4. Polizzotto, *The Elect Nation*, p. 79.
5. *Ibid.*, p. 80.
6. For Gianfrancesco Pico's defence, *ibid.*, p. 81.

Eighteen

1. Cappelli, 'Fra Girolamo Savonarola', p. 406.
2. L. Landucci (trans. A. de R. Jervis), *Diary from 1450 to 1516 by Luca Landucci continued by an unknown hand till 1542 with notes*, London, 1927, p. 102.
3. Savonarola, *Predica I sopra Amos e Zaccaria* (17 February 1496).
4. *Ibid.*
5. *Ibid.*
6. *Ibid.*
7. Savonarola, *Predica VIII sopra Amos e Zaccaria* (24 February 1496).
8. Savonarola, *Predica XXVI sopra Amos e Zaccaria* (13 March 1496).
9. *Ibid.*
10. Savonarola, *Predica XXXII sopra Amos e Zaccaria* (23 March 1496).
11. Savonarola, *Predica IX sopra Amos e Zaccaria* (25 February 1496).
12. Savonarola, *Predica XLVIII sopra Amos e Zaccaria* (10 April 1496).
13. For the Pratica, see Gherardi, *Nuovi Documenti*, p. 136.
14. Savonarola, *Predica XLVIII sopra Amos e Zaccaria* (10 April 1496).
15. Gherardi, *Nuovi Documenti*, pp. 140–2.

16. Savonarola (ed. V. Marchese), *Lettere inedite di fra Girolamo Savonarola e documenti concernenti lo stesso*, in *Archivo Storico Italiano*, App. VIII, Florence, 1850, p. 125.
17. *Ibid.*, n. 172 (wrongly dated by Marchese).
18. Savonarola, *Lettere*, p. 108.
19. *Ibid.*, p. 106.
20. Villari, *La storia*, vol. 1, p. 461.
21. *Ibid.*, vol. 1, docs, pp. xxx, cxxxiii.
22. *Ibid.*, vol. 1, docs, pp. xxxvi, clix.
23. Cinozzi, *Estratto d'una epistola*, p. 6.
24. Villari, *La storia*, vol. 1, docs, pp. xxxi, cxxxvi.
25. G. Savonarola, *Prediche sopra Ruth e Michea*.
26. *Ibid.*
27. *Ibid.*

Nineteen

1. Landucci, *Diario fiorentine*, p. 138.
2. Guicciardini, *Storia d'Italia*, vol. 1, p. 261.
3. *Ibid.*, pp. 256, 262.
4. *Ibid.*, p. 263.
5. Villari, *La storia*, vol. 1, p. 484.
6. Savonarola, *Predica XXVI sopra Rut e Michea* (28 October 1496).
7. Savonarola, *Predica XXVII sopra Rut e Michea* (1 November 1496).
8. Savonarola, *Predica XXVIII sopra Rut e Michea* (2 November 1496).
9. Pseudo-Burlamacchi, *Vita*, p. 99.
10. Villari, *La storia*, vol. 1, docs, pp. xxxiii, cxlii.
11. Savonarola, *Predica VI sopra Ezechiele* (23 December 1496).
12. Landucci, *Diario fiorentine*, pp. 144, 145.
13. Pseudo-Burlamacchi, *Vita*, p. 113.
14. Landucci, *Diario fiorentine*, p. 168.
15. Pseudo-Burlamacchi, *Vita*, p. 114.
16. G. Ciappelli, 'Il Carnevale del Savonarola', in Garfagnini (ed.), *Studi Savonaroliani verso il V centenario*, Florence, 1996.
17. Savonarola, *Prediche sopra Ezechiele*, quoted by Ridolfi, *Vita*, vol. 1, p. 279.

Twenty

1. Savonarola, *Predica XXXII sopra Ezechiele* (4 March 1497).
2. G. Gruyer, *Les illustrations des écrits de Jérôme Savonarole publiés en Italie au XVe et au XVI siècle, et les paroles de Savonarole sur l'art*, Paris, 1879, p. 195.
3. Savonarola, *Predica XXVI sopra Ezechiele* (26 February 1497).
4. B. Parenti, 'Storia fiorentina', in J. Schnitzer, *Quellen und Forschungen zur Geschichtes Savonarolas*, vol. 4, Leipzig, 1910, p. 7.
5. Savonarola, *Predica XIII sopra Amos e Zaccaria* (6 March 1496).
6. H.P. Horne, *Alessandro Filipepi, Commonly called Sandro Botticelli, Painter of Florence*, London, 1908, p. 272.
7. 'Simone detto il Cronaca', Vasari, *Le Vite*, vol. 4, p. 453.
8. See G. Gentile, *Proposta per Michelangelo Giovane: Un Crocifisso in legno di tiglio*, Florence, Museo Horne, 1994.
9. G. Milanesi, *Le Lettere di Michelangelo Buonarroti*, Florence, 1875.
10. Ascanio Condivi, *Vita di Michelagnolo* [sic] *Buonarroti*, Florence, 1926, p. 98.
11. Vasari, *Le Vite*, vol. 1, p. 275.
12. S. Filipepi, 'Estratto della Cronaca di Simone Filipepi', in P. Villari and E. Casanova, *Scelta di prediche e scritti di Fra Girolamo Savonarola*, Florence, 1889.

13. Duffy, *Saints and Sinners*, p. 197.
14. Landucci, *Diario fiorentine*, p. 163.
15. Vasari, *Le Vite*, vol. 3, p. 317.
16. See R. Hatfield, 'Botticelli's *Mystic Nativity*, Savonarola and the Millennium', in *Journal of the Warburg and Courtauld Institutes*, 58, 1995, LVIII, 1995, pp. 89–114.
17. Horne, *Alessandro Filipepi*, pp. 294–301.
18. R.M. Steinberg, *Fra Girolamo Savonarola, Florentine Art and Renaissance Historiography*, Athens (Ohio), 1977.
19. See Padovani (ed.), *L'età di Savonarola. Fra Bartolommeo e la Scuola di San Marco*, Venice, 1996.
20. Steinberg, *Florentine Art*, p. 13.
21. Vasari, *Le vite*, Florence, 1881, p. 179.
22. G.M. Cao *et al.*, *L'età di Savonarola: I luoghi, la Storia, l'arte*, Pistoia, 1996.
23. Levey, *Florence: a Portrait*, p. 241.
24. Vasari, *Le vite*, p. 569.
25. Pseudo-Burlamacchi, *Vita*, p. 166.

Twenty-one

1. Guicciardini, *Storie fiorentine*, p. 152.
2. Cappelli, 'Fra Girolamo Savonarola', p. 374.
3. Gherardi, *Nuovi Documenti*, p. 149.
4. *Ibid.*, p. 153.
5. Savonarola, *Predica XXVIII sopra Ezechiele* (last sermon of Lent 1497).
6. Villari, *La storia*, vol. 2, p. 14.
7. *Ibid.*, vol. 2, p. 22.
8. Ridolfi, *Vita*, vol. 1, p. 291.
9. Landucci, *Diario fiorentine*, p. 148.
10. *Ibid.*, p. 150.
11. *Ibid.*, p. 152.
12. *Ibid.*
13. Savonarola, *Lettere*, p. 128.
14. Villari, *La storia*, vol. 2, docs, p. xxxix.
15. Gherardi, *Nuovi Documenti*, p. 163.
16. Savonarola, *Lettere*, p. 145.
17. *Ibid.*, p. 141.
18. *Ibid.*, p. 146.
19. Savonarola (ed. Marchese), *Lettere inedite*, n. 155.
20. Villari, *La storia*, vol. 2, docs, pp. vii, xlii.
21. Savonarola, *Lettere*, p. 154.
22. *Ibid.*, p. 167.
23. *Ibid.*, p. 156.
24. Cappelli, 'Fra Girolamo Savonarola', p. 382.
25. Savonarola, *Lettere*, p. 180.

Twenty-two

1. Cappelli, 'Fra Girolamo Savonarola', p. 135.
2. Landucci, *Diario fiorentine*, p. 155.
3. Villari, *La storia*, vol. 2, p. 9 and docs, p .iii.
4. Guicciardini, *Storie fiorentine*, p. 139.
5. Savonarola, *Lettere*, p. 178.
6. Landucci, *Diario fiorentine*, p. 157.
7. Villari, *La storia*, vol. 2, pp. 61–2.
8. *Ibid.*, vol. 2, docs, p. xxxv.
9. Savonarola, *Lettere*, p. 181.
10. Pseudo-Burlamacchi, *Vita*, p. 92.
11. Cappelli, 'Fra Girolamo Savonarola', p. 135.
12. Gherardi, *Nuovi Documenti*, p. 176.

Twenty-three

1. Guicciardini, *Storia d'Italia*, vol. 1, p. 295.
2. Ridolfi, *Vita*, vol. 1, p. 319.
3. Landucci, *Diario fiorentine*, p. 161.
4. Cappelli, 'Fra Girolamo Savonarola', p. 142.
5. *Ibid.*, p. 142.
6. Gherardi, *Nuovi Documenti*, p. 176.

7. Landucci, *Diario fiorentine*, p. 162.
8. Savonarola, *Prediche sopra l'Esodo*.
9. *Ibid*.
10. *Ibid*.
11. Villari, *La storia*, vol. 2, p. 95.
12. Landucci, *Diario fiorentine*, p. 163.
13. Pseudo-Burlamacchi, *Vita*, p. 115.
14. Guicciardini, *Storia d'Italia*, p. 296.
15. Gherardi, *Nuovi Documenti*, p. 180.
16. Savonarola, *Prediche sopra l'Esodo*.
17. Villari, *La storia*, vol. 2, p. 102 and docs, p. lxvi.
18. Savonarola, *Prediche sopra l'Esodo*.
19. Villari, *La storia*, vol. 2, docs, p. liiii.
20. Savonarola (ed. Marchese), *Predica VII sopra l'Esodo* (2 March 1498).
21. Savonarola, *Lettere*, p. 202.
22. Guicciardini, *Storia d'Italia*, vol. 1, p. 296.
23. Villari, *La storia*, vol. 2, p. 98.
24. *Ibid*., vol. 2, docs, pp. xiii, lxii.
25. Landucci, *Diario fiorentine*, p. 165.
26. Polizzotto, *The Elect Nation*, p. 93.
27. Burchard, *Diarium*, vol. 2, p. 462.
28. Savonarola (ed. Marchese), *Lettere inedite*, n. 40.
29. Savonarola, *Prediche sopra l'Esodo*.
30. Savonarola, *Predica VIII sopra l'Esodo* (3 March 1498).
31. Savonarola, *Predica XX sopra l'Esodo* (16 March 1498).
32. Savonarola, *Predica XXII sopra l'Esodo* (18 March 1498).

Twenty-four

1. Villari, *La storia*, vol. 1, p. 329.
2. *Summa Theologica, Quaestio 172, de causa prophetia*.
3. *Ibid.*, *Quaestio 171, de prophetia*.
4. *Ibid.*, *Quaestio 171, de prophetia*.
5. The most easily accessible edition of *De veritate prophetica dyalogus* is the translation (1997), with an invaluable preface by Claudio Leonardo.
6. Villari, *La storia*, vol. 1, pp. 329–30.
7. Schnitzer, *Savonarola*, vol. 2, p. 563.
8. Ridolfi, *Vita*, vol. 2, p. 22.
9. G. Savonarola (ed. C. Leonardi), *De veritate prophetica dyalogus*, trans. O. Bucci as *Verita della profezia*, Florence, 1987, p. 178.

Twenty-five

1. J. Nardi, *Istoria di Firenze*, Florence, 1858, vol. 1, p. 101.
2. Ridolfi, *Vita*, vol. 1, p. 341.
3. F.T. Perrens, *Jérôme Savonarola, d'après les documents originaux*, Paris, 1856, vol. 1, p. 481.
4. Villari, *La storia*, vol. 2, p. 115.
5. *Ibid.*, vol. 2, p. 116.
6. Gherardi, *Nuovi Documenti*, p. 194.
7. C.L. Lupi, (ed.), *Nuovi documenti intorno a fra Girolamo Savonarola*, in *Archivio Storico Italiano*, 3rd series, vol. 3, pp. 33–53.
8. Villari, *La storia*, vol. 2, pp. 117–21.
9. Savonarola, *Prediche sopra l'Esodo*.
10. See A. Brown, 'Savonarola, Machiavelli and Moses: a Changing Model', in *Florence and Italy: Renaissance Studies in Honour of Nicolai Rubinstein* (eds P. Denley and C. Evans), London, 1988.
11. Lupi, *Nuovi documenti*, p. 54.
12. Savonarola, *Prediche sopra l'Esodo*.

Twenty-six

1. Commines, *Mémoires*, vol. 3, p. 302.
2. Gherardi, *Nuovi documenti*, p. 204.
3. *Ibid.*, p. 205.
4. Cappelli, 'Fra Girolamo Savonarola', p. 146.
5. Villari, *La storia*, vol. 2, docs, p. lx.

6. I. Del Lungo, *Fra Girolamo Savonarola: Nuovi Documenti* in *Archivo Storico Italiano*, new series, Florence, 1863, part ii, p. xviii, n. 36.
7. Guicciardini, *Storia d'Italia*, vol. 1, p. 296.
8. Villari, *La storia*, vol. 2, docs, p. lxi.
9. Del Lungo, *Fra Girolamo*, n. 36.
10. Villari, *La storia*, vol. 2, p. 132.
11. *Ibid.*, vol. 2, p. 132–4.
12. *Ibid.*, vol. 2, docs, p. clxx.
13. *Ibid.*, vol. 2, docs, p. cclxii.
14. *Ibid.*
15. *Ibid.*, vol. 2, docs, p .lxix.
16. *Ibid.*, vol. 2, docs, p. cclxxii.

Twenty-seven

1. Savonarola (ed. Marchese), *Lettere inedite*, n. 24.
2. Villari, *La storia*, vol. 2, p. 138.
3. *Ibid.*, p. 139.
4. Savonarola (ed. Marchese), *Lettere inedite*, n. 24.
5. *Ibid.*
6. Lupi, *Nuovi documenti*, pp. 55ff.
7. Villari, *La storia*, vol. 2, p. 142.
8. Gherardi, *Nuovi Documenti*, p. 217.
9. Pseudo-Burlamacchi, *Vita*, p. 123.
10. Gherardi, *Nuovi Documenti*, p. 219.
11. Villari, *La storia*, vol. 2, p. 149.
12. Landucci, *Diario fiorentine*, p. 168.
13. Villari, *La storia*, vol. 2, p. 152.
14. *Ibid.*, p. 159.

Twenty-eight

1. Landucci, *Diario fiorentine*, p. 169.
2. *Ibid.*, p. 170.
3. Villari, *La storia*, vol. 2, docs, p. ccxxxvi.
4. *Ibid.*, p. 165 and docs, p. ccxxxiii.
5. *Ibid.*, p. ccxxvi.
6. Landucci, *Diario fiorentine*, p. 171.
7. Pseudo-Burlamacchi, *Vita*, p. 140.
8. Luschino, *Cedrus Libani*, Ch. ix.
9. Pseudo-Burlamacchi, *Vita*, p. 144.
10. *Ibid.*, p. 144.
11. Villari, *La storia*, vol. 2, p. 177.

Twenty-nine

1. Landucci, *Diario fiorentine*, p. 171.
2. Lupi, *Nuovi documenti*, p. 65.
3. Villari, *La storia*, vol. 2, docs, p. cxlix.
4. Landucci, *Diario fiorentine*, p. 172.
5. Gherardi, *Nuovi Documenti*, p. 231.
6. Ridolfi, *Vita*, p. 381.
7. Landucci, *Diario fiorentine*, p. 172.
8. *Ibid.*
9. Villari, *La storia*, vol. 2, p. 193.
10. *Ibid.*, p. 204.
11. Landucci, *Diario fiorentine*, p. 173.
12. Villari, *La storia*, vol. 2, docs, p. cv.
13. *Ibid.*, p. ccxiv.
14. Perrens, *Jérôme Savonarola*, p. 93.
15. Landucci, *Diario fiorentine*, p. 174.
16. Lupi, *Nuovi documenti*, p. 75.

Thirty

1. Pseudo-Burlamacchi, *Vita*, p. 154.
2. For this third trial, Villari, *La storia*, vol. 2, docs, p. clxxxiv.
3. Villari, *La storia*, vol. 2, docs, p. clxxxv.
4. *Ibid.*, vol. 2, docs, p. clxxxvii.
5. *Ibid.*, vol. 2, docs, p. clxxxix.
6. *Ibid.*
7. *Ibid.*, vol. 2, docs, p. cxii.
8. *Ibid.*
9. Ridolfi, *Vita*, vol. 1, p. 297.
10. Parenti, *Storia fiorentina*, p. 277.

11. S. Filipepi, *Estratto della Cronaca di Simone Filipepi*, in Villari and Casanova, *Scelta di prediche e scritti*, p. 508.
12. Villari, *La storia*, vol. 2, p. 234.
13. For this letter, see K. Meier, *Girolamo Savonarola aus grossen Theils handschriftlichen Quellen*, Berlin, 1836, p. 389.
14. For the condemnation, see Villari, *La storia*, vol. 2, docs, p. cclxxxvii.
15. Eliot, *Romola*, p. 541.

Thirty-one

1. An unbiased court using canon law of the period would have acquitted him, claims Luotto; cited by Weinstein, *Savonarola and Florence*, p. 9.
2. G.D. Mansi, 'Monumentum Historicum Appendix', in *Stephani Baluzii Miscellanea*, Lucca, 1761, vol. 1, pp. 583ff.
3. Pseudo-Burlamacchi, *Vita*, p. 155.
4. Landucci, *Diario fiorentine*, p. 176.
5. Pseudo-Burlamacchi, *Vita*, p. 155.
6. *Ibid.*, p. 156.
7. *Ibid.*, p. 157.
8. Pseudo-Burlamacchi is the most immediate account, with other details given by Landucci, Parenti, Cerretani and Nardi. See also Villari, *La storia*, vol. 2, p. 233.
9. Landucci, *Diario fiorentine*, p. 177.
10. Nardi, vol. 1, p. 161.
11. Pseudo-Burlamacchi, *Vita*, p. 162.
12. Landucci, *Diario fiorentine*, p. 177.

Thirty-two

1. Filipepi, *Estratto*, p. 507
2. Landucci, *Diario fiorentine*, p. 181.
3. Machiavelli, *Discorsi*, vol. 1, ii, p. 120.
4. Filipepi, *Estratto*, p. 493.
5. Zambotti, (ed. G. Pardi), *Diario ferrarese*, vol. 24, vii, 2, p. 281.
6. Polizzotto, *The Elect Nation*, p. 101.
7. F. Gregorovius, *Lucrezia Borgia nach Urkunden und Korrespondenzen ihrer einigen Zeit*, Stuttgart, 1925, doc. 51.
8. *Ibid.*, doc. 48.
9. Gardner, *Dukes and Poets*, p. 434.
10. J. Fisher, *Defensio Regis Assert*, in *Omni Opera*, Wurzburg, 1597, cap. 1, vols 108–9.
11. J. Musson, *The Development of Reformation Thought and Devotion in England . . . with particular reference to the works of, and those associated with, Fra Girolamo Savonarola*, unpublished thesis, Warburg Institute, 1938, p. 39.
12. Varchi, *Storia fiorentina*, vol. 1, p. 366.
13. *Ibid.*
14. The best account is Polizzotto, *The Elect Nation*, Ch. 7.
15. Varchi, *Storia fiorentina*, vol. 1, p. 178.
16. Polizzotto, *The Elect Nation*, p. 376.
17. Varchi, *Storia fiorentina*.
18. Ridolfi, *Vita*, vol. 2, p. 58.
19. N.H. Milman, *Savonarola, Erasmus and other Essays*, London, 1870, p. 73.
20. J.A. Symonds, *Renaissance Italy*, London, 1875–6, vol. 1, p. 471.
21. Villari, *La storia*, vol. 2, p. 260.
22. Quoted approvingly by Ridolfi, *Vita*, vol. 2, p. 71.
23. *Ibid.*, vol. 2, p. 72.
24. Ivan Illich (1926–2002) argued that the modern West's godless civilisation was a corruption of Christianity set in motion by the Church's institutionalisation, and that the West's only hope lay in a new understanding of religion centred on the parable of the Good Samaritan.

Bibliography

Contemporary Sources

Anon, *Alessandro VI e Savonarola (Brevi e lettere)*, Turin, 1950

Aquinas, St Thomas (ed. T. Gilbey), *Summa Theologica*, London, 1963–80

—— (ed. T. Gilby), *Philosophical Texts*, Oxford, 1951, 1955

Burchard, J. (ed. L. Thuasne), *Diarium sive rerum urbanum comentarii*, Paris, 1883–5

Burlamacchi, P. ('Pseudo-Burlamacchi'), *Vita del P.F. Girolamo Savonarola, riveduta poco dopo ed aggiunta dal P.F. Timoteo Botonio*, Lucca, 1764

Cambi, G. (ed. I. San Luigi), *Delizie degli eruditi toscani: Istorie*, ii, vol. 21, Florence, 1785

Capelli, A. (ed.), 'Fra Girolamo Savonarola e notizie intorno il suo tempo', *Atti e Memorie delle R.R. Deputazioni di Storia Patria per le provincie Modenesi e Parmensi*, 4, 1869

Cerretani, B., 'Storie fiorentine', in J. Schnitzer, *Quellen und Forschungen zur Geschichte Savonarolas*, vol. 4, Munich, 1902–4

Cinozzi, P., *Epistola de vita et moribus Ieronimo Savonarolae*, in Villari and Casanova, *Scelta di prediche e scritti de Fra' Girolamo Savonarola con nuovi documenti intorno alla sua vita*, Florence, 1898

Commines, P. de (ed. J. Calmette and G. Durville), *Mémoires*, Paris, 1924, 1925

Del Lungo, I., *Fra Girolamo Savonarola: Nuovi Documenti in Archivo Storico Italiano*, new series 18, part i, pp. 318 and part ii, pp. 3–41

Filipepi, S., 'Estratto della Cronaca di Simone Filipepi', in P. Villari and E. Casanova, *Scelta di prediche e scritti de Fr' Girolamo Savonarola*, Florence, 1889

Fisher, J., *Defensio Regis Assert*, in Omni Opera, Wurzburg, 1597

Gherardi, A. (ed.), *Nuovi Documenti e Studi intorno a Girolamo Savonarola*, Florence, 1887

Giannotti, D., *Della Repubblica fiorentina*, Florence, 1727

Guicciardini, F. (ed. V. de Caprariis), *Opera*, Milan, 1953

—— (ed. C. Panigaglia), *Storia d'Italia*, Bari, 1929

—— (ed. C. Panigaglia), *Storie fiorentine*, Bari, 1931

—— (trans. A. Brown), *Dialogue on the Government of Florence*, Cambridge, 1994

Landucci, L. (ed. I. del Badia), *Diario fiorentine del 1450 al 1516 continuato da uno anonimo fino al 1542*, Florence, 1883

—— (trans. A. de R. Jervis), *Diary from 1450 to 1560 by Luca Landucci continued by an unknown hand till 1542 with notes*, London, 1927

Lupi, C.L. (ed.), *Nuovi documenti intorno a fra Girolamo Savonarola*, in *Archivio Storico Italiano*, 3rd series, 1866

Luschino, Fra Benedetto, *Vulnera Diligentis*, Florence, 2002
——, *Cedrus Libani*, in Marchese, *Archivo Storico Italiano*, App. VII, Florence, 1849
Machiavelli, Niccolò (ed. A. Panella), *Le Istorie fiorentine*, Florence, 1843
——, *Il Principe*, Florence, 1857
——, *Discorsi sopra la prima deca di Tito Livio*, Florence, 1857
——, *Lettere* (ed. F. Gaeta), Milan, 1961
Mansi, G.D., 'Monumentum Historicorum Appendix', in *Stephani Baluzii Miscellenea*, vol. 1, Lucca, 1761
Nardi, J., *Istoria di Firenze*, Florence, 1858
Pardi, G. (ed.), *Diario Ferrarese dall' anno 1409 sino al 1502, di autori incerti*, in *Rerum Scriptores Italicarum*, vol. 24, vii, 1, Bologna, 1928
Parenti, P., *Storia fiorentina*, in J. Schnitzer, *Quellen und Forschungen zur Geschichtes Savonarolas*, vol. 4, Leipzig, 1910
Pico della Mirandola, G. (ed. J. Quétif), *Vita R.P. Fr. Hieronymi Savonarolae Ferrarensis Ord. Praedicatorum*, Paris, 1674
——, *Ioannis Pici . . . Vita*, trans. Sir T. More and also A.S.G. Edwards in A.S.G. Edwards, K. Gardiner Rodgers and C.H. Miller, *The Complete Works of St. Thomas More*, Yale, New Haven and London, 1997
Pius II (trans. F.A. Gragg), *Commentaries*, Northampton, MS, 1941–50
Savonarola, G. *Compendium Revelationum*, in Pico della Mirandola (ed. Quétif), *Vita R.P. Fr. Hieronimi Savonarolae Ferrarensis Ord. Praedicatorum*, Paris, 1674
—— (ed. V. Marchese), *Lettere inedited di fra Girolamo Savonarola e documenti concernanti lo stesso*, in *Archivo Storico Italiano*, App. VIII, Florence, 1850
—— (ed. G. Guasti), *Poesie*, Florence, 1862
—— (ed. G. Baccini), *Prediche*, Florence, 1889
—— (ed. P. Villari and E. Casanova), *Scelta di prediche e scritti con nuovi documenti intorno alla sua vita*, Florence, 1898
—— (ed. F. Cognasso), *Prediche Italiani ai fiorentini*, Perugia–Venice, 1930
—— (ed. R. Ridolfi), *Le Lettere*, Florence, 1933
—— (ed. R. Ridolfi), *Prediche sopra Ezechiele*, Rome, 1955
—— (ed. R. Ridolfi), *Prediche sopra Giobbe*, Rome, 1957
—— (ed. C. Leonardi), *De veritate prophetica dyalogus*, trans. O. Bucci as *Verita della profezia*, Florence, 1987
—— (ed. A. Verde), *Sermones ad primam Divi Joannis epostolam*, Rome, 1989
Vaglienti (eds. G. Berti, M. Luzzati, E. Tongiorgi), *Storia dei suoi tempi, 1492–1514*, Pisa, 1982
Varchi, B., *Storia Fiorentina*, Florence, 1843
Vasari, G., *Le vite de' più eccellenti pittori, scultori ed architetti*, Florence, 1881
Violi, L., *Le Giornate* (ed. G.C. Garfagnini), Rome, 1986
Zambotti, B. (ed. G. Pardi), *Diario ferrarese dall' anno 1476 sino al 1504 in Rerum Scriptores Italicarum*, vol. 24, vii, 2, Bologna, 1934

Later Sources

Aquarone, B., *Vita di fra Jeronimo Savonarola*, Alessandria, 1857
Armstrong, E., 'English Purchases of Printed Books from the Continent, 1465–1526', in *English Historical Review* (1979)

Arrasse, D., Dempsey, C., De Vecchi, P., Galizzi Koegel, A., Paolucci, A. and Strinati, C., *Botticelli de Laurent le Magnifique à Savonarole*, Paris, 2003

Bacon, F. (ed. J.R. Lumby), *History of the Reign of King Henry VII*, London, 1888

Balan, P., *Storia d'Italia*, vols 4–6, Modena, 1895, 1896

Bertozzi, M. (ed.), *Alla corte degli Estensi. Filosofia, arte e cultura a Ferrara nei secoli XV e XVI*, Ferrara, 1994

Bowra, M. 'Songs of Dance and Carnival', in E.F. Jacob, *Italian Renaissance Studies*, London, 1960

Brown, A., 'Savonarola, Machiavelli and Moses: a Changing Model', in P. Denley and C. Evans (eds), *Florence and Italy: Renaissance Studies in Honour of Nicolai Rubinstein*, London, 1988

Burckhardt, J., *Civilisation of the Renaissance in Italy*, London, 1944

Cao, G.M., Pons, N. and Tarquini, A., *L'Età di Savonarola: i luoghi, la storia, l'arte*, Pistoia, 1996

Cassuto, U., *Gli Ebrei a Firenze nell' età del Rinascimento*, Florence, 1918

Chesterton, G.K., *St Thomas Aquinas*, London, 1933

Ciappella, G., 'Il Carnevale del Savonarola', in Garfagnini (ed.), *Studi Savonaroliani*, Florence, 1996

Cittadella, L.N., *La nobile famiglia di Savonarola in Padova e in Ferrara*, Ferrara, 1867

Claudin, A., *Histoire de l'imprimerie en France au xve siècle et au xvie siècle*, Paris, 1900

Cloulas, I., *I Borgia*, Rome, 1988

Condivi, A., *Vita di Michelagnolo* [sic] *Buonarroti*, Florence, 1926

Cordero, F., *Savonarola: voce calamitosa 1452–1498*, Rome and Bari, 1986–8

Delaborde, H.F., *L'expédition de Charles VIII en Italie*, Paris, 1888

Duffy, E., *Saints and Sinners: A History of the Popes*, London, 1997

Eliot, G., *Romola*, Oxford, 1994

Ettlinger, L.D., 'A Fifteenth century View of Florence', in the *Burlington Magazine*, 94, London, 1952

Fletcher, S. and Shaw, C. (eds), *The World of Savonarola: Italian Elites and Perceptions of Crises*, Burlington, USA, 2000

Fusero, C., *I. Borgia*, Milan, 1966

Gardner, E.G., *Dukes and Poets in Ferrara*, London, 1904

Garfagnini, G.C., *Savonarola, 1498–1998. Studi Savonaroliani verso il V centenario*, Florence, 1996

Garin, E., *Giovanni Pico della Mirandola: vita e dottrina*, Florence, 1937

——, *L'Umanesimo Italiana*, Bari, 1952

Gentile, G., *Proposta per Michelangelo Giovane: Un Crocifisso in legno di tiglo*, Florence, Museo Horne, 1994

Ghisalberti, M. *et al.* (eds), *Dizionario biografico degli italiani*, Rome, 1960–2001

Godman, P., *From Poliziano to Machiavelli: Florentine Humanism in the High Renaissance*, Princeton, 1998

Gregorovius, F., *Lucrezia Borgia nach Urkunden und Korrespondenzen ihrer einigen Zeit*, Stuttgart, 1925

Gruyer, G., *Les illustrations des écrits de Jérôme Savonarole publiés en Italie au XVe et au XVI siècle, et les paroles de Savonarole sur l'art*, Paris, 1879

Gundersheimer, W.L., *Ferrara: the Style of a Renaissance Despotism*, Princeton, 1973

Hale, J.R., *Renaissance Europe 1480–1520*, London, 1971

Hall, M., 'Savonarola's preaching and the patronage of art', in T. Verdon and
     J. Henderson (eds), *Christianity and the Renaissance*, Syracuse NY, 1990
Hatfield, R. 'Botticelli's *Mystic Nativity*, Savonarola and the Millennium', in *Journal of
     the Warburg and Courtauld Institutes*, 58, 1995
Heiss, A., *Les médaillons de la Renaissance*, Paris, 1881–92
Horne, H.P., *Alessandro Filipepi, Commonly Called Sandro Botticelli, Painter of
     Florence*, London, 1908
Jacob, E.F. (ed.), *Italian Renaissance Studies*, London, 1960
Kent, F.W., 'Lorenzo di Credi, his patron Iacopo Bongianni and Savonarola', in the
     Burlington Magazine (September) 1983
Kristeller, P., *Early Florentine Woodcuts*, London, 1968
Lazzari, A., *Il primo duca di Ferrara. Borse d'Este*, in 'Monumenti della Deputazione di
     Storia Patria per l'Emilia e la Romagna', sezione di Ferrara, 1945
Levey, Michael, *Florence: A Portrait*, London, 1996
Lucas, H., *Fra Girolamo Savonarola*, London, 1899
Luotto, P., *Il Vero Savonarola*, Florence, 1900
Mallet, M., *The Borgias*, London, 1969
Masséna, V., Prince d'Essling, *Les livres à figures Vénitiens*, Paris, 1909
Meier, K., *Girolamo Savonarola aus grossen Theils handschriftlichen Quellen*, Berlin,
     1836
Meltzoff, S., *Botticelli, Signorelli and Savonarola, Theologia Poetica and Painting from
     Boccaccio to Poliziano*, Florence, 1987
Meneghin, V., *Bernardino da Feltre e i Monti de Pietà*, Vicenza, 1974
Milanesi, G., *Le lettere de Michelagelo Buonarroti*, Florence, 1875
Milman, H.H., *Savonarola, Erasmus and other Essays*, London, 1870
Mitchell, R.J., 'English Students at Ferrara in the XV Century', in *Italian Studies*, I,
     Manchester, 1938
Musson, J., *The Development of Reformation Thought and Devotion in England
     . . . with particular reference to the works of, and those associated with, Fra Girolamo
     Savonarola*, unpublished thesis Warburg Institute, 1989
Padovani, S. (ed), *L'età di Savonarola. Fra Bartolomeo e la Scuola di San Marco*, Venice,
     1996
Partner, P., *The Pope's Men: the Roman Civil Service in the Renaissance*, Oxford, 1990
Pastor, L. von, *The History of the Popes* (trans. F.I. Antrobus), London, 1938–61
Pelizzari, A., *Un asceta del Rinascimento (Della vita e delle opere di Girolamo
     Benivieni)*, Genoa, 1906
Perrens, F.T., *Jérôme Savonarola, d'après les documents originaux*, Paris, 1856
Picotti, G.B., *Alessandro VI*, in *Dizionario Biografico degli Italiani*, vol. 2, Rome, 1960
Polizzotto, L., *The Elect Nation: the Savonarola Movement in Florence 1494–1545*,
     Oxford, 1994
——, 'Savonarola and the Florentine oligarchy', in Fletcher and Shaw (eds), *The World
     of Savonarola*
Ranke, L. von, 'Savonarola und die florentinische Republik gegen Ende des funfzehnten
     Jahrhunderts', in *Historische-biographische Studien, von L. von Ranke*, Leipzig, 1878
Ridolfi, R., *Studi Savonaroliani*, Florence, 1935
——, *Vita di Girolamo Savonarola*, Rome, 1952
——, *Vita di Niccolò Machiavelli*, Rome, 1954

Rimondi, R., *Estensi: storia e leggende, personaggi e luoghi di una dinastia millenaria*, Ferrara, 2004

Ross, J., and Hutton, E. (eds), *Poesi volgari de Lorenzo de' Medici*, Edinburgh, 1912

Roth, C., *The Last Florentine Republic*, London, 1925

Rubinstein, N., 'Politics and Constitution at the end of the Fifteenth Century', in *Italian Renaissance Studies*', ed. E.F. Jacob, London, 1960

Sauto, A., 'La casa dove nacque e abito fra Girolamo Savonarola', *Studi Savonaroliani, Atti e memorie della Deputazione Provinciale Ferrarese di storia patria*, n.s. vol. 7, 3, Ferrara, 1952–3

Scapecchi, P., 'Bartolomeo frate e pittore nella Congregazione di San Marco', in *L'età di Savonarola*, ed. Padovani

Schnitzer, J., *Savonarola: ein Kulturbild aus der Zeit der Renaissance*, Munich, 1924

——, *Quellen und Forschungen zur Geschichtes Savonarolas*, Munich, 1902–4

Schutte, A.J., *Printed Italian Vernacular Religious Books: A Finding List*, Geneva, 1983

Sebregondi, L., 'Santo, eretico, precursore della Riforma: la diffusione dell'imagine di Girolamo Savonarola', in *Atti del convegno Girolamo Savonarola l'uomo e il frate*, Spoleto, 1999

——, *Diffusione e fortuna dell'iconografia de Girolamo Savonarola 1495–1998*, Florence, 2002

Segarizzi, A., *La Vita e le opere di Michele Savonarola*, Padua, 1900

Shaw, C., *Julius II, the Warrior Pope*, Oxford, 1988

Soranzo, G., *Il tempo di Alessandro VI papa e di Fra G. Savonarola*, Milan, 1960

Steinberg, R.M., *Fra Girolamo Savonarola, Florentine Art and Renaissance Historiography*, Athens (Ohio), 1977

Symonds, J.A., *The Renaissance in Italy*, London, 1875–86

Trexler, R.C., 'La prostitution florentine au XV siècle: patronages et clientes', in *Annales* 36, 1981

Tuohy, T., *Herculean Ferrara*, Cambridge, 1996

Verde, A.F., 'La Congregazione di San Marco dell' ordine dei frati Predicatori. Il "reale" della predicazione Savonaroliana', in *Memorie Dominicane*, 14, 1983

—— (ed), 'Epistolario di Fra Santi Rucellai', in *Memorie Dominicane*, n.s. 34, 2003

Villari, P., *La storia di Girolamo Savonarola e de' suoi tempi* (rev. edn), Florence, 1898

Weinstein, D., *Savonarola and Florence: Prophecy and Patriotism in the Renaissance*, Princeton, 1970

Index

in French invasion 104, 106
and Maximilian 161
opposes Savonarola 134, 153, 160, 232
placates Savonarola 155–6
reaction to excommunication 188
Lombard Dominicans 29, 70, 137, 138,
    182, 187
Lorenzo di Credi 176, 177
Lorenzo the Magnificent vi, 180
Louis XII 271, 273
Luschino, Bettuccio 123–4
Luther, Martin/Lutherans 273–4, 279
Lyons 76–7, 84

Machiavelli, Niccolò vi, 28, 39, 63, 98,
    224
    and Alexander VI 65
    and Lorenzo de' Medici 49, 50
Malegonelle, Antonio 223
Manfredi, Manfredo 95, 106, 180–1, 194,
    199
Mansi, Giovanni 263
Mantua 14, 22, 46
Marchese, Fra' Vincenzo 176, 280
Mariano da Genazzano, Fra' 40, 55–6,
    184, 206–7
Marseilles 162, 163
Maruffi, Silvestro 218, 248, 252
    killed 264–7
Maximilian I 104, 161–2, 164, 229,
    255
Mazzinghi, Domenico 230–1, 247
medallions/coins 67, 94, 173
Medici, Cosimo de' 38
Medici family 48, 77, 89, 224, 278,
    279
    fall of 90, 93, 96
    supporters of 129, 163, 166–7, 276
Medici, Giovanni de' 78
Medici, Giuliano de' 21, 80, 182
Medici, Lorenzo de' 21, 27, 28, 47,
    48–58, 48, 59–60, 89, 93, 214
    death 60–1
Medici, Lorenzo de' (Piero's cousin) 78,
    104, 116
Medici, Piero de' 39, 74, 77, 78, 87–8,
    108

capitulates to French 79–80
coup attempts 137, 138–9, 180, 182,
    192–3
    see also Piero plotters' trial
death 273
Savonarola denounces 75
support for 180
tyranny of 63, 70–1, 79
medicine 4–6, 11, 15
Mei, Fra' Francesco 166
mercenaries 51, 78, 108, 131, 276
Michelangelo vi, 33, 78, 126, 172, 173,
    178, 272, 276
Milan 23, 73–4, 145, 161, 221, 273
Modena 2, 22, 46
Monte Cavo 69
Monte della Pietà 124–5, 126
Monte delle Fanciulle 51, 61
Montpensier, Compte de 106
More, Thomas 85
Morelli, Lorenzo 104
Il Moro *see* Lodovico il Moro
Myers, Frederick 52
Mystic Crucifixion (Botticelli) 174–5
Mystic Nativity (Botticelli) 175, 178

Naples 23, 41, 70, 74–6, 77, 258–9
    army of 100
    French invasions of 88, 89, 102–5,
    273
Nardi, Jacopo 119, 219–20
'New *Piagnoni*' 280–1
Neri, Philip 279
Nesi, Giovanni 117–18, 123, 187–8
Niccolini, Agnolo 259
Niccolini, Jacopo 265
Niccolò III 2, 3, 5
Nicholas V, Pope 6

Onestà 37–8
Orleans, Duke of 78
Orsini family 63, 100
Ostia 66, 100
Otranto 63, 76

Padua 4
Pagagnotti, Monsignor 266